The

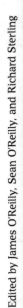

Ultimate

Journey

Edited by James O'Reilly, Sean O'Reilly, and Richard Sterling

inspiring
stories of
living &
dying

Barbara Kingsolver,

Mary Morris, Barry Lopez,

Sogyal Rinpoche,

Rachel Naomi Remen, M.D.,

Pico Iyer, and many more

CRITICAL ACCLAIM
FOR TRAVELERS' TALES

"The *Travelers' Tales* series is altogether remarkable."
—Jan Morris, author of *Journeys, Locations*, and *Hong Kong*

"For the thoughtful traveler, these books are an invaluable resource.
There's nothing like them on the market."
—Pico Iyer, author of *Video Night in Kathmandu*

"I can't think of a better way to get comfortable with a destination
than by delving into *Travelers' Tales*...before reading a guidebook, before
seeing a travel agent. The series helps visitors refine their interests and
readies them to communicate with the peoples they come in contact
with...."
—Paul Glassman, Society of American Travel Writers

"*Travelers' Tales* is a valuable addition to any pre-departure reading list."
—Tony Wheeler, publisher, Lonely Planet Publications

"*Travelers' Tales* delivers something most guidebooks only promise: a real
sense of what a country is all about...."
—Steve Silk, *Hartford Courant*

"*Travelers' Tales* is a useful and enlightening addition to the travel book-
shelves...providing a real service for those who enjoy reading first-person
accounts of a destination before seeing it for themselves."
—Bill Newlin, publisher, Moon Publications

"The *Travelers' Tales* series should become required reading for anyone
visiting a foreign country who wants to truly step off the tourist track
and experience another culture, another place, first hand."
—Nancy Paradis, *St. Petersburg Times*

"Like having been there, done it, seen it. If there's one thing traditional
guidebooks lack, it's the really juicy travel information, the personal
stories about back alleys and brief encounters. The *Travelers' Tales* series
fills this gap with an approach that's all anecdotes, no directions."
—Jim Gullo, *Diversion*

TRAVELERS' TALES

The Ultimate Journey

inspiring stories
of living and dying

Edited by
James O'Reilly, Sean O'Reilly,
and Richard Sterling

TRAVELERS' TALES

SAN FRANCISCO

Cover design: Michele Wetherbee
Interior design: Susan Bailey and Kathryn Heflin
Cover photograph: © Bill Ross/Corbis.
Special Research: Joanie Crété and Rajendra S. Khadka
Series Editors: James O'Reilly and Larry Habegger
Page layout: Patty Holden using the fonts Bembo and Boulevard

Distributed by Publishers Group West, 1700 Fourth Street, Berkeley, CA 94710.

Library of Congress Cataloging-in-Publication Data

The ultimate journey: inspiring stories of living and dying/edited by James
    O'Reilly, Sean O'Reilly, and Richard Sterling.—1st ed.
       p.   cm.
    ISBN 1-885211-38-4
    1. Death. 2. Near-death experiences. I. O'Reilly, James. II. O'Reilly, Sean.
III. Sterling, Richard.
BD444.U48 2000
128'.5—dc21   99-042251
                                                            CIP

First Edition
Printed in the United States of America
10 9 8 7 6 5 4 3 2 1

Of all the world's wonders,
which is the most wonderful?

That no man, though he sees others
dying all around him,
believes that he himself will die.

—THE MAHABHARATA

Table of Contents

Part Two
ENCOUNTERS

Part Three
RITUALS

Part Four
SHADOWS

Part Five
BLESSINGS

The Ultimate Journey: An Introduction

Death, vast and mysterious, surrounds us whether we give it little thought or a great deal of thought. Seasons come and go, family, friends, strangers, and enemies all die, young and old, the sick and the strong alike. The world turns. Your heart beats. And you wonder, where did your beloved go? Where is he now? Does she see me, hear me? The life of the body ends at death, but the soul? Does love, which towers over all we do in our brief lives, endure? Are we immortal or are we petals on a flower, or both? Your heart beats again, in an immense galaxy, in an ocean of night vaster than the ability to comprehend. The world turns again. Your lungs fill, and in their emptying, you wonder who fills them, over and over and over? Who or what gave you the breath of life, who will take it away? Who is at the forge, working the bellows of all beings?

This book is a conversation with great writers about living and dying. They all have something important to say about near-death experiences, the culture of death around the world, and the meaning death has for the conduct of one's life. A little boy comes out of a coma with a startling message. A couple survives certain death in Afghanistan, but doesn't understand how. A woman struggles to grasp the meaning of visions she has in Brazil. A writer in India discovers that he really doesn't want to know the hour of his death. A Tibetan Buddhist describes the marvelous death of his master and its lessons for all of us. A physicist relates an amazing out-of-body experience. A blind Frenchman returns from the brink of death in Buchenwald free of all fear, able to see more clearly than those with sight. An explorer in Greenland encounters a place that is simply beyond strange. A musician makes a practice of comforting the dying. During a Day of the Dead celebration in Mexico, a pilgrim encounters an old woman who knows more than seems possible. A priest helps a young woman find forgiveness and start life over again. A mortician buries his father. A traveler witnesses a sky burial in the holy city of Lhasa. A writer discovers the hidden gift of a fatal disease. A woman goes to Rwanda to help the survivors of genocide recover hope and faith. A teacher discovers the identity of the "angel" who greeted her following two near-fatal accidents. Moments of synchronicity, the numinous, the marvelous, the strange, abound in these pages.

Why would a travel publisher want to produce a book about death? The answer is simple—travel mirrors the journey we all face, the journey on which we are already booked. When we travel, we cut ties, leave family and home behind, to face new worlds. Much like death, travel changes us, leavening our pride, changing our assumptions—in short, transforming us. Death is the final train leaving at midnight.

Soon after we began working on this book, we realized that "death" was such a huge and fascinating subject, we could happily compose ten books instead of one. During this long process our editorial team gathered at Sleeping Lady retreat center in the Cascades, near Leavenworth, Washington. The beautiful setting for our sessions, one might think, was in stark contrast to the subject matter. But in fact, the mountains, the rivers, the forests, and the books and stories we read and discussed formed more of a symphony to us than a lugubrious undertaking. As we neared the end of our preliminary editorial work, our unanimous sentiment was that we felt privileged—uplifted—to have read so much about the final journey. We felt that our lives and indeed our own deaths had in many ways been affected by these stories.

We think that this will be true for you too, and the more you read of *The Ultimate Journey*, the more you will let go of whatever fears you may harbor about your demise, and come to feel that the moment of death itself is no more to be dreaded than a visit to the dentist. It is, according to the thousands of people who have experienced "clinical" death and come back to life, merely a passage, not an end. A journey, if you will, into a bigger life, a journey from reality into Reality.

—JAMES O'REILLY

PART ONE

MYSTERIES

DAVID YEADON

* * *

The Bridge

Life is deep and mysterious
whether we notice or not.

I THINK I TRAVEL BECAUSE I'M ALIVE. AND I DON'T MEAN THAT TO sound glib. I mean that I really should be dead. A part of me still thinks that maybe I did die years ago when I was an ambitious urban planner working with the Shah of Iran and his wife, the Empress Farah, on the future master plan for the city of Tehran, and that someone else (another me?) took over my body and mind and has been living here happily ever since.

It's a short story, but still a disconcerting one. Even as I write it now I feel the old tremor through my fingers.

Anne and I were high up in the Elburz Mountains of Iran. This dramatic range acts as a 14,000-foot wall separating the desert of Tehran and the south from the lush jungled hills bordering the Caspian Sea. We'd had a few lazy days of meandering, trying to learn a little more about this anomalous country and its long history. We were returning back over the mountains on the "old road," a narrow unpaved trail that promised more adventure than the carefully graded curves and tunnels of the new road a couple of hundred miles to the west. Everything was going fine. There was no traffic, and we felt very much at peace among the peaks and high valleys.

We were descending a steep pass, the road curling and twisting through a broken stretch of country. Around a sharp bend we approached a one-lane bridge with no retaining wall on either side—just a vertical drop of 300 feet or so into a shadowy ravine. A dramatic place. Then suddenly, with no warning, an enormous Mack truck came barreling across the bridge spewing rocks and dust. He, like us, assumed he had the road to himself and was trying to gain acceleration for the long climb up the pass. By this time we were actually on the bridge, which seemed hardly wide enough for one car, let alone two vehicles heading straight for each other. We realized he couldn't possibly brake without careening off the bridge. We also knew the same applied to us, and there wasn't time to stop anyway. But I did brake. I didn't know what else to do. And—like watching a slow-motion film—we could see our car skidding sideways right toward the wall-less edge of the bridge and the ravine. We both closed our eyes, and I remembered two silly things quite distinctly: a beautiful color of bright purple inside my closed eyelids, and feeling a strip of torn leather on the steering wheel and wondering why I'd never repaired it. We were still skidding; I could hear the gravel hissing under the sliding tires. We waited, eyes still closed, for the collision with the truck or for the fall into the ravine—or both. We were absolutely calm. No screams. Just acceptance.

What seemed like minutes later, but can only have been a second or two, we opened our eyes to find ourselves moving slowly forward, down the center of the bridge. The car seemed to be driving itself. We pulled to a stop and looked behind us. There was no truck, no dust. We got out of the car and listened. There was no sound—no indication that the truck had ever been there at all. We were absolutely calm; no fear, no shaking, no aftereffects of shock. We just kept looking around and then looked at each other. We even looked over the bridge to see if the truck had tumbled into the ravine. Nothing.

We got back into the car and drove on. We didn't speak for a long time. Then Anne said: "That did happen, didn't it?"

"It happened," was all I could think to say. Though *what* had actually happened we couldn't understand. All we knew was that something very strange had taken place, and we were still alive. And then we were weeping. Great big sobs. And then laughing and then very quiet for most of the journey back to Tehran.

Many people experience some climactic event that makes a radical change in their lives. Well, this was ours. We still don't know what happened; we don't know how we survived, when it is obvious even now, having written it all down for the first time, I'm none the wiser. Wiser, that is, about the event itself. But we both became much wiser in other ways that completely transformed our lives.

We began to understand with greater clarity the fragility and wonder of life itself; we knew from that moment we would try to live our lives to the full, doing what we felt, deep down, we should be doing, no longer putting things off until we had accumulated enough capital or confidence or security to feel "free." We had found freedom on that bridge. We needed for nothing after that. Even though there were difficult years in material and other ways, we never had any real doubts about what we were doing with our lives. It didn't always make sense, particularly to others. But somehow that singular experience had bored a hole into our souls, and certainty flowed out and just kept on flowing.

David Yeadon has written and illustrated many books, including New York: The Best Places, Backroad Journeys of Southern Europe, Lost Worlds: Exploring the World's Most Remote Places, *and* The Back of Beyond: Travels to the Wild Places of the Earth, *from which this story was excerpted. He is a contributing editor at* National Geographic Traveler *and lives with his wife, Anne, in Mohegan Lake, New York.*

✦ ✦ ✦

A Minor Resurrection

What can death be?

EMBROIDERED WITH GOLD LIKE A WEDDING SARI, THE SKY ABOVE Tiruvannamalai around sunset had weight and substance, almost undulated in the breeze above the huge carved *gopura* of the temple. I easily found the part of the bazaar that specialized in pots and pans. Kerosene tapers burned like flecks fallen from the flaming yellow banner fluttering over our heads, throwing off a thousand reflections across the walls of copper tureens, jugs, and woks, and dancing around a hundred steel *dekchis*, chapati irons, and rice double boilers. A faint aroma of *bhang* hung in the air, along with a dozen spices, incense, and wood smoke. Shadows clustered in the gathering gloom, and in these, men in *lungis* and undershirts conspired, puffing *beedies*, gossiping. Housewives, proud in rustling saris of Kanchipuram silk, strode from stall to stall, finally hammering out deals for frying pans or ladles or aluminum saucepans large enough to serve soup to multitudes. A turbaned man with a mustache like buffalo horns strolled by, dragging a sad, moth-eaten dancing bear muzzled and leashed. The man looked dangerous; the bear had big black tears hanging rigid in the corners of its eyes.

There were no yogis in sight.

I asked a vendor about Yogi Ramsuratkumar. The vendor tried

very hard to sell me a copper saucepan, coming down to a price so reasonable I would have bought it had I not pictured myself lugging it around India for years. I reminded him I had asked about the yogi, not the saucepan. The man sighed, knowing he'd done his best. He pointed across the dusty lane.

"Yogi is there," he said.

"Where?" I saw nothing.

"There only. You see...."

I walked across to what appeared to be a vacant stall. On a bench in the shadows sat a powerfully built man, perhaps in his late sixties—it was hard to tell—with a huge, graying beard. His dirty robes had something of ancient Rome about them. He was flapping a circular fan of some sort of dried leaf attached to a wooden handle, powerfully, urgently, as if the heat really bothered him. His hand moved in a blur below his face. A large, soiled rag worn bandanna-style was drenched in perspiration.

"Yogi Ramsuratkumar?" I asked, suddenly nervous.

He looked up with bright eyes that were full of an impish amusement, smiling and nodding his head.

"Oh!" he kept repeating. "Oh!" He stood, putting the fan aside and grasping both my hands like some dotty old uncle I hadn't visited in years. "Oh! You have come!"

I confessed it was true.

"From where?" he asked, an odd intelligence entering his voice and eyes.

His English was excellent, and, judging by the pale skin and the accent, he was certainly not from these parts, not a Southerner. His body, too, was different: large-boned, with sizable muscles in the legs, big feet, and large but slender and well-formed hands. A Bengali, I decided, mainly because he resembled the poet Tagore.

He bade me sit next to him and proceeded to fumble with a packet of Wills Filters and light a cigarette, smoking it furiously through his fist, the other hand working the fan again. I noted an old cloth bag at his feet, from which protruded three more similar fans.

"I didn't know yogis smoked."

He merely laughed, puffing and fanning with even more concentrated intensity. The actions seemed connected. He did not look like someone enjoying a cigarette so much as someone using an asthma inhaler.

I lit up a cigarette myself, but felt oddly uncomfortable smoking it next to the yogi. I soon dumped it surreptitiously, asking him if he always smoked. He had just lit a second cigarette from the previous butt.

"Only here," he replied.

I felt the curious sensation you get when you suspect someone can read your mind, or, stranger still, can inscribe on it what you are currently reading there yourself.

When his other hand was not fanning, I noticed, it was performing a rapid motion like counting the beads of an invisible rosary. Indeed, he was all motion. In anyone else it would have seemed neurotic, anxious, but with him it gave the impression of someone who needed to vent excess energy.

I asked where he lived and what he did during the day.

"This beggar lives out there," he replied, indicating the barren wasteland surrounding Arunachala. "He does whatever God asks."

"What *does* God ask?"

"What this beggar does is not important," he answered firmly. "What is it that *you* wish?"

I told him that I just wanted to meet him.

He laughed insanely and long, as if he'd never in his life heard anything so preposterous. I wondered if maybe he *was* just a beggar. Except he seemed more like a king in exile.

"Oh! Oh! Oh!" he gasped, coughing. "Is it so?"

"Yes. I'm really interested in what you people do. Where I come from everyone thinks that a man's duty is to work in the world…with others—you know, make it a better place and all that."

This definitely amused him. "Is it so?" he repeated.

"They'd say you were escaping responsibilities, you know—running away."

"There are many tasks in this world," he suddenly said, his voice calmer now. "Many jobs that must be done by those who God wishes to do them…"

He went on to say, without once mentioning himself, that negative forces clustered around people in important positions, such as political leaders, and it was vital that they be protected from such negative forces while doing their jobs, otherwise wars and catastrophes would result. I gleaned from this that Yogi Ramsuratkumar's job was to build auras of protection around such people by exerting some sort of influence to insure that positive forces determined major events.

This struck me as an important job. It also struck me as absurd. Did it exist beyond his imagination? And if it did exist, why wasn't it very successful—considering the number of wars and catastrophes that were happening even as we spoke? I couldn't trap him like this, however, since he never referred to himself as anything but a beggar, a vehicle for God's inscrutable will. Who knew how much worse things might have been without whatever it was he did, after all?

"There was a great teacher" was about all he'd say regarding the past. "The teacher took this beggar and made him function for the will of God. Just as a broken automobile can be repaired so the driver can drive it again. Is it true? The driver must drive—yes? So his automobile should function? A broken automobile is of no use to anyone—is it not so?"

I agreed. He wouldn't say who the "great teacher" was. I asked how one built an "aura of protection." He laughed once more, tickled to death. *At least*, I thought, *I'm providing the evening's entertainment.*

Without warning, he swatted a fly on the bare counter of the vacant stall with his powerful hand. He picked the creature up by a wing and give it to me. I tentatively accepted it, trying to appear grateful, and examined the insect in the palm of my hand to see if there was something I had missed. Mangled, oozing, one wing buckled into a squashed abdomen, it looked like any other dead fly I'd ever encountered.

The yogi watched me intently, puffing and counting those invisible beads, a big, generous smile swelling through his high cheekbones.

"Very dirty," he said, nodding at the fly. "Put it there." He indicated the spot where the fly had just met its abrupt end. A tiny stain was still visible on the wood.

I tipped the speck down near the stain.

"What can death be?" the yogi asked.

I shrugged, not about to offer an answer to that.

"It is a question we are interested in—is it not so?" I nodded.

"Watch." He pointed to the fly.

I watched the raisinlike blob, hearing the yogi's breathing become faster and faster—until it suddenly stopped. He then held up his right hand a yard or so from the fly, becoming incredibly still. This stillness was all the more dramatic after his perpetual motion—and it really *was* stillness. As I continued to watch, the fly started twitching, shaking its buckled wing out, then getting up, testing its legs with a few unsteady steps. A second later, it flew away.

> S hining, yet hidden,
> Spirit lives in the cavern.
> Everything that sways, breathes,
> opens, closes, lives in Spirit;
> beyond learning, beyond every-
> thing, better than anything;
> living, unliving.
>
> It is the undying blazing
> Spirit, that seed of all seeds,
> wherein lay hidden the world
> and all its creatures. It is life,
> speech, mind, reality, immortality.
> It is there to be struck. Strike it,
> my son!
>
> Take the bow of our sacred
> knowledge, lay against it the
> arrow of devotion, pull the
> string of concentration, strike
> the target.
>
> —*Upanishads*

The yogi remained motionless for another minute, then immediately became his old self again, lighting up and fanning.

My first thought was just how dead the fly had been. Surely I had seen enough dead flies to know the difference. This fly had been crushed, split open.

"How did you do that? I asked.

He looked over through the gloom, the whites of his eyes sparkling. "Life is a force," he said quietly. "Death is the absence of that force—is it not so?"

"I suppose…"

"Fly needs less force than the human—is this true?"

"Probably…"

"Can this beggar not give the fly enough force to live?"

I asked how he could transfer his life force and how the fly could repair the damage to its body even if it received new life force.

"Is it not so that God can do anything he wishes?"

"Yes, but…" I stopped, because I had the distinct impression that the answers I was looking for weren't available. No words from this yogi were going to explain anything at all.

"Why do you not wish to see this beggar?"

I didn't want to seem ungrateful. I knew that whatever he was doing, coming to the bazaar when he did, I would probably not understand, either. I told him I was glad he had spared some time to talk to me. Once more he laughed uproariously.

"Can I give you anything?" I inquired.

This got a chuckle, too. Then he said, "This beggar needs nothing. God gives him what he deserves…but he deserves nothing really—is it not?"

I held out my pack of cigarettes. He laughed, looking at it as if observing something about it that I couldn't see. Then, almost coyly, he took a cigarette.

I told him to keep the whole pack, but he bluntly refused, looking somewhat embarrassed.

Then I asked about the holy mountain, Arunachala, and why it was holy. He seemed baffled, reluctant to answer. I asked if there was any cosmic advantage in walking to its summit. There usually is with holy mountains. Quite forcefully, he replied that it was better to walk around it.

"Around it?"

"Good exercise—is it not so?" he said.

"Which direction?"

This clearly did not matter. I thanked him, feeling I'd overstayed my welcome, and asked if I could come back tomorrow.

"Why would you want to see this filthy old beggar again?"

"I like this filthy old beggar…"

"Oh! Oh!" He sighed, grasping my hands. "God is too good to this old beggar."

"Does Indira Gandhi have an aura of protection?" I asked, standing to leave.

"What God wills must be so—is it not?"

"Is she a client of yours?" *Client* seemed as good a term as any.

"What use is a filthy old beggar to a queen?"

It was an odd reply, one I thought about often in the years ahead. I thought of it the day Indira lay in a pool of blood and India seemed poised on the brink of an abyss.

I left Yogi Ramsuratkumar there, amid the pots and pans, beneath a seething night brimful of mysteries. My heart was well and truly splashed across the heavens as I walked back up to the silent ashram. Some moments you would not trade, even for another hundred years of life.

Paul William Roberts graduated from and taught literature at Oxford University. After stints in India and Hollywood, he settled with his wife and children in Toronto, where he has been the recipient of numerous screenwriting, journalism, and fiction awards. His travel writing has appeared in Harper's, Condé Nast Traveler, The Toronto Star, *and many other publications, and he is the author of* River in the Desert, In Search of the Birth of Jesus, Demonic Comedy: Some Detours in the Baghdad of Saddam Hussein, *and* Empire of the Soul: Some Journeys in India, *from which this story was excerpted.*

BARRY LOPEZ

* * *

Pearyland

*Maybe there really is
a twilight zone.*

I APOLOGIZE FOR NOT BEING ABLE TO TELL YOU THE WHOLE OF this story. It begins at the airport at Søndrstrømfjord in Greenland and it happened to a man named Edward Bowman. He'd just come down from Pearyland, by way of Qânâq and Upernavik, then Nûk. About a hundred of us were waiting around for planes, his out to Copenhagen, with Søndrstrømfjord socked in. He'd been at the airport for six days; I'd been there just a few, with four Inuit friends from Clyde Inlet, on Baffin Island. In those days—just out of law school—I was working with Canadian Eskimos, helping to solidify a political confederation with Eskimos in Greenland.

We were all standing by, long hours at the airport. Some people went into town; but the notion that the weather might suddenly clear for just a few minutes and a plane take off kept most of us around, sleeping in the lounges, eating at the restaurant, using the phones.

Bowman was at work on a master's degree in wildlife biology at Iowa State, though by that time he may have already abandoned the program. His thesis, I remember well, had to do with something very new then—taphonomy. He was looking, specifically, at the way whitetailed deer are taken apart by other animals after they die, how they're funneled back into the ecological community—how bone

13

mineral, for example, goes back into the soil. How big animals disappear. Expanding the study a little brought him to Pearyland. He wanted to pursue in northern Greenland some threads of what happens when large animals die.

I should say here that Bowman wasn't eager to talk, that he didn't feel compelled to tell this story. He didn't avoid my questions, but he didn't volunteer much beyond his simple answers. His disinclination to talk was invariably polite, not unlike my Inuit friends, whose patience I must have tried all those years ago with my carefully framed questions and youthful confidence.

Did he go up there just to look at dead animals? I asked him. In a cold place where carcasses decay very slowly? Partly, he said, his interests became more complicated. Pearyland is an arctic oasis, a place where many animals live despite the high latitude—caribou, wolves, arctic hares, weasels, small animals like voles and lemmings, and many birds including snowy owls. Bowman said he'd tried to get grants to support a summer of study. Of course, he was very curious about the saprophytic food web, the tiny creatures that break down organic matter; but, also, no one understood much about Pearyland. It was remote, with a harsh climate and very difficult and expensive to get to.

No funder was enthusiastic about Bowman's study, or his curiosity. (He told me at one point that part of his trouble in applying for grants was that, after working with the deer carcasses in Iowa, he just had an instinct to go, but no clear, scientific purpose, no definite project, which finally presented the larger institutions with insurmountable problems.) Eventually, he was able to cobble together several small grants and to enlist the support of a foundation in Denmark, which enabled him to buy food and a good tent. For his travel north to Qânâq he was going to depend on hitching rides on available aircraft. With the last of his funds he'd charter a flight out of Qânâq for Bronlund Fjord in early July and then arrange for a pickup in mid-September. All of which he did.

When we met, the only cash he had was his return ticket to Copenhagen, but he was not worried. Somehow, he said, everything would work out.

Now, here is where it gets difficult for me. I've said Bowman, unlike most white men, seemed to have no strong need or urge to tell his story. And I couldn't force myself to probe very deeply, for reasons you'll see. So there could be—probably are—crucial elements here that were never revealed to me. It's strange to think about with a story like this, but you'll be just as I was—on your own. I can't help it.

What Bowman found at Bronlund Fjord in Pearyland was the land of the dead. The land of dead animals.

When he arrived, Bowman made a camp and started taking long walks, six- or seven-mile loops, east and west along the fjord and north into the flat hills, into the willow draws. The fjord stood to the south—open water at 82°N in July, which surprised him; but that is the nature of arctic oases. Summer comes earlier there than it does farther south, and it lingers a bit longer. In winter it's relatively warmer. Some days, Bowman said, he wore only a t-shirt.

Bowman's treks brought him within sight of many animals in the first few days, but he wasn't able to get near them. And, a little to his wonder, not once on these long walks did he come upon an animal carcass, not even a piece of weathered bone.

The only thing he worried about, he told me, was polar bears. He saw seals regularly in the fjord, so he expected bears would turn up; but he saw no tracks or scat, not even old signs. He wasn't afraid of being attacked so much as of having a bear break into his food. He had no radio, so he ran the risk of starving before the plane came back. For this reason alone, he said, he had agreed to take a gun, which the Danish government insisted he carry. How he learned where he was, that he'd camped in the land of the dead, was that one morning he went for the rifle and it wasn't there.

Of course, no one was around, so its loss made no sense to him. He looked underneath everything in his camp, thinking, absent-minded, he might have left it at his defecation pit, or taken it down to the shore of the fjord. Or that in his sleep he'd gotten up and taken the gun somewhere and thrown it away. He said he entertained this last possibility because he was never comfortable with the idea of having the gun; and who could know, he said to me, what the dreaming mind really wanted done?

The day after he missed the gun he saw a few caribou close by, less than a half mile away. He was eating breakfast, sitting on an equipment crate, watching the wind ripple the surface of the fjord and tracing with his eye a pattern in the purple flowers of a clump of saxifrage. The animals' hard stare caused him to turn around. He gazed back at them. Four animals, all motionless. It struck him then that in that first week or so he hadn't seen any caribou or musk oxen grazing or browsing.

He reached for his binoculars, but in that same moment the caribou dropped off behind a hill. He saw no other animals the rest of the day, but the following morning the caribou were back in the same place. This time, he sat very still for a long while. Eventually the caribou walked down to where he was, only about twenty yards away.

"Where is your place?"

Bowman said when he heard these words he thought it was the animals that had made them, but when he turned around he saw, far off near the edge of the water, a man, an Inuk.

"What place are you from?"

It was hard for Bowman to understand that this man's voice was coming to him clearly even though he was standing far away. He didn't know what to answer. He didn't think the man would know about Indiana, so he said he was from very, very far away, to the west and south.

"What do you want here?"

Bowman told me he wished to answer this question in such a way that he would not offend the man because he had a strong feeling he might be hindered in his study here (which, he pointed out again, was nearly aimless). Or possibly harmed.

"I want to listen," he said finally.

"Do you hear the wind? Meltwater trickling down to the fjord? The arctic poppies turning on their stalks in the summer sunshine?"

"Yes. I listen to all this."

"Do you hear the songs of my brothers and sisters?" asked the man by the fjord.

"I'm not sure," answered Bowman. "I don't think I've heard any singing. Perhaps if I listened better."

Cumulus
Status

At that moment, Bowman turned quickly to look at the caribou. They'd come much closer. Swinging still further around, he caught sight of two wolverine, that odd lope of theirs, as they came bounding toward him from the west. Then the Inuk was right next to him, sitting on another crate, looking out over the waters of the fjord. Bowman couldn't make out his face from the side.

"I'm the caretaker here," the man said. Bowman could see now that he was about forty, fifty. "What do you want? What is 'Indiana'?" he asked.

Bowman, startled, described where Indiana was. Then he tried to explain what he did as a biologist, and that he was specifically interested in what happened to animals after they died. After that, he told me, he shouldn't have said anything more, but he went on until he ran out of things to say.

"The dead come here," the man said when Bowman was finished talking. He stood up. Bowman saw he was short, only five feet four inches or so, his short-fingered hands massive, the veins prominent, his forehead receding into a line of close-cropped, raven-black hair. "You've come to the right place," he said. Then he walked away. Although he walked slowly, soon he was very far away.

The caribou were gone. The wolverine were still there, watching him, but after a while they, too, disappeared.

Bowman did not see the man again for four or five days, and then he just saw him at a great distance, walking along the low edge of the sky.

One morning Bowman crawled out of his tent and saw an arctic fox resting on its haunches, looking at seals in the fjord. When he awoke, he took his binoculars and studied the tundra in every direction, writing down whatever he saw—arctic hare, musk oxen, snow geese. He ate, then took a lunch and his pack and went for a long walk. He made lists of all the flowers, the tracks he came upon, the animals he saw; and he fought against a feeling that he was not accomplishing anything. Every day he wrote down the temperature and he estimated the speed and direction of the wind and he made notes about the kind of clouds he saw in the sky. Altostratus. Cumulonimbus.

One day the man came back. "Why aren't you trying to hunt?" he asked. "How come you don't try?"

"When I was a young man I hunted with my father in Indiana. I don't do that now." Bowman told me he wanted to be very careful what he said. "I don't hunt here, in this place, because I brought food with me. Besides, I don't know these animals. I have no relations with them. I wouldn't know how to hunt them."

"No hunting here, anyway."

"I know this is your country," Bowman said cautiously, "but why are you here?"

"Caretaker. Until these animals spirits get bodies and are ready to go back, a human being must be here, to make sure they aren't hungry. If the animals want something—if they want to hear a song, I learn it. I sing it. Whatever they want, I do that. That's my work."

"Have you been here a long time?"

"Eating—it's not necessary." After a moment he said, "They are feeding on the sunlight."

"When they are ready, where do they go?"

"All everywhere. They go home. They go back where they're from. But too many, now, they don't come here. They are just killed, you know. No prayer." He made a motion with his fist toward the ground as though he were swinging a hammer. "They can't get back there then. Not that way."

"Which ones come back?"

The man regarded Bowman for a long moment. "Only when that gift is completed. Only when the hunter prays. That's the only way for the animal's spirit to get back here."

"Do they come here to rest?"

The man looked at Bowman strangely, as if Bowman were mocking him with ignorant questions. "They get their bodies here."

"But only if they are able to give their lives away in a certain manner, and if the hunter then says a prayer?"

"Yes."

After a while the man said, "Many religions have no animals. Harder for animals now. They're still trying."

Bowman did not know what to say.

"Very difficult, now," said the man.

"What do you hear in this place?" the Inuk asked abruptly. "Do you hear their songs? Do you hear them crying out?"

"In my sleep," Bowman ventured. "Or perhaps when I am awake but believe I'm sleeping. I hear a sound like a river going over a wall, or wind blowing hard in the crown of a forest. Sometimes I hear heartbeats, many heartbeats overlapping, like caribou hooves."

"The soul of the animals calling out for bodies, bodies calling out for their souls."

"The bodies and the souls, searching."

"Yes. They come together, falling in love again like that. They go back, have children. Then one day someone is hungry, someone who loves his family, who behaves that way. Wolf, human being— the same. That's how every- thing works."

"Is there another place," asked Bowman, "where the animal souls go if they are just killed?"

The Inuk looked at Bowman as if he weren't there and got up and walked away.

He didn't come back and Bowman didn't see him again.

A long the path
I pass oases
for the spirits of lovers
long dead, not yet born, present
for the moment.
They come here to frolic
sing, and soar, and love
unencumbered by the
        impositions of inches
or light years, seconds
or centuries, hunches
or convictions.
We have met here before,
        you and I
as cheetahs on the Serengeti
trees beside the Amazon
icebergs in the Arctic because
all places, times, realities
are one.
Today I am travelling
I hear a sound, and turn.
Is it you?
                —Thomas Handy Loon,
                "Precipice of Longing,"
                written in Afghanistan

The animals around Bowman's camp grew less shy. They began to move past him as though he were growing in the ground or part of the sky. The caribou all walked in the same, floating way, some pairs of eyes gleaming, some opaque, looking at the plants and lichens, at the clouds, and staring at rivulets of water moving across the tundra.

Bowman saw his gun one morning, leaning against a crate.

During his last days, he said, he tried to sketch the land. I saw the drawings—all pastels, watercolors, with some small, brilliant patches of red, purple, and yellow: flowers, dwarf willow, bearberry. The land was immense. It seemed to run up against the horizon like a wave. And yet it appeared weightless, as if it could have been canted sideways by air soft as birds breathing.

The pilot came and took him out to Qânâq, nearly five hundred miles. Two days later he began traveling south. Now, with the rest of us, he was waiting for the weather to clear.

Bowman told me this story over three days. He said it only a little at a time, as though he were not certain of it or me. I kept trying to get him to come back to it, but I wasn't insistent, not rude. I had many questions. Did the animals make sounds when their feet touched the ground? Did he see airplanes flying over? Was he afraid ever? What was the Inuk wearing?

The hardest question, for I had no other reason than my own inquisitiveness to pursue him, was asking whether he had an address where I might reach him. He gave me an address in Ames, where the university is, but by the time I wrote he'd moved away; and like so many young people—he was twenty-three, twenty-four—he did not leave a forwarding address.

Sometimes when I am in a library I look up his name. But as far as I know he never wrote anything about this, or anything else.

The last day of September the fog lifted suddenly, as though it had to go elsewhere. Bowman's plane, which had been there on the ground for eight days, left for Copenhagen and an hour later I flew with my friends back to Frobisher Bay, on Baffin Island.

Barry Lopez is the author of Arctic Dreams, Crow and Weasel, Field Notes, Of Wolves and Men, Crossing Open Ground, *and* Field Notes, *from which this story was excerpted. He is the recipient of the National Book*

Award, the John Burroughs Medal, the Christopher Medal for Humanitarian Writing (twice), and the Award in Literature from the American Academy of Arts and Letters.

MELVIN MORSE, M.D., with PAUL PERRY

✶ ✶ ✶

Tell All the Old People

Many people have already scouted
the territory ahead.

"YOU HAVE GOT TO TELL ALL THE OLD PEOPLE SO THAT THEY WON'T be afraid to die!"

I nearly choked with emotions as the little boy before me spoke these words. I remembered when I first saw him. His name was Chris. It had been four years earlier when his limp body was brought to the hospital by helicopter. He had nearly drowned after his father lost control of the sedan he was driving and plunged over a bridge and into the freezing waters of a river near Seattle. His brother and mother were in the car too. All were dazed by the impact and stunned by the horror of sinking in the dark waters.

The impact had knocked the father unconscious. The mother was left to find a way out of the rapidly filled automobile. She unfastened her seatbelt and kicked at the passenger window. Nothing happened. Then, as she told me later, "I felt an indescribable sensation go through my body, and as this happened, I was given the physical strength to kick out the window." She did this despite three compression fractures sustained during impact.

Chris's mom, Patti, swam out through the passenger window, got to the surface, and grabbed the ski rack that was attached to the top of their car. Somehow, Chris's six-year-old brother, Johnny, had also gotten out of the car, and was floating down the river, unconscious. Johnny was almost out of reach before Patti was able to grab him and push him to the top of their car, which was about a foot underwater. The father and little Chris remained trapped inside. For a terrifying moment Chris struggled as the water enveloped him. Then he lost consciousness and "went to heaven." He was submerged in the icy water for almost fifteen minutes. As we spoke in the living room of his house, he told me again in his childlike way what that voyage was like.

"When I died, I went into a huge noodle," said Chris, who was four years old when the accident happened. "It wasn't like a spiral noodle, but it was very straight, like a tunnel. When I told my mom about nearly dying, I told her it was a noodle, but now I am thinking that it must have been a tunnel, because it had a rainbow in it, and I don't think a noodle has a rainbow.

"I was being pushed along by a wind, and I could kind of float. I saw two small tunnels in front of me. One of them was animal heaven and the other one was the human heaven. First I went into the animal heaven. There were lots of flowers and there was a bee. The bee was talking to me and we were both

Like Out of Body Experiences, Near Death Experiences appear to be a universal phenomenon. They are described at length in both the eighth-century *Tibetan Book of the Dead* and the 2,500-year-old *Egyptian Book of the Dead*. In Book X of *The Republic* Plato gives a detailed account of a Greek soldier named Er, who came alive just seconds before his funeral pyre was to be lit and said that he had left his body and went through a "passageway" to the land of the dead. The Venerable Bede gives a similar account in his eighth-century work A *History of the English Church and People*, and, in fact, in her book *Otherworld Journeys* Carol Zaleski…points out that medieval literature is filled with accounts of Near Death Experiences.

—Michael Talbot,
The Holographic Universe

smelling flowers. The bee was very nice and brought me bread and honey because I was really hungry.

"Then I went to human heaven. I saw my grandmother (who had died years earlier). Then I saw heaven. Human heaven was beautiful. It was like a castle, but not one of those grungy old places. This was not a golden castle, it was just a regular old castle. As I looked at heaven, I heard music. The music was very loud and it stuck in my head. I started looking around at it, and then all of a sudden I was in the hospital. Just like that I woke up, and there were nurses standing around me. It was just that easy."

I laughed when he got to the "easy" part. As I reviewed his case history, I could see that keeping him alive wasn't easy at all. He had been underwater over ten minutes until Dennis Johnson, a carpenter who had witnessed the accident, dove repeatedly to the sunken car and pulled the young boy from the backseat. He then towed Chris to shore and revived him with mouth-to-mouth resuscitation. "I knew he was dead when I reached shore," said Johnson. "He wasn't breathing, but I had to try to bring him back to life anyway." This selfless act of heroism won Johnson a Carnegie Medal for Heroism and a Washington State Patrol Award of Merit, an honor usually reserved for state troopers. Chris was then airlifted to the nearest hospital, where further heroics were required to keep him alive.

Chris's father was the last one to be pulled from the car. He was airlifted to Harborview Hospital where extensive efforts were made to resuscitate him. He died despite the efforts.

Now, four years later, Chris was sitting in the living room of his home casually playing what sounded like avant-garde jazz on a portable keyboard. His mother said he had shown little interest in music before the accident, but afterward she had to buy him a keyboard so that he could play the hauntingly beautiful tune he had heard while traveling through the "huge noodle."

I had been invited to hear Chris's story. An acquaintance of Chris's mom was familiar with my work in near-death studies and thought that I would be interested in talking to her son about his experience at the threshold of death. Even though I have heard hundreds of children describe their near-death experiences, chills ran up my spine as I listened to Chris play the music of his experience. I taped the piece that Chris played and later had a professor of music listen to it. He said it sounded like an advanced piece of jazz being played by a child who had not yet developed the hand-eye coordination necessary to read music and play it. It sounded nothing like the kind of music I would associate with church or death.

I was deeply absorbed in the spiritual concert that was taking place.

Suddenly Chris stopped.

"I have to ask you a question," he said with the sophistication of someone ten years older. "How do I know that what happened was real? How do I know that I really went to heaven? How do I know that I wasn't just making it all up?"

I had focused on that very question myself for ten years. From the day that I heard my first near-death experience and a little girl patted me on the hand and confidently told me, "You'll see, Dr. Morse, heaven is fun," I have sought to answer the very question that Chris was asking me.

I looked around the living room as everyone waited patiently for my response. Even with the years of research I have done on this topic, this is a difficult question for me to answer. I cleared my throat and smiled nervously at Chris.

"Chris, what happened to you is as real as it gets."

Melvin Morse, M.D., and Paul Perry have written the best-sellers Closer to the Light, Transformed by the Light, *and* Parting Visions: Uses and Meanings of Pre-Death, Psychic, and Spiritual Experiences, *from which this story was excerpted. Morse is a practicing pediatrician in Seattle, Washington. Perry is the former executive editor of* American Health *magazine and lives in Scottsdale, Arizona.*

⋆ ⋆ ⋆

Restless Ghost

Who you gonna call?

THE WITCH DOCTOR PLACED HIS HAND ON MY TREMBLING SHOUL-
der and assured me I would be safe. "Mister, don't be scared. Fatima
only attacks women. She's not interested in you." Meanwhile, my
adopted sister was semiconscious on the living room couch, sweating profusely and speaking in tongues.

"Besides," he continued, "this sort of thing is common. It's nothing to get excited about."

Is it common for a woman to be possessed by a vindictive ghost?
Well, that depends on where you are. I was in Sulawesi, living with
an affluent Indonesian family that consisted of my Ibu (mother),
Bapak (father), and two bright and engaging teenage sisters—Sari
and Wati. Like most things in Indonesia, my introduction to the
spirit world occurred over food.

It was a normal evening. I ate my dinner of *sambal*, rice, and spicy
fish, as the rest of the family watched television.

After taking a few bites, though, I suddenly noticed a strange,
eerie silence in the house. For the first time since my arrival three
months earlier, the entire family was quiet. Titi, the normally chirp-
ing pet cockatoo, held his beak shut. The cats were completely still,
and my sisters were not engaging in their normal evening-time

gossip. Even the volume of the constantly blaring television set seemed subdued.

Then, in the space of about two seconds, something extraordinary happened. The cats screeched at the top of their lungs, Titi began to squawk, and Wati let out a quick, high-pitched, blood-curdling yelp before passing out on the couch.

I was stunned, but the rest of the family didn't even seem surprised. Bapak gently laid Wati down and put her head on a pillow while Ibu took out prayer beads and chanted some mysterious Arabic incantations, continuously stroking Wati's hair. Sari got some rubbing lotion. All of them appeared concerned, but not overly so. Rather than a pressing emergency, I felt they were going through a normal, though troubling, routine.

Suddenly, Wati opened her eyes. Except, she wasn't Wati.

Her dilated pupils shone with a harsh glare, and my sister's normally pleasant face had dissolved into a hard mask of stern, unyielding features. She opened her mouth, groaned, and then collapsed again into unconsciousness.

Bewildered, I finally regained my voice. "What's going on?" The family, oblivious to me until now, turned around, startled. Sari spoke first. "Don't worry, Brett. This happens from time to time. It's, it's…" She looked around nervously for help.

My mother laughed reassuringly. "It's a ghost, Brett. But don't be concerned, she only likes women. She won't attack you." Rather than provide the relief that was intended, it heightened my worries. "A ghost? There's a ghost?" I could feel my face turning white.

Wati was lying down peacefully now, and Ibu began to rub lotion on her temples, chanting prayers under her breath. Bapak picked up the telephone and walked into the kitchen. Sari answered my question.

"About two years ago, Wati went on a trip to Selajar, an island south of here. While she was there, she disrupted this evil spirit's grave. Ever since then, the ghost refuses to leave Wati alone. But don't worry, Brett. It's no big deal. Most people get possessed from time to time." I remembered what I had learned in my orientation training back in the States. It had included such laughably profound gems as "Don't judge your host culture," and "Try to understand things from their point of view." Their point of view? It's normal to be possessed by a ghost? I tried to come up with a different theory. Maybe Wati was having a seizure or heart palpitations. Maybe it was a severe mental illness. She certainly wasn't faking.

All I could stammer was, "Does this happen often?" My father entered the room to hang up the telephone. He exchanged glances with Ibu. They seemed more worried about me being upset than their daughter being unconscious. Bapak turned toward me. "This is the third time for Wati. But don't worry, Brett, I'm sure the ghost will go back to Selajar soon. I just spoke with the *dukun*. He'll help Wati get rid of this intruder." Meanwhile, my sister seemed to be resting comfortably, though her lips moved, shaping words with no sound.

Although I was worried about Wati, I was excited about meeting a witch doctor face-to-face. I hoped to see a real exorcism with holy water, chants, fire, and other eye-popping special effects. I expected an iron-willed old man, his body etched with tattoos and perhaps a bone through his hair, ready to do bloody battle with the spirit world. Instead, about an hour later, a skinny young man wearing an "Alien Nation" t-shirt and Levi's jeans knocked on the front door. With his baby face, he seemed barely out of high school, though I later found out that he was twenty-seven and considered a junior *dukun*. His boss was busy and would come that evening if there were any serious problems. I noticed his motorcycle had a "Nirvana" bumper sticker on its fender and almost asked him if Kurt Cobain was working on anything new. Maybe a duet with Jimi Hendrix? As he walked in, the *dukun* noticed my worried expression, which contrasted so completely with the rest of the family. He tried to reassure me. "Don't worry, mister. Spirits usually stay away from white people." While I was deciding whether to be relieved or insulted, the young *dukun* went up to Wati and began massaging oils into her skin. This semiwakened her and they began to speak softly. She spoke a strange language, full of grunts and hisses, which only the visitor seemed to understand.

"She is speaking Bahasa Ambon, the language of ancient Moluccas," Sari whispered to me.

After a few moments, Wati collapsed again and the *dukun* turned to the family.

"It's Fatima again. She didn't go back to Selajar like I instructed her last time because she is still angry with Wati." He sighed. "This woman has had a very bad life—and a very bad afterlife. When she was a child, the Portuguese captured her at home in the Moluccas. She was transported to Ternate, where she served as a slave for at least fifteen years. Then, without warning, she was put onboard another ship. Perhaps to work somewhere else. She doesn't know." He shrugged. "Fatima's ship was wrecked off the coast of Selajar. Because she had no burial and no one to remember her, this poor woman has been wandering around that island for over four hundred years. I think I can convince Fatima to leave, at least for a while, and then Wati will have to learn some spiritual exercises to strengthen her defenses."

The word bogey was first used in 1836 and is a semiproper name for the devil. The word is derived from Bugis, the name given to the feared pirates and traders of Sulawesi. Thackeray wrote "The people are all naughty and bogey carries them all off," and even today, parents in Europe and North America still invoke the bogeyman at bedtime, warning that if children misbehave the bogeyman might come and snatch them away. In 1865 the word was bastardized once again into bugbear, a hobgoblin reputed to devour naughty children.

—*Footprint Indonesia Handbook edited by Joshua Eliot*

I was spellbound, but my family just nodded like he had diagnosed the flu. "Like I told you last time," the *dukun* continued, "the most important news is that this is not a very dangerous ghost. She's just an ordinary spirit."

Though she might be trying to have a little fun, Fatima will not kill Wati. She'll leave as soon as she gets bored. After giving this reassurance, the *dukun* went back to work on my sister. He carefully positioned sweet-smelling incense and lumps of black dirt in strategic locations around the room. Then he leaned over the couch, rubbed Wati's head, and chanted some Arabic prayers. The entire ceremony was subdued and quiet. Slowly, my sister's eyes opened and she looked hazily out at the rest of us. Ibu went to get her some water while Bapak walked the *dukun* out. As he left, the *dukun* turned to me. "I know white people are usually very scared of ghosts, so maybe I shouldn't tell you this." Curious, I moved in closer.

"I was surprised, since this sort of spirit usually only likes women. However, she was very interested in you. In fact, Fatima asked me about you several times. She said that you remind her of her Portuguese master. As you can imagine, she didn't like you very much." He started his motorcycle and laughed. "I wouldn't worry, though. She probably won't bother you at all." Probably? For the next few weeks, I slept with the lights on. However, Fatima was never heard from again.

At least, not yet.

Brett Harris is an economist who served a two-year stint with the East-West Center in Honolulu.

THERESE SCHROEDER-SHEKER

✷ ✷ ✷

Death and the
Chalice of Repose

This is midwifery at the other end of life.

FROM LATE DECEMBER 1992 TO DECEMBER 1995, A LARGE AND
specialized team of musician-clinicians practicing the art and science of prescriptive music has attended just under 850 deathbed
vigils in every medical setting possible in Missoula, Montana. With
voice and harp, they worked in teams of two, positioning themselves
on either side of the dying patient, who was usually reclining in
bed, and attentively worked with musical deliveries that would support and facilitate the unbinding process that is central to a conscious, peaceful, or blessed death.

This palliative-medical work is a contemplative practice with
clinical applications, and is called *music-thanatology*. The sole focus of
the music-thanatology team is to lovingly attend the physical and
spiritual needs of the dying with *prescriptive music*. The deliveries
revolve around a lightly nuanced body-systems phenomenology, in
which the dynamic physiological changes in the patient's nervous,
respiratory, circulatory, and metabolic systems are observed. Within
those clinical observations in the deathbed vigil setting, the musician-clinicians surround and anoint the dying patient with music
that will support either heating or cooling, stimulating or soothing
processes in the physical body. These concrete bodily experiences

alter, color, or affect the emotional, mental, and spiritual dimensions in the individual. Unlike pharmacological dosages or protocols, no two prescriptive music deliveries can ever be the same, even if all the patients were dying of the same kind of disease. Prescriptive music is always delivered live, because it is attenuated to the changing state of the one who is dying, their breathing and respiratory rates and patterns. This cannot be accommodated with previously recorded music, no matter how beautiful and substantial the repertoire or the artistry.

Simply put, we've never yet met a single dying person who hasn't had a profound bodily experience in meeting and preparing for their own death, no matter how ready or reticent they are to "let go." When all interventional medical procedures and routes have been exhausted, and the end of life requires palliative care, music-thanatology has proven itself as a singularly effective practice, for patients, for their loved ones, and even for the physicians and nurses who have been their providers. It is such intimate work that not everyone requests it, but approximately 18 percent of the entire dying population in this city are in fact served by this modality. At St. Patrick Hospital, music-thanatology is a standard component of supportive care and is offered to anyone who requests it. The modality is not "pushed" on anyone who wants to be alone.

At one level, the work is a startlingly practical expression of spiritual practice, one that can be lived by any committed musician-clinician, regardless of religious or nonreligious personal identity. Each person has a body of meaning and values, and that is what is understood as spirituality in a medical setting, not our descriptions as humanists, Jews, Christians, Buddhists, or Muslims. The clinical practice involves *interiority* and *presence-of-being* at the deepest levels, along with an ever-increasing musical capacity. From this contemplative perspective of interiority, the work with the dying can be alternately described as *musical sacramental midwifery*. We say *musical* because the materia medica is actually created from the raw materials of tone, melody, harmony, pitch, duration, and timbre. (The materials become compound medicines, and, in that music is simultaneously physical and nonmaterial, the medicine moves right at the threshold where "spirit" and "matter" intersect.) We say *sacramental* in the original sense of the Greek word *mysterion*; how and when each of us die (*transitus*) is always a mystery, and unique in each human autobiography, if we have the courage and love to be present to witness it. We say midwife because *we* understand death as part of the fullness of life, a movement that is sacred *in* human biography regardless of the particular personal story, and worthy of being met with the same attentive care that is involved in bringing new life into the human community. Additionally, for many patients, surviving loved ones, and clinicians, death is not an end, but a birth or transformation to another state or level. The intention of the music-thanatologist is simply and unconditionally to serve the patient's passage with prescriptive music, regardless of their beliefs, identities, or orientations. However, we know that a medical practice devoted exclusively to the needs of the dying requires a profound depth and commitment, not a mere technical fingertip or laryngeal proficiency. That is why the contemplative dimension of this work is so central: anything less spells "burn out" for the clinician within a very short time.

The historical inspiration for this work comes from the Western tradition of monastic medicine. Among many other courses, academic and contemplative, music-thanatologists do study the earliest Cluniac monastic-medical practices that were described in the eleventh century monastic customaries of Bernard and Odo. They also study the regular courses that would be expected in a biomedical model.

The actual clinical inspiration for this work came through a thoroughly contemporary experience that occurred in a geriatric home more than two decades ago. I have been involved in the musical deathbed vigil in one way or another constantly since then, and during these two decades, it has grown into a full-scale, multi-institutional clinical practice and a graduate-level school now located within St. Patrick Hospital. People often ask about the first vigil, the one twenty years ago. It was only an hour or two, but it changed my life, and subsequently, the deaths of many others. The first nineteen years of this work evolved in Denver hospitals, with the assistance and support of Regis University and the graduate school of theology at St. Thomas Seminary, but emerged as a palliative-medical national pilot program in the little university town of Missoula, Montana. The majority of our students enter the program as non-harpists and nonsingers, and leave after having become truly musical. They are transformed, ready, and desiring to serve the needs of the dying in whole new ways. Here is the original story that drew them to us. It is one of intimacy, reverence, and beauty.

I have come to understand that the first time I was ever actually present and alone with someone who was in fact dying is also the first time that I ever really experienced *silence,* and an indescribably delicate kind of light. The man had emphysema; he was struggling, frightened, unable to breathe. No more mechanical ventilations, tracheotomies, or surgical procedures could resolve his disintegrated lungs. He could take no more in, could swallow no more, and, in his complete weariness, there was almost nothing he could return to the world. The room was filled with his fear and agony. I climbed into his hospital bed and propped myself behind him in midwifery position, my head and heart lined up behind his, my legs folded near his waist, and I held his frail body by the elbows and suspended his weight. At first I held us both in interior prayer, but soon began leaning down to his left ear and singing Gregorian chant in an almost inaudible pianissimo: "The Kyrie" from the *Mass of the Angels,* the "Adoro te devote," the "Ubi caritas," the "Salve Regine."

He immediately nestled in my arms and began to breathe regularly, and we as a team, breathed together. It was as if the way in

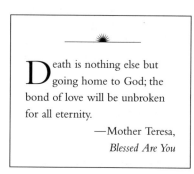

Death is nothing else but going home to God; the bond of love will be unbroken for all eternity.
                    —Mother Teresa,
                    Blessed Are You

which sound anointed him now made up for the ways in which he had never been touched or returned touch while living the life of a man. The chants seemed to bring him balance, dissolving fears, and compensating for those issues still full of sting. How could they do anything less? These chants are the language of love. They carry the flaming power of hundreds of years and thousands of chanters who have sung these prayers before. It seemed that the two of us were not alone in that room. Long after his heart ceased to beat, I was allowed to hold him. Almost twenty years later, the silence that replaced his struggle and that was present in his room has continued to penetrate the core of my life, birthing stages of hearing that even now flower at unexpected times and places.

When you are really peacefully present with someone whose time has come, all that matters is that they shine through the matrix. People ask if a midwife knows fear or sorrow: None of that exists if you are *with* the dying person. It's *their* time, not yours. Any burden or sorrow or wounds of your own disappear. You hold the person and keep vigil while they quietly, almost invisibly, shimmer an indescribable membrane of light. If there is no tenderness in the room, this film dissolves unnoticed. If a midwife is practicing inner emptiness, and is capable of profound stillness, she/he can guard this gossamer film for a moment or an hour. When a dying person's stillness fills an entire room, you can gently let go and lay them to rest. Then you thank them, again and again, for affirming what is so bright.

The mandatory practice of silence and inner emptiness creates a spiritual reservoir that teaches the importance of alternating sound with periods of silence. Hildegard of Bingen suggests that hearing is *receiving*, and as such, the reception of some rare experiences (one hears both sounds and souls) can cause the hardness of your heart to be shattered. When that kind of hearing has penetrated your center with a seemingly luminous wound, the place where you've been pierced can *only* be filled with an entirely new kind of love.

This new radiance must be returned and sung continually, or you burn. This burning is a grace, and it is this kind of singing that anoints a dying person: it is audible warmth and has the silver sound. This warmth helps someone slip from a body of pain into a birth canal.

It is clear that all work with death and dying is about the reception of spirit into matter, and the dissolution of matter into spirit. A conscious death changes everyone involved. The one singing vigil breathes in light, but the one who has just crossed the threshold becomes a source of luminosity. These transformative moments weave shining vestments for our living: we wear them when we celebrate. Together, the living and the dying form choirs of celebrants who bridge the two worlds by dissolving and creating themselves in the mystical body of Christ or the Rainbow body of Buddhism: in either case, the activity is a source of light for the universe.

Every death is exceptional, but it is the ability to hear and draw inspiration from the burning reservoir of silence that allows you to sing vigil for any person who asks you to come. You walk into the room, wondering: Can I put aside my baggage today? Can I be still? Can I make room to receive? Can I hear what they need? In the end, you thank them, again and again, for transforming you fully into your life of song.

Therese Schroeder-Sheker is Academic Dean at the School of Music-Thanatology with the Chalice of Repose Project, St. Patrick Hospital, Missoula, Montana. She is also a recording artist.

SYDNEY LEA

✦ ✦ ✦

Presences

Sometimes listening is the
better part of seeing.

BECAUSE THE FISH MUST HAVE WEIGHED FIVE POUNDS; BECAUSE
she'd been game beyond words; because she was a brown trout; because each little spot on her flanks wore its own pale halo; because
of her shape's sleekness as I held her in the riffle till she recovered
and swam back into deeper, unbroken water; because this was the
fish I'd traveled for—I lay down in the Wyoming sun to nap.
September-cool: not a cloud, not a biting bug.

The cottonwood deadfall on the gravel bar had composted, so
that the trunk, once rough, now made a fine pillow. I put down my
head, all full of the recent perfection. Because the moment had been
the stuff of dreams, only dream could be adequate to it.

And I was tired: from the hike to the river; from the minutes in
its water, which scarcely looked to be moving, but which was impe-
rious when you stood in it; from the concentration that such a fish
demands. I stretched out, convinced that some spiritual benchmark
in my life had established itself, and that whatever might afterward
befall me, I'd have it as an abiding reference.

What you see in today's dream, it's often said, relates directly to
something in today's not-dream. Joey and I had roamed this
country for a week, dawn till dark, without encountering so much

as fresh sign of bear; but as I reclined, the sunlight just warm enough on my face, the sand smoother than any bed, the cottonwood pillow almost itself a part of slumber, the grizzly came.

We'd imagined him for days, and that was apparently enough, was a way of seeing him.

I don't mean that the animal was visible, nor that my sleep was really sleep so much as that half-wakefulness in which sensory detail seems both ordinary and eloquent of a different, a visionary realm.

I knew of the bear's presence because of the wind, which had doubtless been there all along—there as I approached the pool where the big fish and some smaller others were sipping those blue-wings; there as I laid down the cast and my fly drifted over the brown trout's lie and she shot up to have at it.

But in the midst of the stalk and the battle, my mind didn't register the sound, huge air forcing its way through high gaps. Though the air didn't move on the beach where I lay, the passes above were full of somber glissandi, like the musical theme in a frightening film that portends The Awe-Inspiring Thing. And what out here would that thing be besides *Ursus arctos horribilis?*

Even now I believed I could hear the scuff of his pads on the sand-beach, the faint cough of surprise at my scent. He needn't charge but simply and casually walk, all mammoth head and shoulders, to where I lay; then he'd paw me from under the dead-fall like a grub.

No sense for me to bolt—this is an animal that can outsprint a bloodhorse—especially in my heavy, ridiculous waders. You're supposed to climb, because a grizzly doesn't do the same. But the only tree within fifty yards was the fallen one under which I huddled now, almost awake. This was still mostly a dream, I could pray, and so maybe in slumber I looked dead. Because that's the last recourse when the grizzly addresses you: play dead. Joey and I had joked about this. Sure: play dead while 800 pounds of mammal thunders over the earth, the froth from his maw trailing in the breeze, glinting in the last of the sun you'll ever see.

All nonsense, of course. I woke to a water ouzel, disappearing now and then under the surface to fossick for bugs; to an eagle's high screams, faint in the windy clamor, to the purr of the river where it swung through an elbow.

Yet there had been a presence. I am sure of it even now. Perhaps it was facile to associate it with bear, but there'd been something.

I once thought to make a cartoon of myself. Its first panel would show me in woods or moving water, grasping a gun or rod; in the thought balloon over my head I'd be sitting before a typewriter. In the second panel, you'd see me before that same typewriter, but the thought balloon would show me standing with gun or rod in woods or moving water. For I am a man, by turns, in the outdoors with his head full of books and words, and a man in books and words with his head full of the outdoors. Yet I hope that at moments these men are merged, even if such moments exist in my poems alone.

One day—about eight weeks after the wind-driven vision of that Wyoming grizzly—I sat for hours, writing at something without much success. In my frustration I began to meditate on what now and then seems the paucity of milestones in my life. Such self-pity is a loathsome defect of my character: what better monument after all might I leave than my children, the second of whom, a daughter, ten years old at the time, had chosen this day for a house party? I'd stayed at home as token chaperone: Erika's guests were all female schoolmates, well behaved, completely capable of amusing themselves as young girls do—with chat, inventive games, humor.

After the first hour of the party, I saw my irrelevance to it, and perhaps my intrusion. So I advised the kids that I'd be in my office if they needed me, as of course they would not.

Perhaps I needed *them*. In the absence of their patter and shuffle—or the presence of my typewriter's mocking silence—I inwardly moaned that this was a day neither fish nor fowl. I might have gotten an angle on some piece of poetry and been by now some way towards its final draft; but no. I might have abandoned the project and taken myself outdoors, but not that either.

And now I recognized that this fall I'd spent less time than usual outdoors, fewer hours pursuing the grouse among draw, covert, side hill. The wild provender in my freezer was not what it's normally been. The end of shotgun season loomed; I'd have to count on a deer. The bare shelves downstairs became, in this mood, an ungainly metaphor.

But surely all this just signaled slow blood. I simply needed some action, and if it could not come in verbal form, I'd go perspire. I find sweat an almost totally reliable curative. Having checked to see that he was at home, I wrote down the number of a neighbor, then told my daughter and her friends I'd be back soon. They nodded distractedly, then turned again to the play they were rehearsing. I made to complain about how they'd dragged their props—cookware and clothing and bedcovers—into the living room, but thought better.

When I unlocked the kennel doors, the dogs nearly bowled me over. The younger and quicker of the pointers threw gravel at the end of our driveway, leaning into the corner down the woods road. I tooted her halfway back on the whistle, not wanting her out of earshot. The retriever, as usual, made a short dash, lifted a leg, then rushed back to be patted, and the old pointer, grown more meditative than her kennelmate with the hardworking years, pottered and nipped, in that inexplicable doggy way, at a few remaining stalks of grass.

I jogged, carefully, the dogs dashing back and forth by my legs. It had sleeted the night before, then lightly frozen. There were patches of ice along the twitch road, which runs downhill from home a few hundred yards. Where it peters out, there's something like a northward trail—made by game, by me and my dogs in our rambles—to the top of Stonehouse Mountain. It climbs 1,800 feet in less than a mile, over slippery, lichen-covered granite. The soil here pushed settlers out almost as they arrived, their labor fragmentarily evident in stone fences that show all through the woods; occasional boulder-banked cellar holes; barn foundations; a rusted bolt or the spirit of a sugar vat or a hinge.

I made my way at a pace just properly taxing, so that the blood coursed in my ears and my breath came in rhythmic heaves. To make them shed their ice and straighten out of my way, I knocked at the bent saplings before me with a staff.

The therapy was working. I dropped my outer shirt by the side of the trail. I'd make a loop, then fetch it on the way home. My undershirt went wet with the forest moisture, but also with my own, which was what I'd been wanting. I thought how the poem left in my typewriter might write itself out here, if I made sure not to think about it.

I'd had certain things happen, or not, for years.

My legs felt strong and my wind full. I was a long way from dead.

High air when I dreamed the bear, and more air to come, I gulped it that morning of my daughter's party. But just now I'm back in a different season from the same climb. Uphill, the woods were between the trillium—which have collapsed into their own cadaverous rankness—and the wild ladyslippers, little smug burghers that salute the birth of true summer.

But never mind such poetical cant for a moment, for I am also recently back from burying Larry, whose lungs had finally been torn down by the cancer in them, and in everything else, it seems, but his brain, which stayed clear to the end.

I first knew Larry when we both were three. He grew into a freckled, blocky Irish boy, tough and volatile. At length the toughness and volatility got mixed up with much too much booze, and he turned into a mean young man—then a middle-aged bum, flim-flam, mess. Five years ago, he phoned me, drunk enough to call at 3 A.M., lucid enough to scream that he was in trouble: he'd awakened the morning before on an interstate highway, unsure whether this was Florida or Georgia or Mississippi, whether the car was bought or stolen or borrowed.

What could he do?

I told him he could opt to die or not to.

For two years, I took other such phone calls, always in the middle of the night, the words slurring through long-distance static. When I got the last of these rescue signals, I summoned up what little hardness I had: "Larry, I don't want to hear from you again unless you haven't had a drink for twenty-four hours." The phone clicked, and I lay awake, wondering if he was as suicidal as he claimed.

A year went by, and I heard from him again. I listened with my best ear as he got through the small talk. His voice had a crispness, greater even than when he'd been a healthy, hell-raising kid, back in our school days.

"You haven't had a drink," I said.

"Not since the last time I talked to you." I could picture the old smile that made his freckles swim.

We stayed in touch, by mail and phone, through the short years after. The poor man couldn't get a break, yet he was sticking it out.

He was a grocery clerk when he was diagnosed.

Larry had felt sick since midwinter, but he'd needed to work long enough to get company medical insurance before he could afford to see a doctor. By then it was too late, though it would probably have been in any case.

"Where *is* the cancer?" I breathed into the telephone, horrified.

"Where *isn't* it?" he answered. "Liver, lung, bone…"

"It makes me lonely all over."

"It'll be all right."

"But it's sad."

"Sure. But there could have been something sadder."

"What?"

"I could have died the way I was."

I didn't see him again; he was gone before I could get to the city where he lay. And, in fact, before he died I came to think of his cancer for some reason as a city itself, slum infested, beyond any law. I pictured the breeze-blown detritus: plastic wrappers, cinders, tabloid pages. I envisioned the morass of grime from which winked broken wine bottles, shards of ruined windshield, those little sharp pop-top keys. The disease was an inner urban sprawl, dark figures in every aperture and alley.

Yet an angel came to that city. An angel and one other.

Before we buried Larry on that cloudless May afternoon a few days ago—all his friends from school years gathered at the plot— his brother told me a strange thing or two. He reminded me first, however, that although his pain was overwhelming, Larry turned down morphine, insisting that his head remain clear.

At 6:45 he told his brother that their mother—dead long since from cancer herself—stood in the room. She was not visible, he explained, but she was there, and she bore a message of assurance.

Just a few minutes later, the mother left and Jesus arrived. Or so Larry claimed; then he turned to that Presence, whatever it was, and said, "I love you."

At seven in the evening exactly, Larry died.

At the same hour, Larry's sister was stabbed seven times by an assailant in her bookshop. She survived; indeed, she was standing among us at the burial ground. And after the funeral, another friend of ours told me how a light had followed him as he walked from his office to his car at seven o'clock. Yet another told how he'd had an appointment

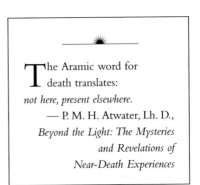

The Aramic word for death translates:
not here, present elsewhere.
— P. M. H. Atwater, Lh. D.,
*Beyond the Light: The Mysteries
and Revelations of
Near-Death Experiences*

that day in Pittsburgh, how he'd misread directions, how he'd pulled over to roadside at the scheduled hour—seven—and concluded that he was lost, forever, beyond recall. Then I remembered the sudden exhaustion that came over me at the identical hour, when my wife and I always read to our three-year-old before putting him to bed. I slept a sleep like death till nine the next morning.

I make no elaborate case here. I seek neither to persuade anyone of anything, nor even to assert that my life has changed—for it likely hasn't: it seems, yes, that they arrive, those spiritual benchmarks in a life; one pledges to attend to them; and at length one goes right on as ever.

Though many of us survivors had drifted out of touch with one another, as with Larry, over the decades, we quickly fell into the old closeness—no, it was a greater closeness, the posturing of male adolescence corrected not only by our aging but also by the dead man's final heroism and serenity. His was the Presence of that day, its genius.

I do not climb for the view alone, since I've got it by heart. Indeed I almost prefer to climb into fog, the kind that cloaked the mountaintop in the forenoon of my daughter's house party. I felt as though I'd stepped into another element altogether, as though I were underwater but able to breathe. Such a thought lifted me back to the Wyoming streamside, to the moment when the brown trout—having taken my little dun, having fought with the courage of wild things against me—quivered for a minute or two in my hand. A moment before I let her go back to her pool. Before the bear arrived.

I can *will* such details into memory, if I choose; but I prefer them to recur by means of some unexpected, unwilled association as they did on Stonehouse Mountain, the day's wetness suddenly transporting me. The spots on the fish's belly and loins reappeared in mind, each brighter than a new-minted coin, each distinct, and—a thousand and more miles away—the air I breathed became freighted with the scent of western rapids and hot stones and fly repellent and bison dung, as well as with the glorious odors of the White Mountains where I lived. And they and the Wyoming mountains I'd visited rolled together, and life seemed all it could ever be.

Coming out of my reverie, I notice a dainty doe's track through the frost that lingered above 2,000 feet. She had crossed the trail on tiptoes; just then I preferred that print to a heel-heavy buck's for a sign. Coarse and heavy myself—bearded, 200 pounds, sweaty, my boots all mire—I was in the domain of delicacy.

I did not worry for my dogs; they'd long since been deer-broken. They champed and thrashed in the understory to either side as I stooped and read the doe's track, fresh enough to fill with fogwater as I beheld it. I closed my eyes, and the fish swam through that water, and the stream out west flowed into it, and it reflected that overhead glory of an early Teton fall, so deep it's something other than blue.

But I was an ignorant man, and I still am.

Uphill forty more yards, two granite slabs leaned together, making a cave. There was no evidence yet of traffic in and out. Come winter, it would shelter a fox or perhaps a second-year cub. Just now,

I fancied it underwater too, and my fish peering from it, suspicious.

At home, the schoolgirls were play-acting. I imagined them as mermaids, or water sprites. Why not? Uninvited to their free-form dramas, I could go on surmising that their visions, like mine, were aquatic today, even though at this time of year I'd normally be pre-occupied—in imagination and action alike—with earth and air. It was still legally hunting season for birds, crouching on the woods-floor, leaping into low sky before my pointers. But water it was, even though there'd be a long, hard winter before the runoff, the spate, the ebb, the occasion to look for a trout nearby.

Perhaps my thoughts ran as they did because I couldn't have hunted in any case. Not only did I have to be roughly within sum-moning distance, nine girls in my house and my wife and our other children away for the day, but also the going would have been too hard for me and my dogs. It's one thing to take an hour or so and follow a trail, however sketchy, to the top of a mountain; it's quite another to break through sodden, icy brush all day.

I'll let the shotgun season die in peace, I concluded, and—that resolve turning me melancholy again—I forged on. The sweat had started to cool, and I was breathing too shallowly. My fish had swum into her cave again, and when I willed her out, she looked different, like an exhibit in some tawdry sporting museum. I let her swim back in.

My younger pointer bitch shot across the trail ahead of me, leap-ing her slower brace-mate, who trotted the other way. Each cast an eye toward me, checking in. "All right!" I called, and they hurried on. Yet I thought suddenly how I'd missed the retriever for a few minutes. He wouldn't have gone far; he never does. But having once lost a dog on such a hike—he got out of hearing, he never came back—I'm more cautious even than I need to be.

I gave four short, quick blasts on the whistle, and waited. Two more minutes went by, and I was mildly unnerved. He is the most reliable, the most companionable, the least rangy of my three. I blasted again, and again I waited. Two more minutes and no retriever.

This went on. I had last seen him fifty or sixty yards back down the trail. I dropped my plan to get to height-of-land; that peak would abide forever, but a dog is mortal, and now suddenly I wanted him more than anything on earth.

My soul ached for a dog…who showed himself in the next instant, by the side of the trail, near where I'd left him a few minutes ago. I scowled and bellowed his name and shrilled at the whistle. He lifted his muzzle momentarily, then, hunching his shoulders and grinning in that manner of a dog embarrassed, he disobeyed me, lowering his head again to whatever it was he sniffed there by the mossy, overturned basswood.

I lifted my stick as if to threaten a beating, but he kept busy with something—something no doubt extraordinary, because he is the most biddable of dogs and never resists me. I stood stock-still for a moment, perplexed: this is a duck dog, a retriever, but he might for all the world have been pointing just then, at whatever it was, flattened to blend with the umbers and beiges of the late-fall carpet.

Suddenly I heard that midrange howl of wind I recalled from the day the dream-bear approached. It must have been blowing between the tops of Stonehouse and Mousley right along, but my crunching bootsoles and my heavy breathing and my water-fantasies must have deafened me to it, even if the trees and the brush were all sideways now in the gale. Since there is scarcely a thing in the New England woods besides the woods themselves to hurt you, I can't say what I felt, hearing that music again: maybe only the vestige of a fear felt in another place.

I walked the few steps to my dog. He had something all right, though he had not taken it up in his mouth. I squatted and saw that it was the severed tail of a red fox, which, despite the dull gray of a cloudy autumn, glinted brightly, its ice-beads like pearls.

The sleet storm of the preceding night had buried whatever sign might have surrounded this foxtail, and there was no trace of the rest of the corpse. Does the animal trot somewhere even now, ridiculous without his fine brush? Or is he dead and devoured almost entirely, nothing left but this muff of hair over frail bone, splendid, bejeweled? And what might have killed him? A fisher, a lucky bear or coyote, a rover dog?

The sound of the wind in the pass was louder and louder, or was it my thoughts that made the crescendo?

It was beautiful, that unbloodied remnant, full with the imminence of white winter, a deep scarlet with undertones of silver. I thought of my daughter Erika, and how I must bring this bolt of fur back to her and her Thespian troupe. I imagined their widened eyes. Perhaps Erika would want to hang it in her room. If not, I thought, I would nail it to the shed wall between the two kennel doors. It would look good there.

But as I reached to take the foxtail up, the wind's roar moved to a still louder pitch, and I could not lift what I meant to lift. I contemplated it, rather—long and sleek, like the body of that trout I'd released. The wind still bore an uncertain burden. I straightened, my eye yet fixed on the dazzling fur before me; but in my lateral vision, there was something I could almost see. I could certainly feel it.

I remain an ignorant man, far too much so to say I was touched then by any spirit from the natural world, the human world, or any imaginable other.

But something was there.

Sydney Lea is author of A Place in Mind, Hunting the Whole Way Home, *and seven verse collections, including* To the Bone: New and Selected Poems. *He teaches in the MFA in Writing Program at Vermont College.*

⋆ ⁎ ⋆

The Survivor

Savage grace leads him forward.

DEAN REYNOLDS CAME FLOATING INTO THE CAFÉ, LOOKING LIKE AN insect in big glasses, a yellow bandanna wrapped around his head. If I hadn't already heard that Dean was a long-term survivor of AIDS, I would never have guessed it. His age was unclear, but what I couldn't mistake was the quality of his energy, festive, gossipy, amused. I liked Dean Reynolds at once.

"Honey, those Zen Buddhists are a bunch of drips," he said, patting my hand and following the waiters' buttocks with his eyes as they flexed past him toward the kitchen.

"Are they really?"

"Ghouls, my dear," Dean assured me. "So judgmental, so serious. I've gone past them now."

Dean told me his story. He had been a Wall Street banker and art maven in New York, a smart-boy party animal, hanging with Andy Warhol and his cronies, making buckets of money and generally running himself into the ground.

"I couldn't stop," he said. "I was spinning, spinning, too much to do and all of it so *exciting*. I mean, who in his right mind would stay home when Andy called? Who'd stay sober when you could do lines and watch the strippers at 54? I was young, I was hot, I was loaded. It was like being at one long fabulous party. But you know what those parties are like at 5 A.M., when half the people have passed out, the place stinks, the sun's coming up, and you just can't face it? Well, my life started to feel like 5 A.M. The music stopped, and there I was, burned out, hung over, completely lost. I needed an excuse to get out. So I got sick."

"On purpose?"

"That's a complex question. Did I get fucked by somebody who was sick on purpose? No. I just got fucked by everybody. But there was a definite connection between my burning out, my needing a reason to leave New York, my emptiness—and my disease. Without question. I got my first lesion on a Thursday, gave notice on a Friday, and moved to a monastery near San Francisco two weeks later. That was five years ago, and it's keeping me alive."

"The monastery?"

"Being free, being away from that world, having permission to live the way I want to live. This disease has been my savior."

"Most people don't buy that," I said, thinking of the patronizing looks I'd gotten when I suggested that this virus had actually saved my life.

"They're scared. It's too much for them to take in. I've seen street kids—I mean real scum-bucket hustlers—come to the hospice with AIDS and turn their lives around. One of them was ordained as a priest a couple of months before he died. This is the fast track to enlightenment, honey."

"Tell me."

"Not that I'm enlightened," Dean continued, "but the fact that I'm sitting here proves something. I was supposed to be dead three years ago. My numbers say I shouldn't be alive. It's almost embarrassing when I go to my doctors now. It's like, 'Sorry I'm proving you wrong,' but the fact of the matter is that they don't know a goddamn thing about what the spirit can do."

"How do you explain it?"

"Little pops," said Dean, snapping his fingers. "Satoris—like something popping in your brain. When I'm least expecting it, not on the *zafu* necessarily—but on a bus, in the hospital, even when

I'm sleeping—there are these little snaps when everything comes together and I feel incredibly light. Suddenly, in those moments. I can see it."

"What?"

"The world as it *really* is. I see love in people's faces, even when there's pain. Your heart breaks and something unbelievably sweet comes out. Everything seems luminous." Dean cut himself short.

"Please," I encouraged, transported by what he was saying.

"When it comes, I can actually see that life is a *rapture*. All of it, even the torment. But words can't really capture the feeling." Dean took a packet of pills from his pocket and swallowed them. "Unfortunately," he contin-

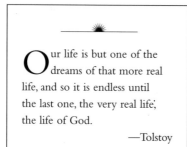

Our life is but one of the dreams of that more real life, and so it is endless until the last one, the very real life; the life of God.

—Tolstoy

ued, "the Buddhists were not amused by me. As soon as I started wanting to venture out, let loose, *live* a little, the axe came down. But when you know you're going to die, you don't care about that dogmatic shit. You're looking at something so much bigger. It's not a hobby; it's a matter of life and death."

"My therapist used to say that when you really see how dangerous life is, you find your way to spiritual practice like a cockroach finds a crack." I said.

"But when your disease becomes your practice, it's even better," said Dean. "Take it from me, I've been pricked and prodded and bled and hosed out from one end of this body to the other. There isn't a hole they haven't pumped or an inch of skin they haven't zapped with radioactivity. But I swear on everything I know and love that it's those satori moments, those little snaps of bliss, that are keeping me alive. My Buddhist friends say it's just more illusion, more attachment, but I love those moments more than anything I've loved in my lifetime, and if it's wrong to be attached to them, well tough. The heart can't survive without hope."

"Even when what you hope for isn't possible?"

"Hope doesn't need an object. Hope is a feeling; it says the world will continue, whether I'm in this body or not. You know the painting of *Hope* in the Tate Gallery?"

"A blindfolded woman playing a harp with one string."

"Yes," he answered. "And do you know why she plays?"

"Because she'd be a fool not to?"

"Exactly," said Dean.

Mark Matousek has written for Details, Harper's Bazaar, The Village Voice, Common Boundary, Poz, Utne Reader, *and many other publications. A former senior editor of* Interview *magazine, he is the author of* Sex, Death, Enlightenment: A True Story, *from which this piece was excerpted.*

Three times in ecstasy
in the month of Aug. 2019

FRED ALAN WOLF

⋆ ⋆ ⋆

Visit to a
Parallel Universe

A physicist explores another realm.

IT HAPPENS FROM TIME TO TIME, USUALLY WHEN I AM NOT EXPECTing it, often after a sleepless period of tossing and turning. The first time it happened was in the fall of 1973. I was a visiting professor at Birkbeck College at the University of London. I had retired about 10 P.M. after returning from my office at Birkbeck. At 2 A.M. I was awake, my mind was filled with physics equations—something to do with parallel universes, other worlds nearly exactly like our own, but somehow different.

Quantum mechanics opens the door to such ideas, and I had been fortunate enough to be at Birkbeck where John Hasted and David Bohm were cochairing the physics department. Hasted was beginning to investigate parallel universe theory to explain some weird paranormal effects that he had observed in his lab. Bohm had been working since the early '50s at the roots of quantum physics, like a patient gardener. Both men must have had their influence on me that night.

I went to the dining table in my apartment so that I wouldn't disturb my sleeping housemate, Nancy. After feverishly writing down a series of seemingly indecipherable hieroglyphics on my paper pad I felt a deep sense of satisfaction and grew drowsy. I went immediately to bed and fell asleep.

Now when I say I "fell asleep," I mean more than you may think. I felt myself falling down a deep and dark well or tunnel. Yet every so often I would stop falling and find myself involved in a scene, as if I were an actor suddenly appearing on a stage. These scenes just appeared and I was enmeshed in them. I was not just an observer but was actually "there." Quickly the scene would change, and I would find myself in yet another scene, entirely different from the one I had just left. These scene changes happened so rapidly that I felt I was descending from one layer of the universe to another, slipping through time and space just as a small pebble slips through the woven mesh of a fabric. As I descended I became more and more aware that I was dreaming. It was dawning on me that I was both snuggled cozily in bed and slipping through space-

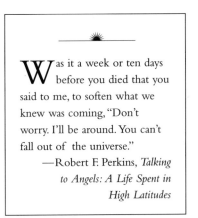

Was it a week or ten days before you died that you said to me, to soften what we knew was coming, "Don't worry. I'll be around. You can't fall out of the universe."
—Robert F. Perkins, *Talking to Angels: A Life Spent in High Latitudes*

time in a dream of uncanny proportions. It was as if my awareness were split in two. To my great surprise I was conscious that I was asleep. What a contradiction! How can you be asleep and conscious at the same time?

Next I found myself awakening, but I was shocked to discover that I had not actually awakened at all: I was dreaming that I was awakening and I knew it! No sooner had I realized that I was still dreaming than I would awaken once more from the dream to dream that I was awakening once again. It was like ascending through a set of Chinese boxes: as soon as I was out of one box I found that I was inside of another, still larger box. I soon realized that I was in control of my dream. I could awaken for real or I could descend to any universe layer I wished and experience my dream consciously. I then decided to explore and instantly found myself in the strangest room that I had ever been in.

The room was shaped like a large cylinder and appeared to have a dirt floor. When I looked up, I saw a clear blue sky shining through what seemed to be an open roof. I found myself standing next to the room's outer wall and began to feel its texture. I was amazed to notice that I could feel the wall and that it felt neither cold nor warm to my touch but instead had a somewhat rough texture, like coarse woven fabric or basket weave. Then something quite strange happened to me.

I noticed that I was rising or floating upward in the room and immediately felt a sense of panic. This anxiety halted my rise and I descended to the floor once more. I "remembered" myself sleeping comfortably back in my earthly abode and breathed a sigh of relief. With my relaxing I immediately began to rise again toward the open roof. Again I felt fear and began to descend. With this new knowledge I experimented with rising and sinking and noticed that all I had to do to descend was feel fear. To rise all I had to do was relax. I was just getting used to my new environment and had ascended fairly close to the blue skylight when I sensed the presence of another person in the room.

Looking down I saw below me the "caretaker," a kindly but blurry-looking old fellow. My vision, I discovered, was as nearsighted as it was normally on earth. The "caretaker" announced himself to me and jovially said, "Hello, you must be new here. Come on down and I'll show you around."

Now, when I say he announced himself to me, I don't mean that he spoke. I just heard him in my mind. I couldn't describe his voice. I wasn't even sure if he was a "he." It was a kind of instant thought communication. I thought and he heard my thought. He thought and I heard his communication. I heard no sound, but I sensed his words as clearly as if he had actually spoken. And he sensed my words in the same apparent manner.

Next we walked side by side out of the room through a nondescript doorway. I found myself walking with him silently and had the feeling that I was in a quiet, beautiful countryside of rolling hills. This is how the surrounding scenery appeared to me. I say I "felt" this was the case because my feelings and my visual sensing of the surroundings were somehow the same. What I felt matched what I saw and vice versa. This is difficult to describe in words.

We continued to walk around and I sensed a great relaxation and peace. The sky was blue and cloudless. There was no sun anywhere. The grass was greener than any grass I had ever seen. I soon noticed that there was a low brick wall, perhaps three feet high, weaving through the hills and greenery. Soon I "heard" voices and saw a large group of people just ahead of us. I realized that the silent "caretaker" was leading me to the people who were sitting comfortably on the low wall and the grassy areas it enclosed.

My entrance into the group stirred no response. I was just another person there. I felt as if I had come to a picnic and yet I noticed that there was no food in sight. And still no one was paying me the slightest bit of attention.

I then began to look around at the faces of my new associates. I must point out how unusual all this was to me, because at any moment I could "remember" myself sleeping in bed at home in Shepard's Bush, London W6. "I" was where I was and "I" was home at the same time. This experience of remembering was exactly the same as when you think back to a past experience, the only difference being that in waking consciousness you can't "return" to your memory. In my altered, or lucid, dream state I not only remembered my sleeping self, I knew I could return any time I wished to.

The reason I was thinking about going home was the bizarre physiognomy I was suddenly gifted with. I merely had to look at a face, any face, and I "saw." More than seeing, I knew. The facts of the personality were an open book to me. I merely looked at a face and it would undergo a series of transformations, each change revealing a new fact. I couldn't look too closely because, frankly, I was frightened by what I saw. On every face was great sadness and pain. The faces were normal when looked at quickly, but when examined for any length of time they became grotesque masks with great striations of contorted pain lines, hideous peelings of unfolding skin layers, and throbbing nerve threads all pulsating on raw skin. Suddenly I realized where I was and announced to myself, i.e., thought to myself, I was on the astral plane of suicides. These people had committed suicide on earth and were waiting to reincarnate—to return to Earth and be reborn. But there was a slight problem. In order for them to return they had to be acceptable to all the "normal" nonsuicidal souls they will share a body with. That is why they were here: to await humanity's decision.

Each of us is a universe of souls, not just a single soul journeying from here to Timbuktu. As the Buddha taught, we are all questions of compromise. Each of us is a universe of past lives, and some of us living now owe a debt of gratitude to the others for allowing us to live again. These suicides were the astral-level component, the parallel-universe level of reality, of past failures in life. We all have in us the lives of past failures, murderers, rapists, saints, and sinners.

This realization appeared to me as a thought, but I had made a mistake. I had thought to myself, not realizing that my thoughts were open books to my fellow "travelers." And even worse, what in all hell was I doing there in the first place? Just then I noticed "her." She was sitting on the wall facing me and, gulp, she was looking directly at me and smiling. I heard her reply, "Oh, you know where you are? Who are you? Where do you come from?" She approached me in an overly

The word *hell* is actually Scandinavian and refers to Hel, the Teutonic queen of the dead and ruler of "the other world." According to Norse myth, "to Hel" is where people went who were good, but not quite good enough to transcend to Valhalla, that heavenly hall reserved for heroes killed in battle and other special folk. Unlike more modern symbols depicting satanic figures and being burned for one's sins, there was nothing evil or scary about Hell (or Hel herself, except her looks). She was said to be deformed, with half of her face human and the other half featureless. Over time allusions to Hel connoted "an abode of the dead," not some place of everlasting punishment.
—P. M. H. Atwater, Lh.D.,
Beyond the Light: The Mysteries and Revelations of Near-Death Experiences

friendly manner. I boasted, "Yes, I know where I am and I can return home any time I want to."

"You can, can you?" she asked with great interest as she came close to me. I was getting frightened. This was my first trip, and I didn't know what danger I might be in by my just being there. Then I looked at her eyes. I don't quite know how to describe what I saw, but her eyes began to spin. They appeared to me as rotating pinwheels of spiraling colors. She was now too close for comfort. I knew then that I had to leave, and I exercised the "leaving ritual," the only one I knew would get me out of there fast. I yelled bloody murder.

I awoke in bed next to Nancy, and this time for real. It must have been past four in the morning, and Nancy wasn't too happy to have me just pop up in bed talking a blue streak. I not only was wide awake, I was fully conscious and quite lucid and gregarious. Loudly I said to her, "Nancy, wake up. I must describe this dream to you now before I forget it." Nancy, hardly believing her eyes or ears, was rudely being shaken from a deep sleep of her own. And dazed but understanding, she listened to the story of my voyage.

It is very important to realize that this "dream" was not just an ordinary dream. I was fully conscious not only during it but in the transition from the astral plane to my bed. My yelling was soundless in the astral realm but gradually became real sound in the physical plane of the bedroom. There was no need for coffee. There was no sleepiness, nor did the dream fade from memory as I became more awake (as most ordinary dreams do). It was simply a matter of recalling actual events in the same manner as you would recall events of the morning over an afternoon lunch.

I hadn't been asleep, and I wasn't simply lying in bed and day-dreaming.

A few weeks later Nancy, her friend Ann, and I went to a Friday evening service of the Druid order presided over by the then chief Druid Dr. Thomas Maughan. Dr. Maughan, now deceased, was a remarkable man. His service was open to any who wished to attend, and he always had an open ear and mind to "voyages" such as mine. After the service Nancy asked me to speak up and tell Dr. Maughan about my dream, and I did. Maughan listened attentively. When I finished, he looked at the group of attendees and reaffirmed that this was no ordinary dream. He asked me what I did for a living. I told him that I was a visiting professor of physics at Birkbeck College. Then, astonishingly, he admonished me for not being more attentive to details when I was there. "You weren't a too careful physicist. You should have talked to the woman, asked her name, gotten her address and phone number," he scolded.

And he was right. I was so struck that I had actually gone to the astral level and had the experience that I failed to take it into account as an experience worthy of physical laws and subject to the same scrutiny as any other physical experience. My own skepticism had defeated my acceptance of its reality. To my rational mind "it was only a dream."

Over the passing years I have had several similar dreams. However, I have never returned to the astral plane of suicidal souls.

Fred Alan Wolf is the coauthor of the revised edition of Space-Time and Beyond, *the author of* Taking the Quantum Leap, *winner of the American Book Award for an original science paperback,* The Dreaming Universe, *and* Star Wave: Mind, Consciousness and Quantum Physics, *from which this story was excerpted. A former professor of physics at San Diego State University, he now teaches and lectures worldwide.*

JON CARROLL

★ ★ ★

What It Means
to Be Dead

Life is a gift—don't question its length.

AFTER THE DEATH OF LINDA MCCARTNEY [THE WIFE OF EX-
Beatle Paul McCartney], I heard someone on television say, with
anger, that her death was tragic because "she had done everything right."

I gathered from context that the speaker meant that Linda
McCartney had eaten food free from additives or hormones, that
she had not used tobacco or drunk alcohol to excess, that she had
exercised regularly and seen her doctor once a year and that, when
the first signs of the disease were detected, she had taken all necessary and appropriate steps.

And I thought of something I had heard a week earlier, a
quote whose source I did not remember: "Americans think death
is optional."

People who do everything right die, and people who do everything wrong die. Death is neither a reward nor a punishment. It is
true that each of us can do things that will improve our chances of
living longer, but that is at best just another form of gambling, like
knowing not to hit on eighteen in blackjack.

There are many flaws in the health care system, but one of them
is not its failure to prevent death. Indeed, it could be argued that the

illusion that death is preventable is at the heart of many of the excesses of the health care system.

How much would you pay to live a minute longer? How about a day longer? How about a year longer, only you'd be unconscious the whole time? Is the length of your life the sole measure of its value?

These are ethical questions, not medical ones. Put it another way: What would you do to live a day longer? Would you steal? Would you commit arson? Would you defraud a blameless widow? Would you kill a confessed murderer?

Up the ante to a year. What would you do to live a year longer? For many people, these are not theoretical questions. Would you take terrible debilitating poisons to ensure that extra year? Would you use your clout to get the experimental medicine, or bribe someone to push yourself to the front of the organ donor line?

What would you do?

Death is not a tragedy. The specific circumstances of a specific death may be tragic. Survivors may feel pain and loss. But I refuse to believe that each life ends in tragedy. And I know that each life ends in death. We don't think about death very well. We think about avoiding it a lot, but that's foolish—it can't be avoided. Looking young doesn't help. Meditation doesn't help. "Doing everything right" doesn't help.

I am persuaded that only gratitude helps.

I bet you have read about advances in genetic engineering, and you have wondered in some vague morning haze about living forever. Suppose death does become optional. Suppose you could live forever, neither more nor less pain-free than you are now, neither more nor less wealthy or happy or wise.

Would you do it? Would you opt for that second hundred years? The planet would get pretty crowded—would you support a ban on new people so the old people would have sufficient resources to live forever? No New People—does that sound like a useful way to run the universe?

What would you do when you were 150? Would you complain about the new music? Would you fret that you'd run out of cool new places to go on vacation? Would you call up your great-great-great-great-grandchild and bore him with stories of When We All Had Cheap Gas and Big Cars?

How about when you were 250? Would you laugh at the callow concerns of yourself at 150?

Maybe we are already living long enough. Maybe that's part of the plan. Linda McCartney found love, prosperity, music, grace. From what we hear, she experienced gratitude for the gifts she had been given. We should all be so lucky.

Jon Carroll is a columnist for the San Francisco Chronicle.

PART TWO

ENCOUNTERS

* * *

Between the Devil and the Deep Blue Sea

Niceness isn't a prerequisite for being a good guy.

ON THE LIGHT CRUISER, U.S.S. *OKLAHOMA CITY*, THE FAMOUS "Gray Ghost of the Vietnam Coast," we were crossing the Java Sea. We were bound south for Jakarta that morning. The equatorial waters were so warm and still that we seemed to be on some quiet pond rather than the farthest reaches of the Pacific. Only our ship disturbed the glassy water. In the distance, clouds rose and formed, and metamorphosed and puffed and spread with startling rapidity. They were mottled with pink and the color fell shining on the sea. The blue of the water, in turn, reached up to the clouds where the colors mixed and mingled and unraveled the horizon, confusing the distinction between sea and sky, making the world a billowy sphere of pink and blue and white for us to glide through.

The sphere was composed of two perfectly matched opposing hemispheres, each reflecting into the other. The sky and clouds shone from the sea, and the sea was visible in the sky. The ship's ripply counterpart shimmered upside down, an undulating alter ego. The ship's eye hung forward and above the prow, where the water was yet undisturbed. To stand there and look down was to see the sky in the sea and the sea in the sky, and yet both still in their proper places, too. One's own face stared up at one looking down and yet still looking up, each into the other, into the other, into the other, "stretching out to the crack of doom," as Macbeth said. To fall in at that place might be to fall into infinity, or the looking glass, or one's self. We sailed in a cosmic house of mirrors, where, after a time, the real and the shade are indistinguishable. The perfect calm had made this dizzy, delirious thing possible. Only a sudden gale, or other rough weather, could have spun this tangled scene apart and torn the real from the tendrils of illusion.

Joseph Conrad called this the "Shallow Sea" because of its submarine mountains and plateaus, rising up within an anchor chain of the surface. Our captain had said that if we found a shallow enough spot we would drop anchor for a few hours and have a swim in the sea and a barbecue on the fantail. And that would be fine. The ship's cooks would bring out their best. The band would play jazz and show tunes. We'd sun ourselves and swim and eat and talk about all the beer we'd drink in Jakarta. And the whores. Beautiful Java whores lolling beneath their big umbrellas or beside their little shepherd's tents, scattered along the beaches like starfish. "Venus's little starfish," we called them.

"I'm gonna fuck a ton o' whores!" bantam Sammy Seacrest crowed.

"How many whores in a ton?" I demanded, as ritual prescribed.

"Two thousand, unless they're small, ha ha!"

"Then I'm gonna fuck two tons of whores, yo ho!"

"Yo ho!" a chorus answered.

The ship's sonar fathometer was in working order but still a bosun's mate stood on the fo'c'sle taking soundings with a plumb line. Standing above the prow, like David about to slay Goliath, his watery reflection mimicking him, he swung the weighted end of his line into a blur, then sent it flying from his hand. The little stone arced through the air and raced ahead of the ship, trailing its slender line. Then, like a fisher bird, it dove to the surface and sought the bottom. As the ship made way the bosun hauled in the line till it hung vertical and called out to the navigator, "By the mark…five!" Five fathoms, thirty feet, from the keel to the bottom. Should we have two fathoms he would call, "By the mark…twain!"

Sam "Malibu" Robinson and I were standing at the lifeline,

drinking mugs of the bad and ubiquitous navy "joe." Coffee to a landsman. Black as night, bitter as death, and hot as Hell, despite its deservedly rotten reputation it seems at times that the U.S. Navy is fueled on this terrible, biting brew. Anyone can tell you that aboard ship no man is ever more than sixty seconds away from an urn full of it. I have heard people joke that it's made from what the coffee dealers sweep up off the floor. Joke or not, I believe it happens sometimes. It really is bad stuff, but American sailors drink gallons of it.

Sam and I were drinking our mugs of mud, making our obligatory complaints about it and trying to look through the sea for the bottom when we heard Seaman Simms holler from aloft, "Go fuck yourself! Eat shit, you motherfucker, eat shit and die! Eat a mile of shit and die!" He bounded down to the main deck and continued his argument with another seaman. I couldn't tell what the argument was about, but it didn't matter, Simms argued about anything. He was always arguing. He was always right and the whole goddamn world was wrong and it could all eat shit and die.

"You know, I hate that sonofabitch," I said to Sam. "I really hate his fuckin' guts."

"You and me and a hundred other guys. If he was in our division we'd have to give him a little 'extra military instruction.'"

"I wish something bad would happen to him," I said, still hearing him bitching at his shipmate. "I hope he gets injured. No, no, I hope he fuckin' drowns today. I hope the bastard goes swimming and drowns!" And I meant it.

Simms finished his tirade and stomped past us. He was twenty years old with blond beach boy good looks and a muscular frame. His face was red and had a look of angry disgust. His eyes bore an injured expression, as if to say, "What's the matter with these assholes? Why don't they shut up and get off my case?"

He stopped near the lifeline and quivered a little. Simms didn't enjoy being angry; he just was. And he always wanted to do things his own way. Whatever he did he would do a good enough job, and he didn't want anybody telling him how to do it, when to do it, or who to do it with. Simms was uncooperative. And that's a maritime and military sin. On shore, individualism is often valued. On a ship, you need cooperation. A ship's company is a family business.

Simms went back aloft to the cable winch he'd been working on and glared at it. That's how he always started a job; he got mad at it. A slow, sustained, internal rage, that was his style. "Bitter as navy joe," is how a bunkmate described it. He stripped off his shirt with determined speed, picked up his tools, and began again on the offending winch. His lower lip pouted and the muscles of his arms bulged as he forced the machine to submit to his will. He stripped off its protective plates and ripped at its insides. When he found the guilty piece he was looking for he tore it out and flung it on the deck. Then, still bare chested, snorting, he paced deliberately back and forth in front of his quarry. He nudged it with his toe. Satisfied that he was alive and it was dead, he picked up the corpse and tossed it overboard.

> "**H**uman being" is more a verb than a noun. Each of us is unfinished, a work in progress. Perhaps it would be most accurate to add the word "yet" to all our assessments of ourselves and each other. Jon has not learned compassion…yet. I have not developed courage… yet. It changes everything. I have seen the "yet" become real even at the very edge of life. If life is process, all judgments are provisional. We can't judge something until it is finished. No one has won or lost until the race is over.
>
> "Broken" may be only a stage in process. A bud is not a broken rose. Only lifeless things are broken. Perhaps the unique process which is a human being is never over. Even at death.
> —Rachel Naomi Remen, M.D.,
> *Kitchen Table Wisdom:*
> *Stories That Heal*

About midday the bottom came to the mark three. The engines reversed, sending a shudder through the cruiser, and then stopped, and the ship glided to a slow halt. Chief Bosun's Mate Smith directed the anchor crew as they dropped the massive hook and the chain thundered through the chute.

I changed into swimwear and met Sam and three others on the

main deck. Sam was dressed in his Malibu jams, Sammy Seacrest was buck naked, and the rest of us were in Government Issue. As cooks set up barbecue grills on the fantail and the ship's band prepared to play, about twenty-five men gathered on deck in a holiday mood and were waiting for the lifeboat to be lowered before we went into the water. Hearty, beer-bellied chief petty officers made jokes and slapped each other on the back. A couple of shy junior officers on their first cruise wondered if they should act decorously in front of "the men" or let their hair down and enjoy themselves. Seamen and apprentices were skylarking and playing grab-ass. And we petty officers admired the scene and told ourselves that it was "us that operate this goddamn ship, ain't it?"

A gunner's mate, sitting on one of the ten-foot gun barrels of the forward turret hollered up to the flying bridge, "Captain, captain, fly the Jolly Roger!" Captain Butcher leaned over the rail and beamed and gave the high sign. He liked playing pirate, too. He gestured to his yeoman. Seconds later the Skull and Crossbones flew up the signal mast and caught an upper level breeze.

"Hurray!" we all shouted. "Shiver me timbers! Hurray!"

Another flag ran up alongside the Roger and snapped open. It was Captain Butcher's personal standard: Popeye with cutlass in hand and an eye patch, and the motto "Press On Regardless."

"Yahoo!" we cheered and applauded.

"Press On, Press On Regardless! Yeah!"

"Haze gray and under weigh, this motherfucker is A-OK!" we chanted.

"She's the Gray Ghost of the Nam coast!"

"Fuckin-ay right!"

Senior Chief Howard, oldest man on board, veteran of the battles of Iwo Jima, Okinawa, Inchon, and a score of duels on the Tonkin Gulf's Yankee Station spilled over with delight and danced a hornpipe. Others jumped up and down, laughing, cheering, exulting.

The lifeboat was in the water now. It was manned by a cox'n in the stern and a swimmer amidships. And in the bow, armed with an M-14 rifle and watching for sharks, was Bosun's Mate Al Trevino, who had a Purple Heart, and whose uncle is Lee Trevino the golfer.

Waving his rifle and shouting he signaled all safe and secure. Several men leaped in and made a great splashing.

"Let's play abandon ship!" Sam yelled.

"Yeah!" the five of us shouted in unison. We raced to the prow to stand above the ship's eye and ran through the navy drill.

"All hands stand by to abandon ship!"

"Ship's position is…"

"Nearest land is…"

"Your mother's name is…"

"Steady men. Go in feet first in case you hit some flotsam."

"Cross your legs to protect the family jewels."

"Arms crossed in front and elbows up to protect your handsome face."

"Eyes on the horizon to keep you vertical all the way down."

"Now, leap through the flaming oil and swim under it to safety, just like it says in the book. Away!"

The sea rushed up and swallowed us with a gulp. Breaking the surface in a froth we swam aft to the stern. Treading water there, we could see through the ocean's perfect clarity to the ship's huge screws. Sammy took a great breath and dove down to the ship's keel where he "tickled her belly." We went forward again to investigate the anchor chain.

Equatorial seas are delicate and changeable. The reflecting half-domes of the Java are as fragile as the mirrors they imitate. They can shatter and take new form suddenly, from placid calm to churning torment without warning. I felt the sea-change before I was consciously aware of it. Then I saw the ship swing on her anchor as she would do in harbor when the tide shifts. A swell of water, from nowhere, rose up under me, lifting me with it, then dropped me back down into a trough. The next swell rolled heavily over my head, forcing brine into my mouth. I heard some shouts of the other men, but I could see no one among the sudden hillocks of water. The current was carrying me toward the starboard quarter of the ship so I went with it, rising and falling with the sea, till I was alongside the hull. There I found I had to swim hard against the growing mountains of water just to stay put. "Hey,"

I hollered to the main deck, trying to sound calm. "Somebody throw me a line."

"Hey, hey someone on deck. Somebody, help!" A swell came from behind. It lifted me up. With the sound of the surf it rushed toward the ship and bashed my body against the steel hull. The flowing water pressed me against the ship, forcing air out of my lungs until the wave was spent. As it receded it took me back with it. Salt burned my eyes. I tried to lift my head to breath but the next wave fell on me, tumbling me over and threw me against the ship again. As the steel hull came at me I held my arms out to cushion the blow but several tons of rushing water bent them like sticks. My lip split against the shock of steel. I drank blood and brine and vomited underwater. A throbbing, spinning buzz filled my head. I clawed the air to rise to it. I could hear the shouting of others as the ocean swirled around them too, but I could now see only shapes and swirls of light and dark.

The ship continued to swing on her anchor till she was nose into the sea. Then the swells dragged me along the side of the hull. They rolled me, scraped me against sharp little barnacles that lacerated my body and cut to the knee bone. I tried to swim against it. I swear I tried with all my might. But I just couldn't swim up those hills of water.

They took me beyond the ship. My body ached from blows and fatigue, and blood seeped out of my scraped arms and legs. The swells wouldn't let me have any air. When I tried to breathe they forced brine down my throat and I vomited and my mouth and nose burned. They hurled their monstrous weight on me and beat me down into the troughs. I couldn't move. My strength was gone. I was sleepy. I always thought that in a matter of life or death I could huff and puff and gather the strength to do whatever was needed. But I couldn't even open my eyes.

To me the world became quiet. The thunder of the sea was muffled and distant. I heard no more shouts. The hammering of the waves became a gentle undulation. I became aware that I could see the depths. I saw where the clear blue water near the surface began to darken and then turn black and become void. "I'm dying," I thought with bemused disappointment. "I'm only twenty-two, and I've never even loved a woman, and I'm dying. I've never loved a woman and I'm dying…I've never loved…" In my soul's eye I looked down upon a white sand beach. It was perfectly clean. No driftwood washed up on it. No fire rings dotted it. No sculpted sand castles, and no footprints betold my passing. I slid sadly, gently, painlessly down toward Death. The sea rolled easily over me now.

I began to feel cold. It started at my feet and moved slowly up. But it was an easy cold. It didn't make me shiver.

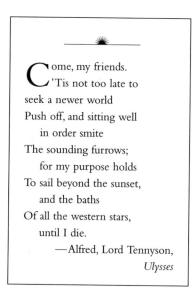

Come, my friends.
'Tis not too late to
seek a newer world
Push off, and sitting well
    in order smite
The sounding furrows;
    for my purpose holds
To sail beyond the sunset,
    and the baths
Of all the western stars,
    until I die.
                —Alfred, Lord Tennyson,
                                    Ulysses

Suddenly, I heard a splashing sound, like a hooked fish fighting for life at the end of a line. Someone pulled my head up out of the water and I began to hear the sea again. "Okay?… Okay?" I heard him say above the roar. My body wouldn't move, it still belonged to Death, but my eyes half opened of their own accord. I recognized Seaman Simms. He had me about the waist in a bear hug. My head leaned against his and we rose and fell with the waves. "We're gonna swim together back to the ship. Okay?" he shouted.

"No," I murmured. To murmur "no" was all I had the strength to do. If he would cheat Death of me, he would do it alone. He hesitated. Maybe he thought of leaving me. He looked past me, through the hostile sea to the ship. A hue of melancholy softened the ever-present anger in his eyes as he judged the task ahead of him. I can't tell you exactly how a man reaches down to the bottom of his soul for strength. But I can tell you that at that moment Simms did. The muscles of his face set and I know, I can swear to it, that he had prepared himself to keep me afloat even if it had to be for the rest of his life. He hugged me very tight and began to swim against the murderous swells. He swam with conviction for 350 yards. He swam without the use of his hands, pushing my dead weight before him. He was wearing fins, but they were speed fins, giving him little advantage. He swam mainly on faith and commitment.

I slipped back into darkness on the way home, but I came to as we reached the starboard quarter. Crewmen had hung a cargo net over the side for men to climb up, but I still had no strength. Simms grabbed a line that somebody had thrown down and tied it around me. Then he slipped, exhausted, under the water. Trevino came by in his boat and caught him by the hair and pulled him aboard. A man on deck began to pull me up out of the water. I don't know who he was. All I could see were his arms, big, muscular, tattooed black arms. I decided that's what angels look like.

I rose from the water by those arms' lengths, and they laid me on the old-fashioned, teakwood-covered deck. I lay there motionless until two men picked me up and carried me below to sick bay. They put me in a bunk in a dark, quiet corner, covered me and left. I lay there between sleep and waking, between death and life, hearing, feeling, thinking nothing. No sound, no smell, no sensation penetrated my senses; no time elapsed. I floated in oblivion or infinity. After a long time an old, familiar sensation ran through me. I heard and felt the comforting, caressing thrumm of the ship's engines as they came back to life. Then the grinding windlasses lifted the anchor from the bottom and pulled it snug into its socket. The Gray Ghost shivered slightly as she gathered way and pitched easily, shaping her course southward, away from the maelstrom. Then I slept.

When I awoke I smelled coffee. Not the coffee you smell in the morning at home, or in restaurants. It was the heavy smell of navy coffee, sharp and burned and bitter. The navy's favorite saying is that "There's the right way, the wrong way, and the navy way" to do anything. That goes for coffee as well as anything else. I opened my eyes to see a hospital corpsman departing, having just given Seaman Simms a mug of joe. Simms was in the bunk across from me.

I wriggled my toes and it hurt. I wriggled my fingers and it hurt.

Anything I moved hurt. Every muscle in my body ached, and the now bandaged barnacle cuts burned. I felt empty, like the sea had torn the kernel out of me and thrown back the useless chaff. I gave a little groan and Simms looked over at me. His usual suspicious, hostile expression was back on his face. I took a little comfort in that, thinking that at least I'd be dealing with the devil I knew. He looked away and took a slurp of his coffee. He rolled it around in his mouth and swallowed, smacked his lips and sniffed. He looked askance back at me.

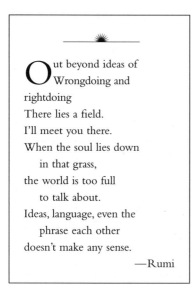

Out beyond ideas of
Wrongdoing and
rightdoing
There lies a field.
I'll meet you there.
When the soul lies down
    in that grass,
the world is too full
    to talk about.
Ideas, language, even the
    phrase each other
doesn't make any sense.
                    —Rumi

He didn't say anything, but he got up and came over to me like he had something to say. He stood there for a moment, suddenly confused or unresolved. He looked like a man standing naked and not knowing what to do with his hands. He sat down on the edge of my bunk, then stared into his coffee for a moment. He looked up at me and, still saying nothing, offered me the big, navy standard, blue trimmed, white china mug.

I struggled to sit up and took the mug from him. I could see and smell that the coffee was made to the usual strength: strong enough to wake the dead and scare the living. Some people would call it cowboy coffee because it's said that you could float a horseshoe in it. The aroma was powerful, almost stingingly bitter and burnt. This was not coffee a man would offer to his wife. But I could feel that the smell alone was bringing my senses back to life. I took a cautious sip. It was hot and thick and strong and it glowed down to my gut, sending out life-giving rays of heat. Its bitterness almost made me shiver and I caught my breath. I heaved in a huge gulp of air. The burned-black coffee taste clung to my tongue and my tastebuds resonated, sang like vibrating harp strings with the old familiar flavor. The powerful potency of the brew was softened ever so slightly by the traditional navy cook's method of preparation. He had added a tablespoon of clean seawater to the five-gallon urn. There is some debate as to whether the seawater should be added before or after brewing, but either approach will take some of the snarl out of the coffee. It's not enough seawater to taste salt, only enough to alter the flavor.

I continued to sip the coffee and with each swallow the empty feeling inside me filled up a little more. I marveled that something so bad could be so good. I drained the cup and finally Simms spoke. "You want some more?" he asked. I nodded. He took the mug and returned with it filled. "I put a little sugar in it," he reported. "Cook said it would give you strength." With that Simms left. I wrapped my hands around the hot mug and hugged it to me. I breathed in the good, bittersweet vapors. "Not a bad guy, that Simms," I thought. "Not a bad guy."

Richard Sterling is a graduate of the University of California, Berkeley, and a veteran of seven years in the U.S. Navy. He is the author of The Fearless Diner: Travel Tips and Wisdom for Eating Around the World, *and* The Eclectic Gourmet Guide to San Francisco. *He's also the editor of* The Adventure of Food, *and* Travelers' Tales Food, *which won a Lowell Thomas award for best travel book. He lives in Berkeley, California.*

MARK KURLANSKY

$\star \overset{\star}{} \star$

Postcard from Death

Lachaim! (To Life!)

I JUST GOT ANOTHER ONE IN THE MAIL, THE THIRD IN A YEAR: A picture postcard of a cemetery. All three cards were of the same Jewish cemetery, and each was sent by a Jew, as though this were the way Jews keep in touch—sending pictures of a graveyard. The cemetery is in Prague, and, yes, it is a picturesque and historic cemetery. But a block away is Europe's oldest functioning synagogue, and although postcards of it are available, nobody has sent me one.

Western Jews go to Central Europe to see death. Since the fall of Communism and the opening of borders to easy, visa-free travel, the growth of Jewish communities has attracted far less interest than the now-accessible concentration camps and cemeteries. Thus Poland, which has more Jewish history but less Jewish life than its neighbors, has become a popular destination for foreign Jews, many of whom profess a hatred for Poland and yet still must see the cemeteries and death camps.

This new obsession is a very un-Jewish thing. There is probably no religion that is less concerned with death. Cemeteries are not supposed to be next to synagogues, because life and death are to be separated. Descendants of priests, the Cohanim, are not to gaze on dead bodies or walk in cemeteries. Christianity, in its Jewish infancy, had as its symbol a fish, signifying the life of Peter; only later, not coincidentally as Christians broke away from Judaism, did they take on the cross, an implement of torture, the symbol of Jesus's agony and martyrdom. I sometimes wonder, as I watch Poland's lucrative new tourist industry, if Judaism is not undergoing a similar transformation.

No one goes to Poland to take in the countryside. The draw is Poland's embarrassment of riches in the field of Holocaust history. Foreigners come to see what is left of the Warsaw ghetto, the Jewish cemeteries, and the death camps: Sobibor, Maidanek, Belzec, Treblinka, Chelmno, Stutthof, Auschwitz-Birkenau. So many tourists are Jewish that local entrepreneurs have had to make their little carved Hasidim dolls less anti-Semitic in order to move them—make the eyes a little less sunken and demonic and ease up on the nose.

Cracow, in southern Poland, has become a tourist center mostly because of its location: it is only a thirty-minute taxi ride from the most famous death camp of them all, which attracts some half a million visitors a year.

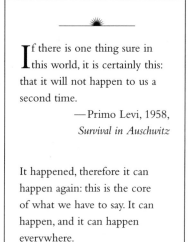

If there is one thing sure in this world, it is certainly this: that it will not happen to us a second time.

> —Primo Levi, 1958,
> *Survival in Auschwitz*

It happened, therefore it can happen again: this is the core of what we have to say. It can happen, and it can happen everywhere.

> —Primo Levi, 1986,
> *The Drowned and the Saved*

When tourists get off the train from Warsaw they are greeted at the platform by eager taxi drivers offering, "Taxi? Hotel? Auschwitz?" When a driver gets an Auschwitz fare he merrily informs the others at the stand, "I'm off to Auschwitz!"

When I went, my taxi driver was extremely jovial, a breach of etiquette for which I instantly hated him. We flew through the hilly countryside in his Mercedes while he talked about what a great car a Mercedes is.

"Yes, the perfect way to go to Auschwitz," I said.

He slammed the dashboard good-humoredly, repeated the joke, and laughed.

The landscape between Cracow and Oświęcim, the town where Auschwitz is located, has probably not changed much since the camp was operating—rolling farmland, yellow strips of harvested hayfields, orchards of branches drooping with the weight of summer apples, towns with traditional log houses, and even some horse-drawn carts. The first thing one sees in Oświęcim is the wide rail-road yard, a junction of so many tracks that it appears to be the outskirts of a major city. The Germans were said to have chosen the spot because of its rail connections. For all those tracks there had been only 12,000 people living there, the majority of whom were Jews. There is said to be one Jew left in Oświęcim, and he, not surprisingly, is a recluse.

Outside the death camp is a parking lot filled with tour buses. Then there is a bookshop and a snack bar and a pretty green spot with rows of two-story brick barracks. Many of the barracks have been turned into national pavilions, each displaying the suffering of its country, some in brutal documentary style, others seeming almost artsy. Auschwitz has become a kind of World's Fair of geno-cide. Every institution with any pretense of moral authority wants the last word on Auschwitz, and there is an international commit-tee that is eternally debating what to do with it. The place remains incomprehensible and its questions as unanswerable as those of Job. The moral voice tends to fall to the greatest victims, who were the Jews. As Polish Jewish journalist Konstanty Gebert said, "The world owes us the right to exist because we have suffered. However, on the pinnacle of suffering there is room for just one." The problem is that there is very little a truly moral voice can say. Meanwhile, Auschwitz survivors do their duty and sit on the committee, forced not only to think about but to visit the site of their nightmares.

Auschwitz shows things that are beyond commentary—human hair, eyeglass frames, piles of toothbrushes, an unremarkable-looking oven; gallows where prisoners were hanged and walls where they were shot and laboratories where they were worked on. Somehow families drift through this. Many of the visitors weep. Others look stunned. Some look like bored tourists shuffling from exhibit to exhibit, taking snapshots to mark each spot. When I was through, my jovial taxi driver was waiting in the parking lot with a somber, sympathetic face. "Makes you sick, doesn't it," he said. "People shouldn't go

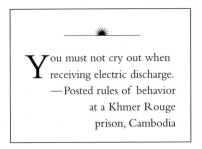

You must not cry out when receiving electric discharge.
— Posted rules of behavior at a Khmer Rouge prison, Cambodia

here. I don't like this place. They killed my grandfather here." His grandfather had been among the Polish political prisoners for whom the Germans had first established the camp.

But as soon as we got away the mood was broken and he was jovial again. I liked this man now. He seemed to like life, and he certainly enjoyed the drive, playing a cassette of German oompah-pah music, which I asked him to change. Again he slapped the dashboard and laughed at the silly irony of it, and switched to a Polish-language recording of "Now It's Time to Say Good-bye for the Summer."

Although many of the tourists at Auschwitz were Jewish and had traveled with the help of Jewish organizations, I wouldn't say I had a Jewish experience there. I would say I had a Nazi experience. There is a need to preserve such places precisely because there is a need to understand what Nazis were, what they did. I don't think Jews are the people who most need this. But they are the ones who are experiencing it the most frequently. There seems to be a tremendous confusion about who defines what a Jew is. How often is a Jewish lecture, a Jewish film, or a Jewish book not about the Holocaust? I have for the past two years been working on a book about European Jewry. People constantly assume I am writing about the Holocaust. No, I say, this is contemporary. They look at me with confusion. I see them thinking,

"What is there to say about contemporary Jews?" Then they invariably start talking to me about neo-Nazis.

I do not believe that Jews, as Gebert stated with intended irony, are owed the right to exist because they have suffered but rather because they have the right to exist. If suffering were the only legacy of Judaism, it would not be worth continuing. What forces Jews ever deeper into the dilemma of identity is historical revisionism, by which another generation of Nazis forces another generation of Jews to focus on the Holocaust. Revisionists are more than maddening quacks insisting the world is flat in the face of overwhelming evidence to the contrary. Where there are denials of the facts of the Holocaust, there are invariably trails that lead to organized neo-Nazis. It must be denied in order to be done all over again. This mentality is amply demonstrated by an anonymous hand that scrawled on the walls of a Paris suburb, "Auschwitz was a lie," and in the same handwriting, "Gas the Jews."

Since the fall of Communism, revisionism has taken on an even more dangerous form. On my first trip to post-Communist Poland, I shared a train compartment with a nineteen-year-old Pole from Cracow. He was very excited to meet an actual Jew. I was his first Jew and he was my first Polish philo-Semite, the weird new breed of Polish anti-Semite. He loved Isaac Bashevis Singer and had read all of his books. Upon learning I was Jewish, he immediately

> So why did the firing squad evolve? I suspect it had something to do with a logical distortion it allowed each participant: if it takes one shot from each of five people to kill a man, each participant has killed one-fifth of a man. And on some cognitive level, it is far easier to decide then that you have not really killed someone or, if you possess extraordinary powers of denial, that you have not even contributed to killing someone.
>
> —Robert M. Sapolsky,
> "Measures of Life: The
> Etiquette of the Firing
> Squad," *The Sciences*

wanted to apologize to me for Gomulka's anti-Zionist campaign of 1968. "That was the greatest disgrace in Polish history," he magnanimously declared. (Later he got down to questioning me about the avariciousness of Jews and the length of their noses.)

The point about the 1968 smear campaign is the claim that the Communists were as bad as the Nazis. If it is accepted that the Communists were as evil as the Nazis, it will not take long for Poles to believe that the Nazis did no worse than the Communists, that the Holocaust was something like Gomulka's 1968 campaign. This is only one of the dangerous games being played by many establishment figures in today's united Germany. When it is written in the opinion pages of the daily *Die Welt* that Erich Honecker was "the greatest German murderer and war criminal," it is hard to believe that there is not some revisionism afoot. Honecker did not murder six million people, cause the deaths of twice that many, author a "final solution," or establish a massive network of killing centers. If the Nazi record can be reduced to that of Erich Honecker, then the neo-Nazis are in business and, as they like to say, "Germany can be proud again."

Thus Jews have good reason to work actively to preserve the memory of the Holocaust. But if today's Nazis can turn today's Jews into a people who are largely focused on the Holocaust, if this focus increases rather than diminishes with each generation, then the cultural and intellectual richness of Judaism will have been diminished, and the Nazis will have achieved a significant victory.

While visiting Auschwitz I saw a little French girl, perhaps eight years old, sit down outside one of the display barracks and refuse to go in. "Come on," pleaded her parents, pointing to the sign identifying the display. "This is about the life of the prisoners."

"I don't want to see that," said the little girl, hunkering down on the wooden stoop. How supremely rational she was. I wanted to sit on the stoop, too. But instead I went in.

Mark Kurlansky is a journalist and author of fiction and nonfiction books. This article was based on his 1994 book, A Chosen Few: The Resurrection of European Jewry. *His other books include* A Continent of Islands: Searching for the Caribbean Destiny, The Basque History of the World, *and* Cod: A Biography of the Fish That Changed the World.

PAUL WINSTON

★ ✶ ★

In Friendship

*André's legacy is one all of
us can leave behind.*

AS A BOY, I LOVED LISTENING TO MY MOTHER'S COLLECTION OF classical recordings. Many of them were operas, and among her favorites were those featuring a French-born coloratura soprano named Lily Pons. Buried in our living room's big record-storage shelves were also many classical and light-classical recordings by a popular conductor and composer of the day, a musician named André Kostelanetz.

He was often maligned by critics. One day I asked a wise friend why some spoke in such a belittling way about him.

"It's simple," he answered. "He sells a lot of recordings, because he seems to know what the public wants to hear. He's very successful. Success can sometimes upset the unsuccessful. On top of that, I'm told he's kind and generous, and has lots of friends and admirers. That's even harder for some folks to bear."

Many years later, at a little hotel I owned in Northern California, Mr. Kostelanetz came to stay. We met, and later stayed in touch through notes and letters.

He always ended with "In Friendship." Over the years, I came to understand that he really meant it. He was not collecting names in a basket. He was expressing a deeply felt warmth toward those he called his friends.

*

André telephoned me one day from Los Angeles. Could I come down and attend a special concert at the Shrine Auditorium?

"Are you conducting?" I asked.

"Yes, I am, but it's a concert for Lily Pons. We were once married, you know. She's not had a concert in years. She's in her 70s, now, and won't sing in public anymore. She doesn't think her voice is good enough. I'm arranging this concert for her. Her voice is still quite wonderful. She doesn't believe me, but it's true. Please come down."

When I flew down, André had arranged a backstage pass for me. I stood in the wings, out of everyone's way, drinking in many great operatic arias for which Miss Pons was world-famous. She was a tiny woman with a huge voice: her range had once been an extraordinary two and a half octaves. That night, she looked like a young girl, singing with tremendous joy, her voice still remarkably beautiful. I was hearing Mom's recordings, live at the Shrine.

André slipped up behind me to watch her take her final curtain calls. The capacity audience was standing, cheering, stamping, applauding. She would rush into André's arms, then turn and go out for another bow.

"Was I all right?" she asked him over and over, in French. He would smile and point toward the sold-out house cheering for her.

"You see?" he whispered to me while she was onstage taking her bows. "She hit notes tonight she thought she could never reach again. She said her upper ranges had been gone for years, but suddenly tonight they were there. She reached them." Over and over, she said to him, "Thank you, André."

Sometime later, I learned that André had paid all the concert's costs himself, to mount what was in effect a farewell performance for Miss Pons. She was someone he cared for deeply. The concert was his gift to her.

I remembered what I'd been told about him years before, and I thought, "Why, he's just being who he is: a kind, generous, loving man who conducts and records for a living but who really lives to give pleasure to others. What a great way to live one's life."

*

Some years later, I received a telephone call from New York, from André's secretary. André, who had just passed on, had earlier arranged for a special memorial at Lincoln Center in New York. He'd told his office to be sure to invite me.

"I am honored by this," I told his secretary, "but, frankly, I rarely attend funeral services, and I'm 3,000 miles away, so…"

"Oh," said his secretary happily, "this isn't a funeral or a memorial service. It's something André arranged personally, something special. I think you'd enjoy yourself."

At the last moment, I decided to attend. I flew into New York and took a taxi to Lincoln Center. I walked into the main lobby and suddenly found myself standing with hundreds of people. We were André's guests: ladies in flowered dresses, men dressed up like peacocks, all attending a party André was giving. Singers, conductors, classical—and popular—music celebrities, business friends, a Who's Who of the musical world.

It was so jolly that I stood still in astonishment. Look who's here! Isn't that…? I was awestruck. An orchestra played show tunes, buffet tables were stacked with things to eat. Everything—flowers, food, music, and especially the guests—was the best, top-drawer. No expense had been spared. Everyone was laughing, talking, eating, dancing. Many lined up to speak at a microphone on a raised platform, to honor André with their memories of him. They told funny or inspiring stories about his generous heart, his many kindnesses.

A man in a lime sport coat walked in, looking as puzzled as I had been. He walked over to me. "Where are the services for André?" he asked.

"This is it," I smiled back at him.

"Why, it's a party!" he said and laughed. "What a wonderful idea! My, isn't this just like André?" I agreed. I wanted to tell a story about André and Lily Pons, but the line at the microphone was long. I saw the lime sport coat greeting friends across the room. Everyone was nodding to him or shaking his hand. Hmmm. I blocked a waiter rushing by me. "Do you know who that man in the lime-green sport coat might be?"

He was definitely a New York waiter. "You puttin' me on?" he snarled. I shook my head vigorously. "That's Aaron Copland," he replied in a rich Bronx tone. I was properly stung, Aaron Copland, a hero of mine, one of America's greatest composers, was right in front of me. He'd shown up, too, for André. "In Friendship," I thought.

If André was too lowbrow for some, what was Copland doing here? Was it the free food? That made me smile. Many of the guests I was staring at could have packed the Met or Carnegie Hall all by themselves.

As I rode back to the airport, I thought: "What was I doing there?" I'd hardly known him. Most of the time it had been he who'd stayed in touch, not me. That stopped me cold: and I thought, "In Friendship." What a great way to live one's life.

Paul Winston attended the University of Southern California, followed by Harvard Law School, and a Rhodes Scholarship nomination. He has written a novel, The Rhone Foundation. *His essays have appeared in the* Christian Science Monitor *and* The Catholic Digest. *His friendship with Andre Kostelanetz goes back to his years at Ventana, Big Sur. Andre came to stay as a guest and they became friends.*

BARBARA KINGSOLVER

$\star \overset{\star}{} \star$

In the Belly of the Beast

Too much attention to weapons poisons us all.

THE TITANS, IN THE STORIES OF THE ANCIENT GREEKS, WERE unearthly giants with heroic strength who ruled the universe from the dawn of time. Their parents were Heaven and Earth, and their children were the gods. These children squabbled and started a horrific, fiery war to take over ruling the universe.

A more modern legend goes this way: The Titans were giant missiles with atomic warheads. The Pentagon set them in neat circles around chosen American cities, and there they kept us safe and free for twenty-two years.

In the 1980s they were decommissioned. But one of the mummified giants, at least, was enshrined for public inspection. A Titan silo—a hole in the ground where an atomic bomb waited all its life to be launched—is now a missile museum just south of Tucson. When I first heard of it I was dismayed, then curious.

What could a person possibly learn from driving down the interstate on a sunny afternoon and descending into the ground to peruse the technology of nuclear warfare?

Eventually I went. And now I know.

The Titan who sleeps in his sleek, deep burrow is surrounded with ugliness. The museum compound, enclosed by an unkind-looking fence, is set against a lifeless backdrop of mine tailings. The grounds are gravel flatlands. The front office is blank except for a glass display case of souvenirs: plastic hard hats, model missile kits for the kids, a Titan-missile golf shirt. I bought my ticket and was ushered with a few dozen others into a carpeted auditorium. The walls bore mementos of this silo's years of active duty, including a missile-shaped silver trophy for special achievement at a Strategic Air Command combat competition. The lights dimmed and a gargly voice rose up against high-drama music as the film projector stuttered, then found its stride, and began our orientation. A ring of Titan II missiles, we were told, encircled Tucson from 1962 until 1984. The Titan II was "conceived" in 1960 and hammered together in very short order with the help of General Motors, General Electric, Martin Marietta, and other contractors. The launch sites are below ground—"safely protected from a nuclear blast." The missile stands 103 feet tall, 10 feet in diameter, and weighs 150 tons. A fatherly sounding narrator informed us, "Titan II can be up and out of its silo in less than a minute, hurling its payload at speeds of over 15,000 miles per hour nearly halfway around the world. This ICBM waits quietly underground, its retaliatory potential available on a moment's notice."

The film went on to describe the typical day of a missile crew, and the many tasks required to keep a Titan in a state of constant readiness. Finally we were told sternly, "Little remains to remind people that for twenty-two years a select group of men stood guard twenty-four hours a day, seven days a week, protecting the rights and freedom we enjoy in these United States." Day and night the vigilant crew monitored calls from their command post, "Waiting..." (a theatrical pause) "for a message that never came."

We filed out of the auditorium and stood in the hostile light of the gravel compound. Dave, our volunteer guide, explained about reinforced antennas that could go on transmitting during an attack (nuclear war disturbs radio transmissions, among other things). One small, cone-shaped antenna sat out in the open where anyone could trip over it. Dave told us a joke: they used to tell the rookies to watch out, this was the warhead. My mind roamed. What sort of person would volunteer to be a bomb-museum docent? The answer: he used to be a commander here. Now, semiretired, he trained cruise-missile operators.

It was still inconceivable that a missile stood erect under our feet, but there was its lid, an enormous concrete door on sliding tracks. Grate-covered holes in the ground bore a stenciled warning: TOXIC VAPORS. During accidents of miscalculations, deadly fuel would escape through these vents. I wondered if the folks living in the retirement community just downhill, with the excruciatingly ironic name of Green Valley, ever knew about this. Dave pointed to a government-issue weather vane, explaining that it would predict which way the poisonous gases would blow. What a relief.

We waited by the silo entry port while a Boy Scout troop emerged. I scanned the little boys' faces for signs of what I might be in for. Astonishment? Boredom? Our group then descended the cool stairwell into the silo. Just like a real missile crew, we put on hard hats to protect ourselves from low-hanging conduits and sharp edges. Signs warned us to watch for rattlesnakes. The hazards of snakes and bumped heads struck me as nearly comic against the steel-reinforced backdrop of potential holocaust. Or, put another way, being protected against these lesser hazards made the larger one seem improbable.

A series of blast doors, each thicker than my body, were all propped open to let us pass. In the old days, you would have had to wait for security clearance at every door in turn before it would admit you and then heave shut, locking behind you. If you turned out to be an unauthorized intruder, Dave explained, you'd get a quick tour of the complex with your face very near the gravel.

Some forty steps down in the silo's bowels, we entered the "No Lone Zone," where at least two people stood guard at all times. This was the control room. Compared with my expectations, undoubtedly influenced by Hollywood, it seemed unsophisticated. The Titan control room was run on cathode-ray tubes and transistor technology. For all the world, it had the look of those fifties spaceship movies, where men in crewcuts and skinny ties dash around trying to figure out what went wrong. No modern computers here, no special effects. The Titan system was built, Dave said, with "we-need-it-now technology." I tried to get my mind around the notion of slapping together some little old thing that could blow up a city.

Dave was already moving on, showing us the chair where the missile commander sat. It looks exactly like a LA-Z-BOY recliner. The commander and one designated enlisted man would have the responsibility of simultaneously turning two keys and engaging the missile, if that call came through. All of us stared mutely at the little holes where those keys would go in.

A changeable wooden sign—similar to the ones the Forest Service uses to warn that the fire danger today is MEDIUM—hung above the controls to announce the day's STRATEGIC FORCES READI-NESS CONDITION. You might suppose it went to ultimate-red alert (or whatever it's called) only a few times in history. Not since the Cuban Missile Crisis, maybe. You would be wrong. Our guide explained that red alerts come up all the time, sometimes triggered by a false blip on a radar, and sometimes (unbeknownst to crew members) as a test, checking their mental steadiness. Are they truly sane enough to turn that key and strike up nuclear holocaust? For twenty-two years, every activity and every dollar spent here was aimed toward that exact end, and no other.

"But only the president can issue that order," Dave said. I believe he meant this to be reassuring.

We walked deeper into the artificially lit cave of the silo, down a long green catwalk suspended from above. The entire control chamber hangs on springs like huge shock absorbers. No matter what rocked and raged above, the men here would not be jostled.

On the catwalk we passed an eyewash facility, an outfit resembling a space suit, and a shower in case of mishaps involving toxic missile-fuel vapors. At its terminus the catwalk circled the immense cylindrical hole where the missile stood. We peered through a window into the shaft. Sure enough it was in there, hulking like a huge, dumb killer dog waiting for orders.

This particular missile, of course, is impotent. It has been relieved of its nuclear warhead. Now that the Titans have been decommissioned, they're being used as launch missiles for satellites. A man in our group piped up, "Wasn't it a Titan that blew up a few weeks ago, when they were trying to launch a weather satellite?"

Dave said yes, it was, and he made an interesting face. No one pursued this line of thought, although questions certainly hammered against the roof of my mouth. "What if it'd been headed out of here carrying a payload of death and destruction, Dave, for keeping Tucson safe and free? What then?" Like compliant children on a field trip, all of us silently examined a metal hatch opening into the missile shaft, through which service mechanics would gain access to the missile itself. A sign on the hatch reminds mechanics not to use their walkie-talkies while inside. I asked what would happen if they did, and Dave said it would totally screw up the missile's guidance system. Again, I felt strangely inhibited from asking very obvious questions: What does this mean, to "totally screw up the missile's guidance system"? That the bomb might then land, for example, on Seattle?

The Pentagon has never discussed it, but the Titan missiles surrounding Tucson were decommissioned, ostensibly, because of technical obsolescence. This announcement came in 1980, almost a decade before the fall of the Berlin Wall; it had nothing to do with letting down the nation's nuclear guard....

The Pentagon was forced to decommission the Titans because, in plain English, the Titans may have presented one of the most stupendous hazards to the U.S. public we've ever had visited upon us. In the 1960s a group of civilian physicists at the University of Arizona worked

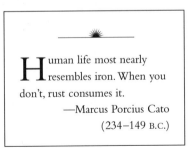

Human life most nearly resembles iron. When you don't, rust consumes it.
—Marcus Porcius Cato
(234–149 B.C.)

out that an explosion at any one of the silos surrounding Tucson would set up a chain reaction among the other Titans that would instantly cremate the city. I learned about this in the late seventies, through one of the scientists who authored the extremely unpopular Titan report. I had months of bad dreams. It was not the first or last time I was floored by our great American capacity for denying objective reality in favor of defense mythology. When I was a child in grade school we had "duck and cover" drills, fully trusting that leaping into a ditch and throwing an Orlon sweater over our heads would save us from nuclear fallout. The Extension Service produced cheerful illustrated pamphlets for our mothers, showing exactly how to stash away in the basement enough canned goods to see the family through the inhospitable aftermath of nuclear war. Now we can pass these pamphlets around at parties, or see the quaint documentary *Atomic Café,* and laugh at the antique charm of such naïveté. And still we go on living in towns surrounded by nuclear choke chains. It is our persistent willingness to believe in ludicrous safety measures that is probably going to kill us....

Our tour finished, we clattered up the metal stairs and stood once again in the reassuring Arizona sun. Mine tailings on one side of the valley, the pine-crowned Santa Rita mountains on the other side, all still there; beneath us, the specter of hell.

Dave opened the floor for questions. Someone asked about the accident at a Titan silo in Little Rock, Arkansas, where some guy dropped a wrench on the missile and it blew up. Dave wished to point out several things. First, it wasn't a wrench, it was a ratchet. Second, it was a crew of rookies who had been sent in to service the missile. But yes, the unfortunate rookie did drop a tool. It bounced and hit the missile's sheet-metal skin, which is only a quarter of an inch thick. And which doesn't house the fuel tank— it *is* the fuel tank. The Titan silo's "blast-proof" concrete lid weighs 740 tons. It was blown 300 yards through the air into a Little Rock cornfield.

Dave wanted us to know something else about this accident: the guys in the shock-absorber-suspended control room had been evacuated prior to the ill-fated servicing. One of them had been drinking a Coke. When they returned they were amazed to see how well the suspension system had worked. The Coke didn't spill.

We crossed the compound to a window where we could look straight down on the missile's nose from above. A woman near me gasped a little. A man asked where this particular missile had been headed for, back in the days when it was loaded, and Dave explained that it varied, and would depend on how much fuel it contained at any given time. Somewhere in the Soviet Union is all he could say for sure. The sight of these two people calmly discussing the specifics of fuel load and destination suddenly scared the living daylights out of me. Discussing that event like something that could really happen. They almost seemed disappointed that it never had.

For years I have wondered how anyone could willingly compete in a hundred-yard dash toward oblivion, and I believe I caught sight of an answer in the Titan museum—in faces that lit up when they discussed targets and suspension systems and megatons. I saw it in eyes and minds so enraptured with technology that they saw before them an engineering spectacle, not a machine designed for the sole purpose of reducing civilizations to rubble.

Throughout the tour I kept looking, foolishly I suppose, for what was missing in this picture: some evidence that the people who ran this outfit were aware of the potential effects of their 150-ton cause. A hint of reluctance, a suggestion of death. In the absence of this, it's easy to get caught up in the internal logic of fuel capacities, circuitry, and chemical reactions. One could even develop an itch to see if this amazing equipment really works, and to measure success in purely technical terms.

The Coke didn't spill.

Outside the silo after the tour, I sat and listened to a young man regaling his girlfriend with further details about the Little Rock disaster. She asked him, "But that guy who dropped the, whatever it was. Did he die?"

The man laughed. "Are you kidding? That door on top was built to withstand a nuclear attack, and it got blown sky-high. Seven hundred and forty tons. That should tell you what happened to the guys inside."

She was quiet for a while, and then asked him, "You really get into that, don't you?"

"Well, sure," he said. "I love machines. It fascinates me what man is capable of designing."

> ━━━━━ ☀ ━━━━━
>
> People must bring a machete, a spear, an arrow, a hoe, spades, rakes, nails, truncheons, electric irons, barbed wire, stones, and the like, in order, dear listeners, to kill Rwandan Tutsis.
>
> —Broadcast on state radio, Democratic Republic of Congo

Since that day, I've had the chance to visit another bomb museum of a different kind: the one that stands in Hiroshima. A serene building set in a garden, it is strangely quiet inside, with hushed viewers and hushed exhibits. Neither ideological nor histrionic, the displays stand entirely without editorial comment. They are simply artifacts, labeled: china sake cups melted together in a stack. A brass Buddha with his hands relaxed into molten pools and a hole where his face used to be. Dozens of melted watches, all stopped at exactly 8:15. A white eyelet petticoat with great, brown-rimmed holes burned in the left side, stained with black rain, worn by a schoolgirl named Oshita-chan. She was half a mile from the hypocenter of the nuclear blast, wearing also a blue short-sleeved blouse, which was incinerated except for its collar, and a blue metal pin with a small white heart, which melted. Oshita-chan lived approximately twelve hours after the bomb.

On that August morning, more than six thousand schoolchildren were working or playing in the immediate vicinity of the blast. Of most of them not even shreds of clothing remain. Everyone within a kilometer of the hypocenter received more than 1,000 rads and died quickly—though for most of them it was surely not quick enough. Hundreds of thousands of others died slower deaths; many would not know they were dying until two years later, when keloid scars would begin to creep across their bodies.

Every wooden building within two kilometers was annihilated, along with most of the earthquake-proof concrete ones, and within sixteen kilometers every window was smashed. Only concrete chimneys and other cylindrical things were left standing. Firestorms burned all day, creating howling winds and unmeasurable heat. Black rain fell, bringing down radioactive ash, staining walls with long black streaks, poisoning the water, killing fish. I can recite this story but I didn't, somehow, believe it until I looked at things a human being can understand: great handfuls of hair that fell from the head of Hiroko Yamashita, while she sat in her house 800 meters from the hypocenter. The pink dress of a girl named Egi-chan, whose blackened pocket held a train ticket out of the city. The charred apron of Mrs. Sato, who was nursing her baby.

The one bizarre, incongruous thing in the museum at Hiroshima, it seemed to me, was a replica of the bomb itself. Dark green, longer than a man, strangely knobbed and finned—it looks like some invention that has nothing to do with people. Nothing at all.

What they left out of the Titan Missile Museum was in plain sight in Hiroshima. Not a sound track with a politically balanced point of view. Just the rest of the facts, those that lie beyond suspension systems and fuel capacity. A missile museum, it seems to me, ought to be horrifying. It had better shake us, if only for a day, out of the illusion of predictability and control that cradles the whole of our quotidian lives. Most of us—nearly all, I would say—live by this illusion. We walk through our days with our minds on schedule—work, kids, getting the roof patched before the rainy season. We do not live as though literally everything we have, including a history and a future, could be erased by two keys turning simultaneously in a lock.

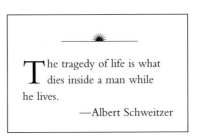

The tragedy of life is what dies inside a man while he lives.
—Albert Schweitzer

How could we? How even to pay our monthly bills, if we held in mind the fact that we are camped on top of a technological powder keg? Or to use Carl Sagan's more eloquent analogy: we are all locked together in a room filled with gasoline vapors, insisting that because *they* have two hundred matches, we won't be safe until *we* have *three* hundred.

The Cold War is widely supposed to have ended. But preparations for nuclear war have not ended. The Titan museum's orientation film is still telling the story we have heard so many times that it sounds, like all ultrafamiliar stories, true. The story is that *they* would gladly drop bombs on us, if they weren't so scared by the sheer toughness of our big missiles. *They* are the aggressors. *We* are practicing "a commitment to deterrence."

Imagine you have never heard that story before. Look it in the eye and see what it is. How do strategic-games trophies and Titan-missile golf shirts stack up against a charred eyelet petticoat and handfuls of hair? The United States is the only nation that has ever used an atomic bomb. Dropped it, on men and women and school-children and gardens and pets and museums, two whole cities of quotidian life. We did it, the story goes, to hasten the end of the war and bring our soldiers home. Not such an obvious choice for Oshita-chan. "To protect the rights and freedoms we enjoy" is a grotesque euphemism. Every nuclear weapon ever constructed was built for the purpose of ending life, in a manner so horrific it is nearly impossible to contemplate. And U.S. nuclear science has moved steadily and firmly, from the moment of its birth, toward first-strike capacity.

If the Titan in Green Valley had ever been allowed to do the job for which it was designed, the firestorm wouldn't have ended a world away. Surely all of us, even missile docent Dave, understand that. Why, then, were we all so polite about avoiding the obvious questions? How is it that a waving flag can create an electromagnetic no-back-talk zone?…

Why did I not scream at the top of my lungs down in that hole?

I didn't, so I'll have to do it now, to anyone with the power to legislate or listen: one match in a gasoline-filled room is too many. I don't care a fig who is holding it.

I donned the hard hat and entered the belly of the beast, and I came away with the feeling of something poisonous on my skin.

The specter of that beast could paralyze a person with despair. But only if you accept it as inevitable. And it's only inevitable if you are too paralyzed with despair to talk back. If a missile museum can do no more than stop up our mouths, with either patriotic silence or desperation, it's a monument the living can't afford. I say slam its doors for good. Tip a cement truck to the silo's gullet and seal in the evil pharaoh. If humanity survives long enough to understand what he really was, they can dig him up and put on display the grandiose depravity of the twentieth century.

I left, drove down into the innocent palm-shaded condominiums of Green Valley, and then, unexpectedly, headed up the other side of the valley into the mountains. When I reached the plateau of junipers and oaks I pulled off the road, hiked into the woods, and sat for a long time on a boulder in the middle of a creek. Water flowed away from me on either side. A canopy of sycamore leaves whispered above my head, while they waited for night, the close of one more day in which the world did not end.

In a poem called "Trinity," Sy Margaret Baldwin explained why she would never go down to the site of the first atomic-bomb explosion, which is opened to the public every year:

> ...I would come face to face with my sorrow, I would
> feel hope slipping from me and be afraid the changed
> earth would turn over and speak the truth to the
> thin black ribbons of my ribs.

Barbara Kingsolver was trained as a biologist before becoming a writer. Her books include poetry, nonfiction, three award-winning novels, and a collection of short stories. This piece was excerpted from her book, High Tide in Tucson: Essays from Now or Never. *She lives with her husband and family in southern Arizona and in the mountains of southern Appalachia.*

ELAINE SOSA

* * *

You Have Suffered Enough

*The compass of the soul always points
in the right direction.*

I HAD AN ABORTION MANY YEARS AGO. I DIDN'T THINK ABOUT IT much at the time. I was twenty years old, unmarried, and totally unprepared to raise a child. I was a child myself.

I knew I was pregnant almost immediately. It happened on a vacation to San Francisco, my first trip west of the Mississippi. A girlfriend and I had come to spend a week in the city. The first thing we did after we checked into our hotel was to head outside to do a little exploring. We walked for a while and finally stopped at a lively bar that caught our eye. The place was packed and everyone seemed to be having a good time.

It took all of about ten minutes to meet him. He was bearded and handsome, and wore snug-fitting Levis with a heavy cotton shirt and tweed blazer. We started chatting. Soon he bought me a drink and then another, and we talked about nothing and everything. I was mesmerized. He was an architect and had lived in the city for several years. He was bright, witty, and sweet. And he was talking to me! As the hours passed, I grew more fascinated with this stranger. It seemed mutual. By the time last call was announced, it was obvious. I found my girlfriend and let her know that our hotel room would be hers for the evening.

We went to his apartment, a wonderful place in North Beach. His creative touches were everywhere. He showed me around and explained several things he had done to the apartment with great delight. When we got to his bedroom and I lay down on the soft, warm waterbed, the realities of my life were a million miles away. I was about to make love to a sensitive and sensual man. Nothing else mattered.

We spent the rest of the week together. My girlfriend had met someone as well that very first night in San Francisco, and the four of us spent a lot of time together. It was almost perfect. Except that I knew. I must have gotten pregnant right away. I had traveled to San Francisco without my birth control pills, and we were not particularly careful. I had been careless before and it had never been a problem. Until now. My lower back ached. My whole body felt different. I was worried, almost sick with worry. But I said nothing.

Within weeks of my return home, my breasts were swollen and painful to the touch. I gained weight, primarily in my stomach. My roommate and I had a Fourth of July party and most of our friends came. Some asked me if I had gained weight while others simply whispered it to each other. My roommate was tactful as always and said nothing. Then I started eating saltines at seven in the morning as I sat on the toilet, stunned that this was happening to me. I went to the doctor and he confirmed what I already knew. I was seven weeks pregnant.

A good friend gave me the name of a gynecologist she knew who performed abortions in his office as part of his practice. I didn't have the nerve to discuss this with the father since I was afraid he would want me to keep the child. After I returned home from San Francisco, we had stayed in close contact over the phone. I had even flown back to see him on the spur of the moment one evening. I had driven myself to the airport, bought a ticket on the next flight and was gone. I knocked on his door later that night and it was magical. But difficult. We lived so far apart from each other. We had our own lives, our own worlds. Neither one of us knew what to do with each other. So I told the nurse at the doctor's office to schedule me for an abortion as soon as possible. I didn't want time to think about it. I was scared to death.

The abortion was performed on a Friday afternoon in the doctor's office. I was ushered into a small room and given a mild sedative. There were several other women in the room. They all looked anxious, which is exactly how I felt. It was dead silent. My name was finally called, and the nurse took me into the room where the procedure would be performed.

The doctor was a handsome young man and seemed very nice. As I lay on the table, I started to cry. I'm not sure why. I didn't want to cause a fuss, so I said that I was fine, just a little tense. I wept quietly throughout the procedure. It was quicker than I expected and not really painful, just strange. I was then moved to another room where I was to stay for a while to be sure I was all right. When it was okay for me to leave, I went to the reception area and paid the bill. As I reviewed it, I noticed that my procedure was referred to as an "aspiration curetage." Was this to make me feel better? Oddly enough, it did.

The doctor had given me some pills in case of pain and advised me to take it easy for a couple of days. It was important that I not hemorrhage. I took no chances at all and stayed in bed for two days, curled up in the fetal position. My roommate never asked any questions, although I was sure she knew. She must have noticed the changes in my body and my behavior since my return from San Francisco. But she said nothing. On Monday I went back to work. I felt fine and was glad that there had been no complications. I was in no physical pain. My other pain was just beginning.

I told virtually no one about my experience at the time, or for years later. I was always afraid of being judged. The abortion might have been the wrong thing to do. If it was, I certainly didn't need anyone telling me so. Ultimately, I came to realize that most of my friends had had a similar experience. No one ever said anything directly about their experience, it just seemed to slip out in conversation. At which time I would say, "Yeah, me too." I learned that some of my friends had dealt with abortion more than once. One had five abortions and another had six. At least I now knew that I wasn't alone. I just seemed to feel worse about it than everyone else. It's not as if the realization of what had happened to me was with me every day. It was more of an occasional sadness, a dull ache that would not go away. And it only got worse. I knew that I had to come to terms with what I had done in order to put it behind me. I decided I would go to confession and tell God that I was sorry, and hopefully, He would listen.

Although I wasn't much of a churchgoer, I managed to find a church near my house that looked suitable. It was big, modern, and impersonal. Unusual, I thought, for a Catholic church. I figured I could be pretty anonymous in there—stop in, say my piece, be absolved, and move on. Sounded easy enough. Until I tried to go. I kicked around in my head what I would say to the priest: that I was young at the time, scared, didn't think. I hadn't really done anything wrong, I'd tell him, it was simply that fear had taken over and acted on my behalf. Some other part of my person, but not the real me. I was innocent. Even though I felt guilty. I wasn't sure why I felt guilty. Probably because I had been brought up to feel guilty, about sex and so many other things. Sometimes I couldn't distinguish good from bad, right from wrong. So I was probably wrong, wrong, wrong.

One afternoon I decided I would go to the church. I drove over and lost my nerve as I was about to enter the parking lot. This happened to me several times. Every time I tried to go I would wind up farther and farther from the church. Some days I couldn't even get into the car, although I had been convinced moments earlier in my house that this would be the day. It was as if some supernatural force was raising its mighty hand and blocking my path. I thought it was hopeless. Yet I knew how very much I needed to do this, because I felt progressively worse. I decided to tell a good friend about the difficulty I was having in the hopes that he could provide some words of encouragement. To my surprise, he had been involved in two abortions himself, by former girlfriends carrying his child. We talked about our shared pain. He also realized just how much I needed to come to terms with my actions and was willing to help.

"Don't worry, if you can't get there yourself, I'll take you there," he said. "Just let me know when you want to go."

Those words were exactly what I needed to hear. My struggle would soon be over. All I had to do was say when.

The next day, I got into my car, drove to the church, entered the parking lot, and got out of the car. By myself. It was three o'clock on a Wednesday afternoon. I didn't think I would find a priest at the church in midafternoon, so I walked over to the rectory and rang the doorbell. A middle-aged woman answered the door. I stared at her and said in a low, shaky voice, "I need to see a priest." The look on my face must have said it all. She asked no questions. She told me to come in and wait in a room off to the left. There was a desk in the room as well as a sofa and chair. A box of Kleenex sat on the desk. A large photograph of the pope looked down from the wall. The room was cold. I hunched over in the chair and waited.

After several minutes the door opened and a man walked in. He was older, with gray hair and rosy cheeks. A small, kind-looking man. He sat on the couch across from me, which was close to the chair I had chosen.

"I'm Father O'Rourke," he said in a heavy Irish brogue. "What can I help you with?"

I think I started with how I had gotten pregnant and what had led me to the abortion. How I had never meant to hurt anyone or to do anything wrong. But I'm not really sure. All I remember is sitting there and words flooding out of my mouth, faster and faster. Tears starting to trickle, and then flowing, down my cheeks. I must have talked and sobbed for about fifteen minutes. I could not stop. Finally he reached over and took my hand and held it very hard.

"My child, you have suffered enough!" he said. "You have more than paid for your sin."

His words stunned me. Was it possible that I had suffered enough? The priest told me that I was forgiven and that I needed to move on with my life. He said some other things, which I didn't hear. I was too busy looking at this sweet, wise man who knew that it was time for my ordeal to be over, and grateful for his kindness.

Elaine Sosa is a former stockbroker who grew weary of going to work at 6 A.M. In 1994 she left Wall Street behind and started "Javawalk," a coffee-walking tour in the heart of San Francisco, as a way to legitimize her coffeehouse addiction. As a tip o' the cap to her hero, Charles Kuralt, she publishes "The Road Sage," an online travel site featuring stories and photos dispatched live from the road.

EDWARD ABBEY

* * *

Dead Man at Grandview Point

A renowned park ranger and writer looks
for a missing man in southern Utah.

THIS MORNING I AM REQUESTED VIA THE SHORTWAVE RADIO TO join a manhunt. Not for some suspected criminal or escaped convict but for a lost tourist whose car was found abandoned two days ago in the vicinity of Grandview Point, about fifty miles by road from my station in the Arches National Monument.

Grateful for the diversion, I throw canteens and rucksack into the government pickup and take off. I go west to the highway, south for three miles, and turn off on another dirt road leading southwest across Dead Horse Mesa toward the rendezvous. There I find the other members of the search party holding a consultation: Merle and Floyd from park headquarters, the county sheriff and one of his deputies, a relative of the missing man, and my brother Johnny who is also working for the Park Service this summer. At the side of the road is a locked and empty automobile, first noted two days earlier.

Most of the surface of this high mesa on which our man has disappeared is bare rock—there are few trails, and little sand or soft earth on which he might have left footprints. There are, however, many washes, giant potholes, basins, fissures, and canyons in which a man could lose himself, or a body be hidden, for days or years.

There is also the abyss. A mile from where we stand is the mesa's edge and a 1,200-foot drop straight down to what is called the White Rim Bench. From there the land falls away for another 1,500 feet or more to the Colorado River. If he went that way there won't be much left worth looking for. You could put it all in a bushel sack.

Learning from the relative—a nephew—that the missing man is about sixty years old, an amateur photographer who liked to walk and had never been in the Southwest before, we assume first of all that the object of the search is dead and that the body will be found somewhere along the more than twenty miles of highly indented rimrock that winds northwest and northeast from Grandview Point.

The assumption of death is made on the grounds that an airplane search by the sheriff failed to find any sign of the man, and that at least two days and possibly more spent in the desert in the heat of August with only what water (if any) he could carry is too much for a man of sixty, unfamiliar with the terrain and the climate.

We begin the search by dividing as evenly as we can the area to be investigated. Assigned the southernmost sector, my brother and I drive down the road another five miles to where it dead-ends close to the farthest reach of the mesa—Grandview Point itself. Here we share our water supply and split up, Johnny hiking along the rim to the northwest and I taking the opposite way.

All morning long, for the next four hours, I tramp along the rim looking for the lost tourist. Looking for his body, I should say— there seems little chance of finding him still alive. I look in the shade of every juniper and overhanging ledge, likely places to find a man besieged by thirst and sun. I look in the gullies and fissures and in the enormous potholes drilled by wind and sand in the solid rock— holes like wells, with perpendicular sides...mantraps.

At times I step to the brink of the mesa and peer down through that awful, dizzying vacancy to the broken slabs piled along the foot of the wall, so far—so terribly far—below. It is not impossible that our man might have stumbled off the edge in the dark, or even— spellbound by that fulfillment of nothingness—eased himself over, deliberately, in broad daylight, drawn into the void by the beauty and power of his own terror...?

"Gaze not too long into the abyss, lest the abyss gaze into thee."

I watch also for a gathering of vultures in the air, which would be a helpful clue. Not for *him*, of course, now perhaps beyond such cares, but for us, his hunters.

The sun burns in a lovely, perfect sky; the day is very hot. I pause when necessary beneath pinyon pine or juniper for rest and shade and for a precious drink of water. Also, I will admit, for recreation: to admire the splendor of the landscape, the perfection of the silence.

The shade is sweet and desirable, the heat very bad, and early in the afternoon, out of water, I give up and return to the truck. My brother is waiting for me and by the lost expression on his face I understand at once that he has found our man.

I radio the rest of the party. Johnny and I wait in the shade of the truck. They arrive; we all wait another hour until the undertaker, who is also county coroner, comes from Moab with his white ambulance, his aluminum stretcher and his seven-foot-long black rubber bag. Then Johnny leads us to the body.

The route is rough and long, across rocky gulches and sandstone terraces impassable to a motor vehicle. We walk it out. About a mile from the road we come to a ledge rising toward the rim of the mesa. Near the top of the rise is a juniper, rooted in the rock and twisted toward the sky in the classic pose of its kind in the canyon country. Beneath the little tree, in the shade, is the dead man.

Coming close we see that he lies on his back, limbs extended rigidly from a body bloated like a balloon. A large stain discolors the crotch of his trousers. The smell of decay is rich and sickening. Although the buzzards for some reason have not discovered him, two other scavengers, ravens, rise heavily and awkwardly from the corpse as we approach. No canteen or water bag in sight.

The nephew makes a positive identification—I can't imagine how. But the coroner-undertaker nods, the sheriff is satisfied, and together with the deputy, the three of them begin the delicate, difficult task of easing the swollen cadaver into the unzipped rubber bag.

Johnny and I retrace what we can of the dead man's course. There is no discernible trail on the slickrock but by walking around his final resting place in a big half-circle we cut sign—intersect his tracks—in a ravine 100 yards away. There on the sandy floor we find his footprints: where he had entered the ravine, where he became panicky and retraced his way not once but twice, and where he had struggled up an alluvial bank to the ledge. From that point he could see the juniper with its promise of shade. Somehow he made his way to it, laid himself down and never got up again.

We return to where the others are waiting, gathered about the black bag on the stretcher, which the undertaker is in the act of zipping shut. The sheriff and the deputy are scrubbing their hands with sand; the undertaker wears rubber gloves.

We are not far from Grandview Point and the view from near the juniper is equally spectacular. The big jump-off is only a few steps south and beyond that edge lies another world, far away. Down below is the White Rim; deeper still is the gorge of the Colorado; off to the right is the defile of the Green River; looking past Junction Butte we can see the barren point where the two rivers join to begin the wild race through Cataract Canyon; beyond the confluence lies the wilderness of the Needles country, known to only a few cowboys and uranium prospectors; on the west side of the junction is another labyrinth of canyons, pinnacles and fins of naked stone, known to even fewer, closer than anything else in the forty-eight United States to being genuine terra incognita—The Maze.

Far beyond these hundreds of square miles of desiccated table-land rise the sheer walls of further great mesas comparable in size and elevation to the one we stand on; and beyond the mesas are the mountains—the Abajos and Elk Ridge forty miles south, the La Sals and Tukuhnikivats forty miles east, the Henrys fifty miles southwest.

Except for the town of Moab, east of us, and the village of Hanksville near the Henry Mountains, and a single occupied ranch on this side of the Abajo Mountains, the area which we overlook contains no permanent human habitation. From the point of view of political geography, we are standing on one of the frontiers of human culture; for the man inside the rubber sack it was land's end, the shore of the world.

Looking out on this panorama of light, space, rock, and silence I am inclined to congratulate the dead man on his choice of jumping-off place; he had good taste. He had good luck—I envy him the manner of his going; to die, alone, on rock under sun at the brink of the unknown, like a wolf, like a great bird, seems to me very good fortune indeed. To die in the open, under the sky, far from the insolent interference of leech and priest, before this desert vastness opening like a window onto eternity—that surely was an overwhelming stroke of rare good luck.

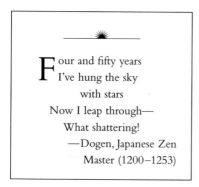

Four and fifty years
I've hung the sky
    with stars
Now I leap through—
What shattering!
    —Dogen, Japanese Zen
        Master (1200–1253)

It would be unforgivably presumptuous to pretend to speak for the dead man on these matters; he may not have agreed with a word of it, not at all. On the other hand, except for those minutes of panic in the ravine when he realized that he was lost, it seems possible that in the end he yielded with good grace. We see him staggering through the fearful heat and glare, across the tilted ledge toward the juniper, the only tree in sight. We see him reach it, at great cost, and there, on the brink of nothing and everything, he lies down in the shade to rest. He would not have suffered much after that; he may have died in his sleep, dreaming of the edge of things, of flight into space, of soaring.

We are ready to go. A few flies are already circling above the dark shape on the stretcher. A few dark birds are floating on thermals far out over the chasm of the Colorado, somewhat below the level of the mesa. It is possible from here to gaze down on the backs of soaring birds. I would like to stay for a while and watch the birds but the others are ready to go, the sun is very hot, the corpse is stinking, there is not enough shade for us all under the one small tree, and the world—the human world—is waiting for us, calling us back. For the time being.

There are eight men here, alive. More or less alive. Four pick up the stretcher and begin the march back to the road and the ambulance. The other four walk alongside to relieve when needed. We soon need relief, for the weight is greater than it looks, and the rock, sand, brush, and cactus make walking with a load difficult. The sun is pitiless, the smell is worse, and the flies are worst of all, buzzing in swarms around the putrid mass in the rubber sack.

The dead man's nephew, excused from this duty, walks far ahead out of earshot. We are free as we go stumbling and sweating along to say exactly what we please, without fear of offending.

"Heavy son of a bitch…"

"All blown up like he is, you'd think he'd float like a balloon."

"Let's just hope he don't explode."

"He won't. We let the gas out."

"What about lunch?" somebody asks. "I'm hungry."

"Eat this."

> And so at last goodbye
> night will fall
> a day will dawn
> love will bloom and mature
> men will age and fall
> fufilled, back into the soil
> and the mountains will
> wear into
> flat plains
> new ones will arise and
> be sculptured
> and God's world goes on
> forever new, forever ancient,
> forever NOW
> —George Simon, *Notebooks*

"Why'd the bastard have to go so far from the road?"

"There's something leaking out that zipper."

"Never mind, let's try to get in step here," the sheriff says. "Goddamnit, Floyd, you got big feet."

"Are we going in the right direction?"

"I wonder if the old fart would walk part way if we let him out of that bag?"

"He won't even say thank you for the ride."

"Well I hope this learned him a lesson, goddamn him. I guess he'll stay put after this…"

Thus we meditate upon the stranger's death. Since he was unknown to any of us we joke about his fate, as is only natural and wholesome under the circumstances. If he'd meant anything to us maybe we could mourn. If we had loved him we would sing, dance, drink, build a stupendous bonfire, find women, make love—for under the shadow of death what can be wiser than love, to make love, to make children?—and celebrate his transfiguration from flesh to fantasy in a style proper and fitting, with fun for all at the funeral.

But—we knew thee not, old man. And there is, I suspect, another feeling alive in each of us as we lug these rotting guts across the desert: satisfaction.

Each man's death diminishes me? Not necessarily. Given this man's age, the inevitability and suitability of his death, and the essential nature of life on Earth, there is in each of us the unspeakable conviction that we are well rid of him. His departure makes room for the living. Away with the old, in with the new. He is gone—we remain, others come. The plow of mortality drives through the stubble, turns over rocks and sod and weeds to cover the old, the worn-out, the husks, shells, empty seedpods and sapless roots, clearing the field for the next crop. A ruthless, brutal process—but clean and beautiful.

A part of our nature rebels against this truth and against that other part which would accept it. A second truth of equal weight contradicts the first, proclaiming through art, religion, philosophy, science, and even war that human life, in some way not easily definable, is significant and unique and supreme beyond all the limits of reason and nature. And this second truth we can deny only at the cost of denying our humanity.

We finally reach the road, which I had begun to fear we would never see—the death march seemed everlasting—and shove stretcher and burden into the undertaker's ambulance, a white Cadillac glittering with chrome and powdered with the red dust of Utah. He slams shut the doors, the undertaker does, shakes a few hands and drives off, followed by the nephew driving the dead man's car.

The air is clean and sweet again. We can breathe. We rest for a while in the shade of the other cars, passing around water bags, smoking, talking a little. Someone tells a bad joke, and the party breaks up. We all go back the thirty-five miles to the highway and from there by separate ways to our separate places, my brother south to Blanding, myself to the Arches.

Evening now, a later day. How much later? I'm not quite sure, I can't say, I've been out here in the heart of light and silence for so long that the numbers on a calendar have lost their meaning for me. All that I can be certain of at this moment is that the sun is down, for there is Venus again, planet of beauty and joy, glowing bright and clear in the western sky, low on the horizon, brilliant and steady and serene.

The season is late—late summer on the high desert. The thunderstorms have been less frequent lately, the tumbleweeds are taking on the reddish tinge of their maturity, and the various grasses— bluestem, fescue, Indian ricegrass, grama grass—which flourished after the summer rains have ripened to a tawny brown; in the slanting light of morning and evening the far-off fields in Salt Valley, where these grasses are most abundant, shine like golden velvet.

The nighthawks, sparse in numbers earlier, have gone away completely. I haven't seen one for a week. But not all the birds have left me.

Southwest, toward Grandview Point and The Maze, I can see V-shaped black wings in the lonely sky, soaring higher and higher against a yellow sunset. I think of the dead man under the juniper on the edge of the world, seeing him as the vulture would have seen him, far below and from a great distance. And I see myself through those cruel eyes.

I feel myself sinking into the landscape, fixed in place like a stone, like a tree, a small motionless shape of vague outline, desert-colored, and with the wings of imagination look down at myself through the eyes of the bird, watching a human figure that becomes smaller, smaller in the receding landscape as the bird rises into the evening— a man at a table near a twinkling campfire, surrounded by a rolling wasteland of stone and dune and sandstone monuments, the wasteland surrounded by dark canyons and the course of rivers and mountain ranges on a vast plateau stretching across Colorado, Utah, New Mexico, and Arizona, and beyond this plateau more deserts and greater mountains, the Rockies in dusk, the Sierra Nevadas shining in their late afternoon, and farther and farther yet, the darkened East, the gleaming Pacific, the curving margins of the great Earth itself, and beyond Earth that ultimate world of sun and stars whose bounds we cannot discover.

Edward Abbey, the legendary author of The Monkey Wrench Gang *and many other critically acclaimed books, was born in Home, Pennsylvania, in 1927, and died at his home is Oracle, Arizona, in 1989.* Desert Solitaire, *from which this is excerpted, established the author as one of the country's foremost defenders of the natural environment.*

★ ⁺ ★

The Solution

Should you turn the other
cheek—or get revenge?

BRIEFLY, BECAUSE HE HAD MET MY WIFE IN DHAHRAN, I TOLD
Dheifallah of my divorce. He was amazed when I told him something of American divorce settlements.

"You've heard of women's liberation, haven't you, Dheifallah?"
chimed in Bob, smiling wickedly.

"That's crazy. I think what you need is man's liberation."

"Listen, America is a good country to be a woman in these days."

"Or criminal. You put killer in jail awhile, then let him out.
When I was in States, man called Son of Sam was killing girls in
New York. They catch him, they put him in jail, maybe they let
him out already. Why?"

"I don't know. Well, I do know—but it's a complicated problem."

"What's complicated? Man kills somebody, you kill him. *Khalas!*"

"You don't have to convince me," said Bob. "I agree with you
100 percent."

I have seldom met an American in Arabia who did not approve
and admire their swift, harsh, and *human* justice. It's human because
it's direct, it's one-on-one, and it's satisfying. It also presents a man
with his choice. As an example of an unsatisfying and inhuman way
of justice, take the American way, as illustrated by the following

113

story, which I proceeded to tell Dheifallah and Bob. The wife of a man of my acquaintance was roller-skating to the liquor store to buy a bottle of wine for dinner one evening when a man from a drug rehabilitation halfway house attacked her and, before he could be stopped, beat her to death with one of her skates. The husband was ready to do the human thing, strangle with his bare hands the animal who had killed his wife, but he never got the chance. The murderer was whisked away by the police and processed through the System: courts, psychiatrists, counselors, state-appointed lawyers, what have you, while my friend vainly tried to keep track of his whereabouts, hoping to catch him somewhere alone for five minutes. But he never got that chance, and eventually the System swallowed the killer up completely; the husband lost track of him. He did locate the man's mother, to ask *her,* if not her son, the unanswerable question *why*, but the mother, half-crazed herself by a life of junk food, TV, bad air, and white-trashdom, only told him what he already knew: that her son was a bad egg, that she was not surprised that in a moment of rage he had murdered a stranger on the street.

Before this appalling tragedy, my friend had never given crime or punishment much thought, except to hold very vague enlightened ideas: if asked, he would say he was against the death penalty. But after he saw his wife a bloody mess on the sidewalk, he knew where he stood. Oh, he was for the death penalty, all right, and he wanted to be the one to deal it out. The matter, however, was taken out of his hands (where, as the party who had suffered the second-greatest wrong, he felt it rightly belonged) and put into the hopper of the penal system, where it would go around and around for years. It was at about this time, when my friend's hot thirst for vengeance had cooled a little, that I told him what a Saudi, in a similar situation—except that Saudis are not crazy and do not kill on the street—would have been able to do.

There would have been four choices available to him. First, he could have killed the man himself.

"Stop right there! That's what I would have done!" cried my friend.

"Well," I said, "wait'll you hear them all. Second, if you were too squeamish to do the job yourself but still wanted him killed, the government would do it for you. Third, since killing the man wouldn't bring your wife back, you could accept a large payment of what is called 'blood money' from the man's tribe."

"A *curse* on his low-life tribe! What's the fourth choice?"

I took a deep breath before I answered. "You could let him go…'into God's hand,' as they say."

Now it was my friend's turn to take a deep breath, and pause a long while. Finally he said, "Yes, I see the beauty of it. Well, what would *you* do?"

Dale Walker lived in Saudi Arabia during its boom years, teaching English as a foreign language. This story is excerpted from his first published work, Fool's Paradise.

LUIS SEPÚLVEDA

✫ ✫ ✫

Hotel Inglés

Oh mama, can this really be the end?

I always come back to Río Mayo, a Patagonian town about 100 kilometres from Coihaique and 200 kilometres from Comodoro Rivadavia. I always come back, and the first thing I do when I get off the bus, truck, or whatever vehicle drops me at the cross-roads is shut my eyes so as not to be blinded by the dust. Then I open them slowly, shoulder my pack, and walk towards an elabo-rately carved wooden building.

It is a noble ruin, a mute witness to better times. Given a shove, the door opens to reveal what remains of the orchestra podium, the bar—its stools covered with brown leather, now mostly eaten by goats—and the portrait of Queen Victoria painted on the wall of the reception hall by somebody with a highly personal understand-ing of anatomy. The eyes of the British sovereign have slid sideways and almost touch her ears, while her flared nostrils, distinctly African in form, occupy half of her face.

"*Salve, Regina*," I say in greeting, and sit myself down to smoke a cigarette before bidding her goodbye. I know for sure that one of the locals will be waiting for me outside. This time it's a woman. Gripping a basket, she watches me with mischievous eyes.

"You're in the wrong place," she says.

"Isn't this the Hotel Inglés?"

"Yes, but it's been shut for ten years, since the gringo died."

"What? When did Mister Simpson die?" I ask, though I already know the story, just for the pleasure of hearing a new version.

"Ten years ago. He shut himself up with five women, you know, women on the game. And he died, the dirty old man."

Five women. The last time I was here, a local told me it was twelve French prostitutes. Perhaps legends dwindle. In any case, what is certain is that when Thomas Simpson found out that cancer was gnawing at his bones and the doctor gave him three months at the most to live, he gave the hotel to his employees and kept only the Presidential Suite for himself. He had some boxes of Havana cigars and a barrel of Scotch sent up to the suite, and he shut himself in with an undetermined number of lively, well-paid ladies, whose task was to hasten his death in the most pleasurable manner.

Within a week, the news of his sweet agony had reached Comodoro Rivadavia. The English community got together and sent a clergyman to put a stop to the scandal, but when the bearer of good news tried to get into the suite, he was stopped by a .45-caliber piece of lead which ripped through one of his legs. Simpson died as he wished to die, and the hotel went to the dogs in no time at all.

Luis Sepúlveda is a Chilean writer who was tortured and exiled from his country because of his beliefs. He is the author of The Old Man Who Read Love Stories, The Name of the Bullfighter, *and* Full Circle: A South American Journey, *from which this story is excerpted.*

✦ ✦ ✦

Fiji Time

Island life has a darker side.

"*BULA!*"

Among native Fijians, "*Bula!*" is the one-word welcome, delivered with enthusiasm and grace, to all who visit the Islands. It's a reception not only to their country, but also to their culture—celebrated for its joyous and leisurely embrace of life.

Travel industry professionals quickly recognized the marketing potential, christening this indigenous attitude: "Fiji time." Brochures designed to lure tourists to these islands are full of glossy four-color photos of white-sand beaches flanked by lofty green-leafed palms on one side, and gentle gin-clear seas on the other. The images are of place, but the implication is tranquility. The brochure text invariably describes time. Fiji Time. "Visit the islands time forgot." "Put a foot in Fiji, and step back a hundred years." "Come to Fiji where your only rigor is relaxation." Thus has "Fiji Time" become a marketing tool—an irresistible invitation to indulge the placid pace of paradise.

For many visitors the transition from Western precision to Fiji time is a skill that must be learned. Some never do. A digital watch can be stopped, but it can never ever run slow. For others, it's precisely this lackadaisical tempo in the tropics that forms the template of "holiday." For them, Fiji time offers a refreshing intermission, an escape from the tightly scheduled daily routines of home.

But for native islanders, there is little alternative. Fiji time is standard issue—pervasive and inescapable. It's genetic, born of climate and culture. Like threads that collectively make cloth, Fiji time is integrally woven into the fabric of this tropical lifestyle.

I chose to get used to Fiji time underwater. In this endeavor, I was not alone. After completing a medical degree, my friend Chris abandoned ship to indulge his passion for coral reefs. On the outskirts of the small town of Savu Savu, he commissioned an open wooden boat and rented a modest house on an idyllic shore worthy of the travel brochures. The front porch overlooks a sheltered bay whose waters sparkle in the sun, and whose beaches are lined by lanky palms gently waving in the breeze. We have breakfast on this porch. And as we sip from tall glasses of freshly squeezed fruit juices, discussion eventually turns to our options for the day.

These are pretty much the same as yesterday, and the day before, and the day before that. In fact for nearly a month, we have started our days sipping a glass of juice, companion to the same dialogue, while admiring the vista off the porch. Then we have gathered our dive gear, boarded Chris's little boat, and somewhere in the bay, slipped quietly into the clear, tepid water, and immersed ourselves in Fiji time.

Life on the reef is rich and diverse. Finely branching corals— pink, green, blue, and yellow—stretch calcium limbs towards the sky. Massive colonies of green corals have slowly grown over the centuries, like sequoias of the sea, forming living mounds nearly the size of our humble house. Collectively, the corals create majestic pinnacles, whose origins rest on the sandy bottom sometimes forty or fifty feet below, and whose sun-driven summits often caress the underside of the sea's surface.

Interspersed in crevices, and undulating near the coral's shallow crown, large schools of tiny fish—orange, lavender, and pink—wiggle their tails and wave their heads in unison, choreographed by the current.

Like the festive *sulus* worn by Fijian men and women, other fish are clad in spots and stripes of radiant colors, as though on daytime loan from the multihued sunsets that punctuate the soft transition into night.

Over the weeks, during our daily indulgence of the reef and Fiji time, the fish, the coral, and their braided routines, have become familiar. In these aquatic communities, as with those on land, existence hinges on an elegant equilibrium—a delicately balanced blend of collaboration and competition.

As our familiarity with the dynamics of reef populations increased, so did our appreciation for the intricacy of Fijian village life. One day early in our stay, the fuel line of our boat's outboard engine became fouled, perhaps with water. We never resolved exactly how or why, and as with so many of life's enigmas, this remains a mystery. But the symptoms were clear. With the boat hauled up on the beach, we pulled off the glistening white plastic cover. As we began to excavate the engine's inner workings, a group of local fisherman gathered to "assist."

In a Fijian village, anyone's affairs, are everyone's affairs. This included our engine. Amused, intrigued, and attentive, the group's individual opinions, vociferously expressed in long strings of mostly vowels interspersed with laughter, eventually evolved to consensus. Our investigations were either politely condemned or condoned by the throng. Although boat engines were nothing new to this crowd, we readily observed that interpersonal relations were often just as temperamental as the motors themselves.

After the surgery was complete, and the cover replaced, Chris pulled the starter cord. The engine sputtered momentarily, and with a unanimous and exuberant *Bula!*, was coaxed back to life. We invited the team back to the porch, where we exchanged introductions and congratulations, followed by a few celebratory rounds of Fiji Bitters.

As with our engine, and the colorful scales of reef fish, a simple cover often cloaks complexity. *Bula!*, we discovered, was equally endowed.

Hospitality is as innate to Fijian culture as the people are indigenous to these islands. Soon after the great motor revival, Chris and

I accepted unending invitations into the homes of our hosts and gradually, the complexion of "Fiji time" was unveiled.

Village life is both individual and collective. Tools, talents, chores, and children are all shared. Older kids attend the needs of younger ones, and often they all carouse the neighborhood, like a playful pack of dolphins. Whichever children end up in the yard at meal time are fed. Often the entire gang sleeps at one home, and the following morning, dressed in fresh clothes to start the day. The soiled garments, independent of ownership, are washed and hung on the line, awaiting their occupants' next arrival.

Personal property is communal property. The phrase "*keri, keri*" is a traditional request that is rarely refused. "*Keri, keri*, your frying pan," for example, means "please lend me your pan." Possessions are shared by obligation. What's mine is yours—by cultural edict. Through this, and other customs, a village takes care of itself, and all its members.

What Fijian life lacks in physical complexity, it compensates for in social and political doctrine. Personal issues are community issues, often resolved by the chief, or elders of the village. And while survival is rarely an issue, personal industry is the foundation of Fiji time. Women, in addition to all the household tasks, labor in the fields growing *dalo*, taro, cassava, and other food crops. Men typically are entrusted with construction, maintenance, and at least in this village, fishing. Interwoven with the work, and in fact supported by it, is the buoyant temperament at whose apex resides the ubiquitous *Bula!*

So it was with some surprise, that as Chris and I completed a delightful day of diving and saw our village fishermen gathered beneath the palms of the shore, not a single *Bula!* was bestowed.

Chris switched off the boat engine, and we quietly glided closer to the beach. The late afternoon sun bathed the trees and the men in a warm yellow light, casting long dark shadows on the sand. Equally dark were the expressions of our friends. Soon we saw why.

I remember the sound of our keel softly grating against the sand as our craft came to rest alongside Tui's small white skiff. Its floor-boards were afloat in a sea of blood. Chris and I quickly jumped to the beach, and in an instant that slowed to an eternity, we were among the men.

Words were not needed. Beneath a small blanket of green palm fronds lay Evuloni, curled up on his left side, as though taking a nap in the shade. A bloodstained towel was draped across his right thigh. Lemecki pulled back the shroud, exposing the wound. A semicircular section of flesh, the size of a young coconut, had been excised, neatly and nearly to the bone.

He and Tui had been spearfishing across the bay. As always, the fish were tied to a line around his waist. This time, however, a small but aggressive shark had swallowed the entire catch, and with it, part of Evuloni's leg.

Kneeling down to check his pulse, Chris desperately asked if someone had called the town's only ambulance. The men solemnly replied yes, but now they were waiting for it to come. I looked at our friend on the ground. He was unconscious, in shock, and quivering like a speared fish. This was no time to wait.

I ran down the unpaved road to a small resort, quickly commandeered a pickup truck, and we all carefully placed Evuloni in the back. Lemecki drove, the others crouched in the rear, cradling their comrade as best they could. The truck was soon only an echo of dust left suspended in the twilight air. The ambulance never did arrive.

That was the last time Chris or I saw Evuloni. He died on the way to the hospital, we were told. Lemecki later speculated that Evoluni had baited the shark deliberately—he was having problems with his wife. The village will look after his wife and two children so young they may not remember their father as they grow.

Later that night, Chris and I sat on the porch where just weeks before we'd hoisted beers with the boys. Moonlight shimmered off the glassy ripples of the bay. Beneath the iridescent surface, reef fish peacefully slept, awaiting the dawn. The palms were now silhouettes against a black sky. Over a soft chorus of crickets and geckos, we quietly talked about the incident. The wound was serious but not in itself fatal. Why didn't Tui stop the bleeding? Why didn't the ambulance come? Why didn't Tui just drive the boat to the clinic near the shore where they were fishing? The questions were for our ears alone. There were no answers.

I had never seen a man die. Nor have I since. And over the course of thirty years of diving the tropics, and numerous visits to Fiji, this remains the single shark attack in my experience. Yes, Evoluni died. But it wasn't the shark that killed him. It was Fiji time.

Joel Simon's photo assignments have taken him to all seven continents, including the North Pole, the Antarctic, and ninety-five countries in between. When not traveling, he's at home in Menlo Park, California, with his wife, Kim, their cat, Ichiban, and an itinerant possum named Rover.

* * *

Choices and Promises

You are your own judge.

ONE EVENING IN JANUARY OF 1974, JEANIE DICUS OF STERLING, Virginia, was lying on the sofa watching television. She remembers feeling strange, then waking up in an ambulance and being told she had had a seizure. Nothing like that had happened to her before nor was there any family history of such a condition. This event was followed by a migraine headache and more seizures. Later, she, her husband, and her daughter drove to Baltimore where her father was a psychiatric consultant at Johns Hopkins Hospital and where they were assured she would receive the finest care. Her case was given to the head of neurology, and she was put on Dilantin and pheno-barbital, normal medications for what appeared to be epilepsy. However, Dicus got much worse and was given yet another drug in addition to the two she was taking. Within three months she had become schizophrenic and was given Valium, as well. She became suicidal and lapsed into one seizure after another. More drugs. More compounding effects, until, by summer, she was engulfed in a catatonic coma that lasted two months. A ward doctor finally noticed what was going on, went to Dicus's father and said, "All her symptoms are the result of the medications, not from mental illness. Stop the drugs." The physician in charge was immediately pulled off the case and shock treatments were applied in an attempt to free Dicus from the coma. By the time this decision was reached, her hands and feet had atrophied and were twisted and paralyzed, her skin was covered with pimples. Electric shocks did make a difference, but during the tenth treatment her heart went into fibrillation—the nurse had forgotten to give her a necessary shot of potassium—and she died:

I was floating above my body. I saw green shower caps. The people in the room all wore those stupid caps. There were five or six caps and they were panicky. Their fear was so thick I could feel it. I kept thinking, Hey, I'm okay, don't worry, but they didn't get my message. This was a little frustrating.

I found myself in the right-hand corner of the room. I lifted my arm and stretched. I had been immobile for so long. It felt like I had taken off a body girdle, and it was so delicious to get out of that cramped body. I felt a wonderful feeling wash over me—a sense of peace and power. I felt love and a sense of wonder as I realized that any question I could come up with would be answered.

There was Jesus. I was stunned and said, "I don't believe in you." He smiled and said the etheric equivalent of tough shit, here I am. Looking at his eyes, I asked, "You mean, you've been with me the whole time and I didn't know?" And his reply was: "Lo, I am with thee, always, even beyond the end of the

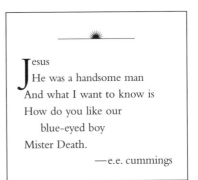

Jesus
He was a handsome man
And what I want to know is
How do you like our
   blue-eyed boy
Mister Death.

        —e.e. cummings

world." Now, I wasn't into *lo* so I said, "Hey, man, this is the seventies and we don't say *lo*. Come on." He kind of grinned, I guess I was amusing him, and answered, "You want to be reincarnated?" "Hey, give me a break," I yelled (only I made no sound). "I just died. Don't I get a chance to rest?" "Take it easy, hold on, it's alright. You can change your mind at any time." I gasped. "I don't even believe in you and now you want me to reincarnate. Help!"

Our conversation continued. He even asked me to kiss his feet. No way. I gave him a bear hug and kissed his cheek. I got the equivalent of a belly laugh. I was so happy with him that words were no longer necessary. We then communicated mind-to-mind. Suddenly I was aware God was coming. I came to know that I had needed a human-looking Christ to relate to so I wouldn't be scared. The Light came and I was given a choice—I could remain trapped in earth, seeing and hearing everything, but unable to help anyone, not even my daughter (I was told this was limbo), or I could stay with God. I chose God.

The White Light in front of me was sorta like a white light bulb only it was so strong. I remember thinking my eyes should be burning, but then I remembered that I didn't have any eyes to burn. God was love and love was light, and it was warm and it permeated every molecule of me. This was so delicious. I was crying with torrents of tears that didn't exist. It was so enormous. I was loved. I didn't feel irrelevant. I felt humble, awed, and amazed. For a long time after my near-death experience, I ended my prayers with, "you are soooooo big!" It was my way of expressing appreciation.

Then I was instantly zapped to a domed room with square screens up and down the walls, on the ceiling—hundreds of television screens. On each screen was a home movie of one event in my life. The good, the bad, the secret, the ugly, the special. Everything was going on at once; nothing was chronological. All was silent. When you looked at the other people or animals, you could hear their thoughts, their feelings, too. And you made the connection between these and the events which ensued. You were filled with, not guilt, but a strong sense of responsibility.

God said to me: "I gave you the precious gift of life. What did you do with this gift?" I answered in a puny, wimpish voice, "I'm only twenty-three. I didn't know I was supposed to do anything. I have a two-year-old daughter. I spend my time and energy on her." It wasn't a good answer, but it was the truth. I was the judge and I was satisfied. I guess that was what God wanted. But the next time this happens, I'm having a list ready. I now have a card on my fridge door that says, "Practice random kindness and senseless beauty." I asked a lot of questions, about sin, murder, and such, and I got a lot of answers. I was told that before we're born, we have to take an oath that we will pretend time and space are real so we can come here and advance our spirit. If you don't promise, you can't be born.

P. M.H. Atwater, Lh.D., is a researcher in the fields of near-death experience and parapsychology. She the author of Children of the New Millennium: Children's Near-Death Experiences and the Evolution of Humankind *and* Beyond the Light: The Mysteries and Revelations of Near-Death Experiences, *from which this story is excerpted. She lives in Charlottesville, Virginia.*

VAL PLUMWOOD

* ⋆ *

Being Prey

*She journeyed into the jaws of Infinity and
returned to tell us what she saw.*

IN THE EARLY WET SEASON, KAKADU'S PAPERBARK WETLANDS ARE
especially stunning, as the water lilies weave white, pink, and blue
patterns of dreamlike beauty over the shining towers of thunder-
cloud reflected in their still waters. Yesterday, the water lilies and the
wonderful bird life had enticed me into a joyous afternoon's idyll as
I ventured onto the East Alligator Lagoon for the first time in a
canoe lent by the park service. "You can play about on the back-
waters," the ranger had said, "but don't go onto the main river
channel. The current's too swift, and if you get into trouble, there
are the crocodiles. Lots of them along the river!" I followed his
advice carefully and glutted myself on the magical beauty and bird
life of the lily lagoons, untroubled by crocodiles.

Today, I was tempted to repeat that wonderful experience despite
the light drizzle beginning to fall as I made my way to the canoe
launch site. I set off on a day trip in search of an Aboriginal rock art
site across the lagoon and up a side channel. The drizzle turned to
rain within a few hours, and the magic was lost. At thirty-five
degrees Celsius, the wet season rains could be experienced as comfortable and welcome: they were late this year, and the parched land
and all of it inhabitants eagerly awaited their relief. Today in the

rain, though, the birds were invisible, the water lilies were sparser, and the lagoon seemed even a little menacing. I noticed now how low the fourteen-foot Canadian canoe sat in the water, just a few inches of fiberglass between me and the great saurians, close relatives of the ancient dinosaurs. Not long ago, saltwater crocodiles were considered endangered, as virtually all mature animals were shot out of the rivers and lakes of Australia's north by commercial hunting. After a decade and more of protection, their numbers are beginning to burgeon. They are now the most plentiful of the large animals of Kakadu National Park, which preserved a major area of their breeding habitat. I was actively involved in the struggle to keep such places, and for me, the crocodile was a patent symbol of the power and integrity of this place and the incredible richness of its aquatic habitats.

After hours of searching the maze of shallow channels in the swamp, I was unable to locate the clear channel leading to the rock art site, as shown on the ranger's sketch map. When I pulled my canoe over in driving rain to a rock outcrop rising out of the swamp for a hasty, sodden lunch, I experienced the unfamiliar sensation of being watched. Having never been one for timidity, in philosophy or in life, I decided, rather than return defeated to my sticky caravan, to explore a clear, deep channel closer to the river I had traveled along the previous day.

The rain squalls and wind were growing more severe, and several times I had to pull my canoe over to tip the rainwater out of it. The channel soon developed steep mud banks and snags, and the going was slow. Farther on, the channel opened up, eventually petering out, blocked by a large sandy bar. I pushed the canoe toward the bank, looking around carefully before getting out in the shallows and pulling the canoe up. I would be safe from crocodiles in the canoe—I had been told—but swimming and standing or wading at the water's edge were dangerous. Edges are one of the crocodile's favorite food-capturing places. I saw nothing, but the feeling of unease that had been with me all day intensified.

The rain eased temporarily, and I picked my way across a sandbar covered with scattered scrub to see what there was of this puzzling place. As I crested the gently sloping dune, I was shocked to glimpse the muddy brown waters of the East Alligator River gliding silently only 100 yards ahead of me. The channel I followed had evidently been an anabranch and had led me back to the main river. Nothing stirred along the riverbank, but a great tumble of escarpment cliffs up on the other side of the river caught my attention. One especially striking rock formation—a single large rock balanced precariously on a much smaller one—held my gaze. As I looked, my whispering sense of unease turned into a shout of danger. The strange formation put me sharply in mind of two things: the indigenous Gagadgu owners of Kakadu, whose advice about coming here I had not sought, and of the precariousness of my own life, of human lives. As a solitary specimen of a major prey species of the saltwater crocodile, I was standing in one of the most dangerous places on the face of the earth.

I turned decisively to go back the way I had come, with a feeling of relief. I had not found the rock paintings, I rationalized, but it was too late to look for them now. The strange rock formation presented itself instead as a telos of the day. I had come here, I had seen something interesting, now I could go, home to caravan comfort.

As I pulled the canoe out into the main current, the torrential rain and wind started up again; the swelling stream would carry me home the quicker, I thought. I had not gone more that five or ten minutes back down the channel when, rounding a bend, I saw ahead of me in midstream what looked like a floating stick—one I did not recall passing on my way up. As the current moved me toward it, the stick appeared to develop eyes. A crocodile! It is hard to estimate size from the small nose and eye protrusions the crocodile leaves, in cryptic mode, above the waterline, but it did not look like a large one. I was close to it now but was not especially afraid; an encounter would add interest to the day.

Although I was paddling to miss the crocodile, our paths were strangely convergent. I knew it was going to be close but was totally unprepared for the great blow that came against the side of the canoe. Again it came, again and again, now from behind, shuddering the flimsy craft. I paddled furiously, but the blows continued. The unheard of was happening, the canoe was under attack, the crocodile in full pursuit! For the first time, it came to me fully that I was prey. I realized I had to get out of the canoe or risk being capsized or pulled into deeper water of midchannel.

The bank now presented a high, steep face of slippery mud, difficult to scale. There was only one obvious avenue of escape, a paperbark tree with many low branches near the muddy bank wall. I made the split-second decision to try to leap into the lower branches and climb to safety. I steered the canoe over to the bank by the paperbark and stood up ready to jump. At the same instant, the crocodile rushed up alongside the canoe, and its beautiful, flecked golden eyes looked straight into mine. Perhaps I could bluff it, drive it away, as I had read of British tiger hunters doing. I waved my arms and shouted, "Go away!" (We're British here.) The golden eyes glinted with interest. I tensed for the jump and leapt. Before my foot even tripped the first branch, I had a blurred, incredulous vision of great toothed jaws bursting from the water. Then I was seized between the legs in a red-hot pincer grip and whirled into the suffocating wet darkness below.

The course and intensity of terminal thought patterns in near-death experiences can tell us much about our frameworks of subjectivity. A subjectively centered framework capable of sustaining action and purpose must, I think, view the world "from the inside," structured to sustain the concept of a continuing, narrative self; we remake the world in that way as our own, investing it with meaning, reconceiving it as sane, survivable, amendable to hope and resolution. The lack of fit between this subject-centered version and reality comes into play in extreme moments. In its final, frantic attempts to protect itself from the knowledge that threatens the narrative framework, the mind can instantaneously fabricate terminal doubt of extravagant, Cartesian proportions: *This is not really happening. This is a nightmare from which I will soon awake.* This desperate delusion split apart as I hit the water. In that flash, when my consciousness had to know the bitter certainty of its end, I glimpsed the world for the first time "from the outside," as a world no longer my own, an unrecognizable bleak landscape composed of raw necessity, that would go on without me, indifferent to my will and struggle, to my life or death.

Few of those who have experienced the crocodile's death roll have lived to describe it. It is, essentially, an experience beyond words of total terror, total helplessness, total certainty, experienced with undivided mind and body, of a terrible death in the swirling depths. The crocodile's breathing and heart metabolism is not suited to prolonged struggle, so the roll is an intense initial burst of power designed to overcome the surprised victim's resistance quickly. Then it is merely a question of holding the now feebly struggling prey under the water a while for an easy finish to the drowning job. The roll was a centrifuge of whirling, boiling blackness, which seemed about to tear my limbs from my body, driving water into my bursting lungs. It lasted for an eternity, beyond endurance, but when I seemed all but finished, the rolling suddenly stopped. My feet touched bottom, my head broke the surface, and spluttering, coughing, I sucked at air, amazed to find myself still alive. The crocodile still had me in its pincer grip between the legs, and the water came just up to my chest. As we rested together, I had just begun to weep for the prospects of my mangled body, when the crocodile pitched me suddenly into a second death roll.

When the tearing, whirling terror stopped again (this time perhaps it had not lasted quite so long), I surfaced again, still in the crocodile's grip, next to the stout branch of a large sandpaper fig growing in the water. I reached out and held onto the branch with all my strength, vowing to let the crocodile tear me apart rather than throw me again into that spinning, suffocating hell. For the first time I became aware of a low growling sound issuing from the crocodile's throat, as if it were angry. I braced myself against the branch ready for another roll, but after a short time the crocodile's jaws simply relaxed, I was free. With all of my power, I used my grip on the branch to pull away, dodging around the back of the fig tree to avoid the forbidding mud bank, and tried once more the only apparent avenue of escape, to climb into the paperbark tree.

As in the repetition of a nightmare, when the dreamer is stuck fast in some monstrous pattern of destruction impervious to will or endeavor, the horror of my first escape attempt was exactly repeated. As I leapt into the same branch, the crocodile again propelled itself from the water, seizing me once more, this time around the upper left thigh. I briefly felt a hot sensation before being again submerged in the terror of the third death roll. Like the others, it stopped eventually, and we came up in the same place as before, next to the sandpaper fig branch. I was growing weaker, but I could see the crocodile taking a long time to kill me this way. It seemed to be intent on tearing me apart slowly, playing with me like a huge growling cat with a torn mouse. I did not imagine that I would survive, so great seemed its anger and its power compared to mine. I prayed for a quick finish and decided to provoke it by attacking it with my free hands. Feeling back behind me along the head, which still held my body in its jaws, I encountered two lumps. Thinking I had the eye sockets, I jabbed my thumbs into them with all my might. They slid into warm, unresisting holes (which may have been the ears or perhaps the nostrils), and the crocodile did not so much as flinch. In despair, I resumed my grasp on the branch, dreading death by slow torture. Once again, after a time, I felt the crocodile jaws relax, and I pulled free.

I knew now that I must break the pattern. *Not* back into the paperbark. Up the impossible, slippery mud bank was the only way. I threw myself at it with all of my failing strength, scrabbling with my hands for a grip, failing, sliding, falling back to the bottom, to the waiting jaws of the crocodile. I tried a second time and almost made it before sliding back, braking my slide two-thirds of the way down by grabbing a tuft of grass. I hung there, exhausted, defeated, *I can't make it, I thought. It'll just have to come and get me.* It seemed a shame, somehow, after all I had been through. The grass tuft began to give way. Flailing wildly to stop myself from sliding farther, I found my fingers jamming into the soft mud, and that supported me. This was the clue I needed to survive. With the last of my strength, I climbed up the bank, pushing my fingers into the mud to hold my weight, reached the top, and stood up, incredulous. I was alive!

✳

Escaping the crocodile was not by any means the end of my struggle to survive. I was alone, severely injured, and many miles from help. During the struggle, I was so focused on survival that the pain from the injuries had not registered. As I took my first urgent steps away from the vicinity of the crocodile, I knew something was wrong with my leg. *The bastard's broken my knee.* I did not wait to inspect the damage, but took off away from the crocodile in the direction of the ranger station.

After putting more distance between myself and the crocodile, I felt a bit safer and stopped to find out what was wrong with my leg. Now I was aware for the first time of how serious my wounds were. I did not remove my clothing to see the damage to the groin area inflicted by the first hold. What I could see was bad enough. The left thigh hung open, with bits of fat, tendon and muscle showing, and a sick, numb feeling suffused my entire body. I tore up some of my clothing to try and bind the wounds up and made a tourniquet for the thigh to staunch the bleeding, then staggered on, thinking only of getting back to the ranger station. Still elated from my escape, I imagined myself, spattered with blood and mud, lurching sensationally into the station. I went some distance before realizing with a sinking heart that I had crossed the swamp above the station in the canoe and that without it I could not get back to the station under my own steam. Perhaps I would die out here after all.

I would have to rely on being found by a search party, but I could maximize my chances by moving downstream toward the swamp edge, about three kilometers away. Still exhilarated by my escape, perhaps now I had a chance of survival. I had recently been reading Robert Graves's memoir of soldiers in the First World War who had been able to walk long distances with severe injuries and survived. Walking was still possible, and there was nothing better to do. Whenever I lay down to rest, the pain seemed even worse. I struggled on, through driving rain, shouting for mercy from the sky, apologizing to the angry crocodile, calling out my repentance to this place for the fault of my intrusion. I came to a flooded tributary and had to make a large upstream detour to find a place where I could cross it in my weakened state.

My considerable bush experience stood me in good stead, keeping me on course (navigating was second nature), and practiced endurance stopped me from losing heart. As I neared the swamp above the ranger station after a journey of several hours, I began to black out and had to crawl the final distance to its edge. I could do no more for myself; I selected an open spot near the swamp edge, and lay there in the gathering dusk to await what would come. I did not expect a search party until the following day, and I doubted I could possibly last the night.

The heavy rain and wind stopped with the onset of darkness, and it grew perfectly still. Dingoes howled, and clouds of mosquitoes whined around by body. I hoped to pass out soon, but consciousness persisted. There were loud swirling noises in the water, and I knew I was easy meat for another crocodile. After what seemed like a long time, I heard the distant sound of a motor and saw a light moving across the other side of the swamp. Thinking it was a boat crossing the swamp to rescue me, I had enough strength to rise up on my elbow and call out for help. I thought I heard a very faint reply, but then the motor grew fainter and the lights went away. Thinking I had imagined the voice, I was as devastated as any castaway who signals desperately to a passing ship and is not seen.

It was not from a boat that the lights had come. Passing my caravan, the ranger noticed there was no light. He had come down to the canoe launch site in a motorized trike to check and, realizing that I had not returned, stopped his motor to listen. He had heard my faint call for help across the dark water, and after some time, a rescue craft appeared. As they lifted me into the boat that was to begin my thirteen-hour journey to Darwin Hospital, my rescuers discussed the need to go upriver the next day and shoot a crocodile. I spoke strongly against this plan: I was the intruder on crocodile territory, and no good purpose could be served by random revenge. The area was full of crocodiles in the water just around the spot I was lying. That spot was under six feet of water the next morning, flooded by the rains signaling the onset of the wet season.

In the end I was found in time and survived against many odds, thanks to the ranger's diligence, my own perseverance, and great good fortune. A similar combination of good fortune and human care enabled me to overcome an infection in the leg that threatened an amputation or worse. I probably have Paddy Pallin's incredibly tough walking shorts to thank for the fact that the groin injuries were not as severe as the leg injuries. I am very lucky that I can still walk well and have lost few of my previous capacities. Lady Luck shows here, as usual, her inscrutable face: Was I lucky to survive or unlucky to have been attacked in the first place? The wonder of being alive after being held—quite literally—in the jaws of death has never entirely left me. For the first year, the experience of existence as an unexpected blessing cast a golden glow over my life, despite the injuries and the pain. The glow has slowly faded, but some of the gratitude for life it left will always be there, even if I remain unsure whom I should thank. The gift of gratitude came from the searing flash of near-death knowledge, a glimpse "from the outside" of the alien, incomprehensible world in which the narrative of self has ended.

There remain many mysteries about the reasons for the attack on the canoe itself, which are unusual in crocodile lore. One issue on which there has been much speculation is the size of the crocodile. It has always been difficult for me to estimate its size because for most of the attack, it was either only partly visible or had ahold of me from behind. The press estimate of fourteen feet—which they arrived at somehow and published widely some five days before I made any sort of statement on the subject—was, I think, certainly an overestimate. One glimpse of the partly submerged crocodile next to the fourteen-foot canoe suggested that it was not as long as the canoe. If the press had an interest in exaggerating the size of the crocodile, the park service, which feared legal liability, had an interest in minimizing it; neither group seemed interested in my views on the matter.

The park service speculated that the crocodile may have been a young male evicted from breeding territory and perhaps embattled by other crocodiles. Their theory is that the crocodile attacked my canoe after a collision by mistaking it for one of these older aggressive crocodiles. From my perspective, however, there are some problems with this account. It is very unlikely that I accidentally struck it with the canoe, as the story assumes and as some press reports claimed. Crocodiles are masters of water, and this one was expecting me and saw me coming. The crocodile most likely observed the passing of my canoe on the way up the channel only a short time before, as it did seem to *intercept* the canoe. Why should a small crocodile of less that ten feet aggressively attack a much larger, fourteen-foot canoe "crocodile" unless we assume that it was bent on suicide? The smaller the crocodile, the more implausible such an attack story becomes. Because crocodiles become sexually mature at around ten feet, the park service's minimization story of a "self-defense" attack by a "small" evicted crocodile is not even internally consistent. My personal estimate is that it was probably a medium crocodile in the range of eight to twelve feet.

Possible explanations for the anomalous attack are almost limitless. Perhaps the crocodile's motives were political, against a species-enemy, human beings are a threat to crocodiles, of a more dire kind than crocodiles are to human beings, through the elimination of habitat. The crocodile may have thought that any human being who ventured alone into these waters in those conditions was offering itself as a sacrifice to crocodile kind. The extreme weather events may have played a role. The crocodile is an exploiter of the great planetary dualism of land and water. As Papua New Guinea writer Vincent Eri suggests in his novel, *The Crocodile*, the creature is a sort of magician: Its technique is to steal the Other, the creature of the land, away into its own world of water where it has complete mastery over it. Water is the key to the crocodile's power, and even large crocodiles rarely attack in its absence.

The crocodile is then a boundary inhabitant and may take a person in a canoe as either of the land or of the water. If a crocodile perceives such a person as *outside* its medium of mastery, the person may not be seen as prey and may be safe from attack. If a person in a canoe is perceived as potentially of the water, as he or she might easily be in an early wet-season day of torrential rain when the boundaries of the crocodile empire are exploding, the person may be much less than safe. Clearly, we must question the assumption, common up until the time of my attack, that canoes are as safe as larger craft because they are perceived similarly as outside the crocodile's medium.

The most puzzling question of all, of course, is why the crocodile let me go. I think there are several factors here. Because it was not a large crocodile that can kill with little effort, perhaps I was marginal prey. The depth of the water and the way it had ahold of my body made it hard for it to keep me under, and it may have let me go the first time to try to get a better grip higher up on my body. Its failure to keep me submerged suggests that it could have underestimated my size, seeing me sitting in the canoe, or overestimated the depth of the rapidly rising water. Maybe it was a stray or a newcomer to the area who did not know the terrain well and was not familiar with the good drowning spots in the shallower back channels. My friend the sandpaper fig allowed me to retain a determined grip on my own medium and contributed essentially to my survival. In another encounter in the territory a few years earlier, an adult man was saved from a fourteen-foot crocodile dragging him off in shallow water by the grasp of a ten-year-old girl pulling the opposite way.

Perhaps, too, the crocodile let go its hold because it was tiring; I experienced the crocodile through the roll as immensely powerful, but that intense burst of energy cannot be sustained long, and must accomplish its purpose of drowning fairly quickly. I have no doubt that had the crocodile been able to keep me submerged after the first roll, there would have been no need for a second. My advice for others similarly placed is the same as that of Vincent Eri, who used the crocodile as a metaphor for the relationship between colonized indigenous culture and colonizing Western culture. If the crocodile-magician-colonizer can drag you completely into its medium, you have little chance; if you can somehow manage to retain a hold on your own medium, you may survive.

I had survived the crocodile attack but still had to survive the contest with the cultural drive to represent such experiences in terms of the masculinist monster myth: the master narrative. The encounter did not immediately present itself in the guise of a mythic struggle: I recall thinking with relief, as I struggled away from the attack site, that I would now have a good excuse for being late with an overdue article and would have a foolish but unusual story for my small circle of walking companions. Nor did the crocodile appear as an implacable monster, although its anger was a mystery. I figured I might have offended it somehow and wished we could have communicated. It had, after all, eventually let me go. Because crocodile attacks, especially in North Queensland, have often been followed by episodes of massive crocodile slaughter in which entire river populations were wiped out, I feared similar reprisals and felt not victorious, but responsible for putting the crocodiles at risk. To minimize this risk, I tried hard at first to minimize media publicity and keep the story for my friends' ears alone.

This proved to be extremely difficult. The media machine headlined a garbled version of the encounter anyway, and I came under great pressure, especially from the hospital authorities whose phone lines had been jammed for days, to give a press interview. We all want to pass on our story, of course, and I was no exception. Often, for the dying, it is not death itself that is the main concern, but the loss of their story, the waste of the narrative that is their life's experience, the crucial ingredients it might contribute to

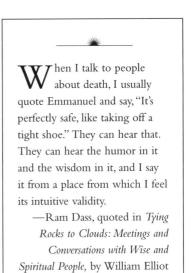

When I talk to people about death, I usually quote Emmanuel and say, "It's perfectly safe, like taking off a tight shoe." They can hear that. They can hear the humor in it and the wisdom in it, and I say it from a place from which I feel its intuitive validity.

—Ram Dass, quoted in *Tying Rocks to Clouds: Meetings and Conversations with Wise and Spiritual People,* by William Elliot

the salty stock of human wisdom. During those incredible split seconds when the crocodile dragged me a second time from tree to water, I had a powerful vision of friends discussing my death with grief and puzzlement. The focus of my own regret was that they would never learn how my story had ended. They would never know about my struggle and might think I had been taken while risking a swim. So important is the story and so deep the connection to others, carried through the narrative self, that it haunts even our final desperate moments.

To the extent that the story is crucial, by the same token the narrative self is threatened with invasion and loss of integrity when the story of the self is taken over by others and given an alien meaning. This is what the mass media tend to do in stereotyping and sensationalizing stories like mine, and this is what is done all the time to subordinated groups, such as indigenous peoples, when their voices and stories are digested and repackaged in assimilated form. As a story that evoked the monster myth, mine was especially subject to masculinist appropriation. The imposition of the master narrative appeared in a number of different forms: in the exaggeration of the crocodile's size, in the portrayal of the encounter as a heroic wrestling match, and especially in its sexualization. The events seemed to provide irresistible material for the pornographic imagination, which encouraged male identification with the crocodile and interpretation of the attack as sadistic rape. The reinterpretation of the experience in these sexual terms and its portrayal in porno films like *Crocodile Blondee* reveal the extent to which sadism is normalized in dominant culture as masculinist sexuality.

Although I had survived in part because of my active struggle and bush experience, one of the major meanings evoked by the narrative was that the bush was no place for a woman. Much of the Australian media seemed to have trouble coming to terms with the idea of women being competent in the bush, but the most advanced expression of this masculinist mindset was *Crocodile Dundee*, which was filmed in Kakadu not long after my encounter. If page-three articles and *Crocodile Blondee* eroticized the crocodile as a male sadist, *Crocodile Dundee* took the more respectable course of eroticizing female passivity and victimhood. The two biggest recent escape stories had both involved active women, one of whom had actually saved a man. However, the film's story line split the experience along conventional gender lines, appropriating the active struggle, escape, and survival parts of the experience for the male hero and representing the passive "victim" parts in the character of an irrational and helpless woman who is incompetent in the bush and has to be rescued from the crocodile-sadist (the rival male) by the bushman hero.

For a long time, I felt alienated from my own story by the imposition of these stereotypes and had to wait nearly a decade before I felt able to repossess my story fully and write about the experience in my own terms. For our narrative selves, being able to pass on our stories in an authentic form is a crucial part of satisfaction in life, a way to participate in and be empowered by culture. Passing on the story is often much more important to people than material possessions; that is why they are capable of making such enormous sacrifices so that the story, the struggle of memory against forgetting, will survive. Retelling the story of a traumatic event can have tremendous healing power. During my recovery, it seemed as if each telling took part of the pain and distress of the memory away. Passing on the story can be a way to transcend not only social harm, but also our own biological death and bodily limitation.

Cultures differ considerably in the opportunities they provide for passing on their stories. Because of its highly privatized conception of the individual, contemporary Western culture is, I think, relatively impoverished in this respect, especially compared with certain indigenous cultures. That is part of the emptiness at its core, an emptiness that must be assuaged with more material commodities and more control. In contrast, many Australian Aboriginal cultures seem to offer rich opportunities for passing on the story, in ways that are reflected in the opportunities for transcendence of individual death provided in the accounts of human identity. In much Aboriginal thinking about death, animals, plants, and humans are seen as sharing a common life force, and there are many narrative continuities and interchanges between humans and other life. To the extent that such a culture provides intense narrative identifications with land and with an ecological and social community based on the history of that land extending over time, a form of individual meaning and narrative continuity is available that enables some degree of transcendence of the individual's death.

In Western thinking, in contrast, the human is set apart from nature as radically other. Religions like Christianity must then seek narrative continuity for the individual in the idea of an authentic self that is nonbodily and above the earth: the eternal soul. This sort of recipe for transcendence of death, however, is bought at a great price, one that can provide narrative continuity for the individual only in isolation from the cultural and ecological community and in opposition to a person's perishable body. This solution to the problem of providing continuity depends on creating a split within the individual and within culture between the immaterial, eternal soul, as the "higher" human essence that continues after death, and the inessential, devalued, and animal body, which dies. Boundary breakdown is an ever-present threat and source of anxiety, reflected in the aura of horror that surrounds deathly decay in the Western tradition, as the forbidden mixing of these hyperseparated categories, the dissolution of the sacred-human into the profane-natural.

If ordinary death is a horror, death in the jaws of a crocodile is the ultimate horror. It multiplies these forbidden boundary breakdowns, combining decomposition of the victim's body with the overturning of the victory over nature and materiality that Christian death represents. Crocodile predation on humans threatens the dualistic vision of human mastery of the planet in which we are predators but can never ourselves be prey. We may daily consume other animals in their billions, but we ourselves cannot be food for worms and certainly not meat for crocodiles.

For the human self as narrative subject, the end of the story is beyond comprehension, outside the framework. For me, it was as if, before the event, I saw the whole universe as framed by my own narrative, as though the two were joined perfectly and seamlessly together. As my own narrative and the larger story in which it was embedded were ripped painfully apart, I glimpsed beyond my own realm a shockingly indifferent world of necessity in which I had no more significance than any other edible being. The thought, *This can't be happening to me. I'm a human being, not meat, I don't deserve this fate!* was one component of my terminal incredulity. Confronting the brute fact of being prey, together with the astonishing view of this larger story in which my "normal" ethical terms of struggle seemed absent or meaningless, brought home to me rather sharply that we inhabit not only an ethical order, but also something not reducible to it, an ecological order. We live by illusion if we believe we can shape our lives, or those of the other beings with whom we share the ecosystem, in the terms of the ethical and cultural sphere alone.

Although I had been a vegetarian for some ten years before the encounter with the crocodile and remain one today, this knowledge makes me wary of the kind of uncontextualized foundation for vegetarianism that suggests that predation is either a negligible anomaly or an unredeemable ethical deficiency in the ecosystem. The presentation of the food chain as a (potentially) peaceful order ideally subject to nonviolent reconfiguration leads ulti-

In the Zen tradition, to die is nothing special. In her foreward to Helen Tworkov's *Zen in America*, Natalie Goldberg tells a marvelous story which exemplifies the calm attitude of a great Zen master when facing the imminent prospect of death:

When a rebel army took over a Korean town, all fled the Zen temple except the abbot. The rebel general burst into the temple, and was incensed to find that the master refused to greet him, let alone receive him as a conqueror.

"Don't you know," shouted the general, "that you are looking at one who can run you through without batting any eye?"

"And you," said the abbot, "are looking at one who can be run through without batting an eye!"

—Sushila Blackman, *Graceful Exits: How Great Beings Die*

mately toward the thoroughly antiecological position that the earth is ethically improved by the elimination of predation. Such an overgeneralized form of vegetarianism can remain consistent only by redoubling the stress on certain radical discontinuities in the categories of plants, animals, and humans. It must situate humans as exclusive possessors of an ideal ethical nature denied to other "lower" plant and animal forms of life and, on pain of starvation, reemphasize the Cartesian consciousness boundary to include in the field of ethical treatment only sentient beings. Other living beings remain outside the sphere of ethical eating and, presumably, ethics. These moves leave largely unquestioned, or merely relocate, the radical discontinuities of the dominant culture, in which the truly human belongs to an ethical order beyond edibility and ecology, while the nonhuman belongs to a hyperseparated edible and ecological order unconstrained by ethics.

In accordance with this dominant view, we have split both ourselves and the world into hyperseparated realms of nature and culture and have acted as if only the last were genuinely human and truly important. To realize a truly ecological identity, we must overcome this radical split, knitting together these hyperseparated realms from both directions, both by extending ecology to the human sphere and by extending ethics to the nonhuman sphere. This means that we must acknowledge not only that ethics applies to those we eat (both plant and animal life), but also the possibility of forms of ethical reciprocity in the food chain. In this case, ethical eating may not always exclude the taking of life, and predation may take forms that are understood in ethical terms. The project of constructing an ethical form for an ecologically sensitive life requires of us ethical evaluation of our ecological identities and relationships but does not suggest that the world would be ethically improved by the elimination of predation. I am a vegetarian primarily because ethical and ecological forms of predation are only exceptionally available in contemporary Western society, with its factory farming and commodified relationships to food.

Resisting the identification of the human with the ethical, and the nonhuman with the ecological, opens a way to bring the spheres of the ethical and ecological, culture and nature, closer together, but it does not make them identical. Paradox envelops their meeting; in that paradox we must somehow make our home as beings of both nature and culture whose ethical life should begin with the recognition that "all our food is souls." Coming to terms with the ethical challenge of other large predators is part of coming to terms with this paradox and with the ethical and the ecological collide; we are forced to face an ecological challenge to the realm of ethics and to try to respond with something more ethical than condemnation or revenge. This is part of the mystery and fascination of our relationship with other large predators.

Large predators like lions and crocodiles are the subjects of an obsessive gaze in contemporary popular culture, and some of this may be derived from the contemporary political agenda of social Darwinism. However, there are also some good reasons for the focus on large predators: They present an important test for us, in both ethical and ecological terms. As ecologists have stressed, the ability of an ecosystem to support large predators is a criterion of its ecological integrity. Crocodiles and other creatures that can take human life also present an important test of ethical and political integrity. The colonizer identity is positioned as an eater of Others who can never themselves be eaten, just as the unmarked gaze of the colonizer claims the power to see but not to be seen. In terms of virtue ethics, the existence of free communities of animals that can prey on humans indicates our preparedness to share and to coexist with the otherness of the earth, to reject the colonizer identity and the stance of assimilation, which aims to make the Other over into a form that eliminates all friction, challenge, or consequence. The persistence of predator populations tests our integration of ethical and ecological identities, our recognition of our human existence in mutual, ecological terms, as ourselves part of the food chain, eaten as well as eater.

Thus the story of the crocodile encounter has, for me, come to have a significance quite the opposite of what is conveyed in the master/monster narrative. For me, it is a cautionary tale about survival and our relationship with the earth, about the need to learn to recognize who we are in different terms that acknowledge our own animality and the ecological as well as ethical context of our lives. I learned many personal lessons from the event, one of which is to

know better when to turn back and to be more open to the sorts
of messages and warnings I had ignored on that particular day. As
on the day itself, so even more to me now a decade later, the telos
of these events lies in the strange rock formation, which symbolized
so well the lessons about the vulnerability of humankind I had to
learn, lessons it seems largely lost to the technological culture that
now dominates the earth. In my work as a philosopher, I see more
and more reason to stress our failure to perceive this vulnerability
and the distortions of our view of ourselves as rational masters of a
tamed and malleable nature. The balanced rock suggests a link
between my insensitivity to my own vulnerability and the similar
failure of my culture in its occupation of the planetary biosystem.
Let us hope that it does not take a similar near-death experience to
instruct our culture in the wisdom of the balanced rock.

*Val Plumwood survived this incident in February 1985. She recently
returned to Australia after a stint as visiting professor of women's studies
at North Carolina State University. Her latest book is* Feminism and the
Mastery of Nature.

PART THREE

RITUALS

⋆ ⋆ ⋆

A Death in the Family

How morticians do it.

MY FATHER DIED THREE YEARS AGO ON AN ISLAND OFF THE COAST of Florida. He was sharing a condo with a woman friend who overestimated the remedial powers of sexual aerobics. Or maybe she underestimated the progress of his heart disease. All of his children knew it was coming. In the first year of his widowhood, he sat in his chair, heartsore, waiting for the other shoe to drop. Then he started going out with women. His sons were glad for him. His daughters rolled their eyes. In the two years of consortium that followed, he'd had a major—which is to say a chest-ripping, down-for-the count-type—heart attack every six months like clockwork. He survived all but one. "Three out of four," I can hear him saying, "but when it's over, you're still dead." He'd had enough. Even now, I think of that final scene in *Doctor Zhivago* when Zhivago's heart is described as "paper thin." He thinks he sees Lara turning a corner in Moscow. He struggles to get off the bus, loosens his tie, and finally makes it to the sidewalk, where, after two steps, he drops dead. Dead chasing love. That was my father—stepping not off a bus but out of a shower in his time-share condo, not in Moscow but on Boca Grande—chasing, just as certainly, love. Chasing it to death.

We are a family of undertakers—five of my eight siblings work in funeral homes that bear my father's name—so when we got the call from his woman friend, my brother and I knew what to do. We had a traveling kit of embalming supplies: gloves, fluids, needles, odds and ends. We had to explain ourselves to the security people at the airlines, who scrutinized the contents of the bag, wondering if we might be able to make a bomb out of embalming fluid or overtake the cabin crew with a box marked "Slaughter Surgical Supplies" that was full of stainless steel instruments they'd never seen before. When we got to the funeral home they had taken him to, the undertaker there asked if we were sure we wanted to do this— our own father, after all—and said he'd be happy to call in one of his own embalmers. We assured him that it would be okay. He showed us into the prep room, that familiar decor of porcelain and tile and fluorescent light—a tidy scientific venue for the horror of mortality, how easily we slip from is to isn't.

It was something we had always promised him, though I can't remember the context in which it was made—the promise that when he died his sons would embalm him, dress him, pick out a casket, lay him out, prepare the obits, contact the priests, manage the flowers, the casseroles, the wake and procession, the Mass and burial. Maybe it was just understood. His was a funeral he would not have to direct. It was ours to do; and though he'd directed thousands of funerals, he had never mentioned his own preferences. Whenever he was pressed on the matter he would only say, "You'll know what to do." We did.

I had seen my father horizontal before, most recently in intensive care units after his coronaries and bypasses, when he was helpless, done unto. But before that there had been the man lying on the living room rug tossing one of my younger siblings in the air; or napping on his office floor at the

> If you know not how to die, do not trouble yourself. Nature will in a moment fully and sufficiently instruct you. She will do it precisely right for you; do not worry about it.
>
> —Montaigne

first funeral home in full uniform—black three-piece, striped tie, wingtips, clean shave; or reclining in the bathtub singing, "From the halls of Montezuma to the shores of Tripoli!" In my childhood he was, like every father on the block, invincible. That he would die had been a fiction in my teens, a fear in my twenties, a specter in my thirties, and, in my forties, a fact.

But seeing him stretched out on the embalming table of the Anderson Mortuary in Fort Myers, with the cardiac blue in his ears and fingertips and along his shoulders and lower ribs and buttocks and heels, I thought, This is what my father will look like when he's dead. And then, as if a door slammed shut behind me, the tense shifted into the inescapable present: this is my father, dead. My brother and I hugged each other and wept for ourselves and for our sisters and brothers back in Michigan. Then I kissed my father's forehead, and we went to work in the way he had trained us.

His was a cooperative body, despite the arteriosclerosis, his circulatory system made the embalming easy. And having just stepped from the shower into his doom, he was clean and freshly shaven. Since he hadn't been sick in the intensive care sense of the word, there were none of the bruises or tubes wrought by medical science. He'd gotten the death he wanted: caught in full stride, hit quickly and cleanly after a day strolling the beach picking seashells for the grandchildren, and maybe after a little bone bouncing with his condomate, though she never said and we never asked and can only hope.

His body bore a kind of history: the tattoo with my mother's name on it that he'd had done as an eighteen-year-old marine during World War II, the perfectly trimmed mustache I used to watch him darken with my mother's mascara when he was younger than I am now, the scars from his quintuple-bypass surgery, the AA medallion he never removed, and the signet ring we gave him for his fortieth birthday, all of us saving money in a jar until fifty dollars had accumulated. I massaged his legs, his hands, his arms so that the fluid that would temporarily preserve him would be properly distributed. Watching the blue clear from his fingertips and heels as the liquid worked its way around his body, I was reminded of how we bury our dead and then become them. In the end I had to say, Maybe this is what I am going to look like dead.

We flew his body back, faxed the obits to the local papers, called the priests, the sexton, the florists, and the stonecutter. We act out things we cannot put into words.

I can remember my father, back in 1963, saying that the reason we have funerals and open caskets is so that we might confront what he called "the reality of death." The participation of the dead human body in its funeral, he used to say, is just as important as the bride being at her wedding, the baby at its baptism. He loved to quote Gladstone, the great Victorian liberal, who wrote that he could measure with mathematical precision a people's respect for the laws of the land by the way they cared for their dead. In 1963, Jessica Mitford had just sold a million copies of *The American Way of Death*, and Evelyn Waugh had lampooned the funeral industry in *The Loved One*. At cocktail parties, people were referring to funerals as "barbaric rituals" and "morbid curiosities," and the mortuary associations were scrambling for cover. Clergy, educators, and psychologists were assembled to proclaim that undertakers' work did in fact serve some purpose, that it was emotion-

---

Jessica Mitford succinctly described modern embalming as bodies being "sprayed, sliced, pierced, pickled, trussed, trimmed, creamed, waxed, painted, rouged, and neatly dressed—transformed from a common corpse into a Beautiful Memory Picture."

To achieve this memory picture, modern embalmers use four methods: (1) *arterial* embalming, in which they inject chemicals into the blood vessels; (2) *cavity* embalming, in which the abdomen and the chest are injected with chemicals; (3) *hypodermic* embalming, in which they inject chemicals under the skin in certain areas; and (4) *surface* embalming, in which they apply chemicals in liquid or gel form directly to the body surface.
    —Kenneth V. Iserson, *Death to Dust: What Happens to Dead Bodies?*

ally efficient, psychologically correct, to do what we'd been doing all along. The track record was pretty good on this. We—the species, not the undertaker—had been doing more or less the same thing for millennia: looking up while digging down, trying to make some sense out of it, disposing of our dead with sufficient pause to say that they'd lived in ways different from rocks and rhododendrons and that those lives were worth mentioning and remembering.

As I watch my generation labor to give their teenagers and young adults some "family values" between courses of pizza and Big Macs, I think that maybe my father had it right. He understood that the meaning of life is connected, inextricably, to the meaning of death; that mourning is a romance in reverse, and if you love, you grieve, and there are no exceptions. And if death is regarded as an embarrassment or an inconvenience, if the dead are regarded as a nuisance from whom we seek a hurried riddance, then life and the living are in for similar treatment.

Thus tending to my father's death, his dead body, had for me the same importance as being present for the births of my sons and daughter. Some expert on *Oprah* might call this "healing." Another on *Donahue* might mention "making good choices." But it is not about choices or functions or psychological correctness. The bodies of the newly dead are not remnant, nor are they entirely essence. They are, rather, changelings, incubates, hatchlings of a new reality. It is wise to treat such new things tenderly, carefully, with honor.

Thomas Lynch is an undertaker in Milford, Michigan, and is the author of Grimalkin & Other Poems, Still Life in Milford: Poems, *and* The Undertaking: Life Studies from the Dismal Trade.

JANET MILHOMME

✦ ✦ ✦

More than Just a Box

Put yourself in the driver's seat.

THE NEW MODELS ARE IN AT PAA JOE'S SHOWROOM. THE EAGLE IS there sporting a look to ruffle some feathers. For those Ghanaians who can afford it, the Mercedes offers an especially heavenly drive. The Barracuda might be dead in America, but the Cod lives on in Accra.

This is, of course, no ordinary vehicle showroom. The transport at Paa Joe's is not from one rutted road to another, but, instead, to another world, the spirit world. The models on display are wildly elaborate caskets that Ghanaians take their final drive in. They are bizarre, colorful, and joyous celebrations of life in sharp contrast to the grim boxed route offered those in the West.

Ghanaian tradition calls for an elaborate postmortem party that the family will go to any length to provide. The behavior of family members, the type of food and refreshments served, the quality of the music and dancing—and the choice of casket—are all important factors which will be judged and commented upon by all who attend.

Coffins are a critical feature of the Ghanaian wake and funeral and are crafted and chosen with incredible care and creativity. They come in an array of styles that symbolize the vitality of the departed's life by representing the tribe, town, profession, interests, achievements or dreams of the person. A beautifully crafted casket brings great honor to the deceased and his family.

Casketmaking is big business in Ghana. Signs along the road advertise the wares of different brands like competing car dealerships. The intricate coffins are created and sold at shops like Paa Joe's, whose sign out front tells people to "BUY YOUR COFFIN HERE."

In a simple showroom, the floor covered with sawdust, customers can choose from a variety of turtles, fish, birds, lizards, and crabs. For centuries, Ghanaian coffins have reflected the trade or status of the deceased. The chief fisherman of a village might be placed in a casket carved in the shape of a fish or perhaps a canoe. A carpenter or contractor might order a coffin designed to look like a house.

The detail and lifelike qualities of the coffins brighten up the sad occasion, leaving the enduring spirit of the departed with all who remain behind. The cocoa pod coffin gleams ripe for the picking. A little figurine at the top of the pod depicts the former cocoa farmer clipping a pod from a tree. The fish casket has a smile. You know that fisherman enjoyed his life.

One of the best features of the Ghanaian system is that people can achieve dreams

In Africa, when some old men tired of trying to get me to understand reincarnation and the notion of the body as a vessel of spirit, they finally organized an outing to the local brewery, a place that held much the same position in their thought as the Garden of Eden might in ours. From here, glamorously excluded by a security fence, you could see returned bottles through a plate-glass window, entering via one door, whirling from machine to machine, gliding magically along a production line, being endlessly refilled with squirting beer, relabelled and pushed out through another door for shipment to a thirsty world. Men watched this ballet, transfixed, for hour after hour.

"Life, death, spirit, and body. Now you have seen," they said.

— Nigel Barley, *Grave Matters: A Lively History of Death Around the World* unrealized in life. One woman had wanted to fly on a big jet airplane, but never had the opportunity. She was buried in her own custom-made 747 coffin.

It's hard to imagine this kind of playful, yet respectful approach in an American showroom. What models would symbolize our lives? Six-foot computer hard drives? Giant TV remote coffins?

In Ghana, though, you can go out in style. Taxi drivers or pedestrians who have always wanted to own one may be buried in a Mercedes, complete with steering wheel and leather interior. Truck drivers can head out on the non-potholed Highway in the Sky in their own big-rig coffin. Some of the options at Paa Joe's include corncobs, fishing boats, books, and doll houses—final resting places for farmers, fishermen, fetish priests, writers, chauffeurs, and mothers.

The elaborate creations are carved from lightweight *wawa* wood in sections that are fitted together and fastened with nails and wooden pegs. Coffins are often adorned with figurines and fetishes, and personalized with symbols, emblems, or special flowers and animals favored by the deceased.

It can take up to two weeks to craft a coffin depending on how elaborate it is. Usually a casket is ordered by a person well in advance of death, and each one is custom made. Each crew member specializes in a certain skill, such as rough cutting, fine carving, finishing, and painting.

For a Ghanaian, death is seen as the time when a person sets out on a long journey to the spirit world, where the ancestors have already gone. There's no more fitting vehicle than a casket representing the essence of interests and achievements culled from hard struggle in life.

That the exquisite works of the casketmakers are placed six feet underground does not seem to bother them. "Is that not the fate of each one of us?" asks one carver. "What difference, then, that my work precedes me to the earth?"

Janet Milhomme is an L.A.-based writer who has traveled extensively in Africa as a journalist and photographer. She was formerly Assistant Editor of Escape *magazine, and is currently at work on two books.*

★ ★ ★

Famadihana Diary

*The author journeys home to Madagascar
to celebrate her mother.*

I TRAVELLED ACROSS THE SEAS TO BE HERE TODAY. THIS DAY WAS long awaited, I would soon be in contact with my mother again. She had died seven years previously and I had not been able to be at her funeral. Tradition had always been so important to her so I knew she would be happy as I have come for her *famadihana*.

The meeting point is at 6 A.M. outside Cinema Soa in Antananarivo. My household woke up at about 4 A.M. to pack the food that had been prepared during the previous week. Drinks and cutlery are all piled into the car. A great number of people are expected as it is also the *famadihana* of the other members of my mother's family.

Fourteen cars and a big taxi-*brousse* carrying in all about fifty people, squashed one on top of the other, turn up. Everybody is excited. It is really great to see faces I haven't seen since my child-hood. Everybody greets each other and exchanges news.

At 8 A.M. we all set off. We are heading towards Ifalimanjaka (meaning "Joy Reigns Here"), in the *fivondronana* of Manjakandriana. Driving through villages with funny names like Ambohidrabiby ("The Town of Animals") brings me back to the time when such names were familiar. We make one stop at Talatan'ny volon'ondry

157

I have been privileged to attend two *famadihanas* in Madagascar. When I describe them to friends I find I have to keep emphasising what a life-enhancing experience this is. I wish we had something similar. In our culture there is the funeral, with all the grieving, maybe a memorial service but the sense of loss is still strong, and…that's it apart from photographs and perhaps an annual visit to the crematorium. When a *famadihana* takes place seven years or so after a death, the family have the chance to remember the dead with happy nostalgia, rather than pain.

On both these *famadihanas*, we felt we were honoured guests at a wonderful party. People were chatting, dancing to the bands, dressed up in their finery, and quite drunk. My strongest memory is of our host perched on the tomb with his camera taking photos of the tourists. A nice reversal of roles! It was not so different to a party at home, but with a special focus. If I were an ancestor, I think this is how I would like to be remembered.

— Hilary Bradt,
"Remembering *Famadihanas*"

for a breakfast of rice cakes and sausages: another opportunity to re-acquaint myself with long-lost cousins with whom I spent the long summer holidays as a child. We used to run around together playing games like catching grasshoppers and then finding carnivorous plants and dropping the insect in to see how long it took the plant to close its top to eat its prey.

We arrive at the tombs at 10 A.M. Faces are bright, full of expectancy. I ask what the day means to them. They all agree that it's a day for family togetherness, a day for joy, for remembrance.

We are in front of my mother's tomb. It is made out of stone and marble, very elegant. The family will have spent more money on keeping that tomb nice and well maintained than on their own house.

Everybody stands around in front of the tomb waiting for the main event to start: the opening of the tomb door. We have to wait for the president of the *fokon'tany* (local authority) to give permission to open the tomb. Although it had been arranged beforehand, he cannot be found anywhere. This wait, after such anticipation, is taken patiently by all—just one of those things.

Mats are laid on the ground on one side of the tomb. The atmosphere of joy is so tangible! Music is blaring out. Permission is finally granted to enter the tomb. The *ray aman-dreny* (the elders) are the first to enter.

The inside of my mother's tomb looks very comfortable with bunk beds made out of stone. It is very clean. There are names on the side of the beds. The national flag is hoisted on top of the tomb as a sign of respect. The conversation goes on happily on the little veranda outside the tomb's door, people chatting about the event and what they have been doing in the last few days.

They start to take the bodies out. Voices could be heard above the happy murmur: "Who is this one? This is your ma! This one your aunt! Here is your uncle! Just carry them around!" The closest relations carry the body but others could touch and say hello. When carrying them, they

Soon the Mentawai villagers [on Siberut, off Sumatra's west coast] disperse. But the baby's body is left in the middle of the *uma*, close to our lineup of mosquito nets, where we will sleep. Only the mother remains kneeling by the body. I can't sleep, though somehow my fellow travelers snooze through the mother's all-night howling. I lay listening to each round of sobs, recalling my mother's funeral and how I would have felt better if I had cried and howled and banged a stick all night rather than trying to maintain my composure. But within hours of my mother's death my family and I had to shelve our grief and decide on a cemetery plot, choose a coffin, pick a tombstone, and worry whether my eighty-year-old great-aunts would need limos to the funeral. Instead of mourning in privacy, I spent the day signing for fruit baskets and flowers. I wish I could have opened my soul that day as the villagers did this night.

—Marlene Goldman,
"Death in the Spirit World"

make sure that the feet go first and the head behind. Everybody carries their loved ones out of the tomb in a line, crying but happy.

When all the bodies are out, they are put on the ground on the front side of the tomb, the head facing east, with their immediate family seated around their loved one. This is a very important moment of the *famadihana*: the beginning of the wrapping of the body. The old shroud in which the body was buried is left on and the new silk shroud put on top of it, following the mummified shape and using baby safety pins to keep it in place. There are three new silk shrouds for my mother which have been donated in remembrance and gratitude. The belief is that she won't be cold and the top shroud befits her, being of top-quality silk with beautiful, delicate embroidery. This is the time to touch her, give her something, talk to her. Her best friend is there, making sure that my mother is properly wrapped, as the ritual has to follow certain rules. Lots of touching as silent conversation goes on, giving her the latest news or family gossip, and asking for her blessing. Perfume is sprinkled on her and wishes made at the same time.

The music plays on, everyone happily sitting around the mummified bodies. Flowers are placed on the bodies. The feeling of togetherness and love is so strong. This occasion is not just for the immediate family, but for cousins, and cousins of cousins, uncles and aunts and everybody meeting, bonded by the same ties, belonging to one unique extended family.

Photographs of the dead person are now put on top of each body. There is a photograph of a couple on top of one body: they were husband and wife and are now together forever in the same silk shroud.

Food is served in the forest area just next to the tombs. The huge feast and celebration begins.

Back to the bodies. We lift them, carrying them on our shoulders. We sing old rhymes and songs and dance in a line, circling the tomb seven times, moving the body on our shoulder and making it dance with us.

The last dance ends. The bodies have to be back inside the tombs by a precise time, and the tomb is immediately closed after a last ritual cleaning. This moment of good-bye is very emotional. The next time the tomb will be opened will not be for happiness but grief because it will be for a burial. *Famadihana* only happens once every seven or ten years.

Everybody returns to the cars and drives to the next meeting place—my uncle's—where a huge party finishes the day. Everyone is happy at having done their duty, *Vita ny adidy*!

It has been a very special day for me. My mother was extremely traditional, spending endless energy and money during her lifetime to keep the traditions. It all makes sense now because this *famadihana* brought so much joy, a strong sense of belonging and identity, and giving a spiritual feeling that death is not an end but an extension into another life, linked somehow with this one.

Misaotra ry neny (thank you, mum).

Seraphine Ramanantsoa was born in Madagascar and came to London at the age of twenty. After studying English literature, she followed a postgraduate course in management studies and then founded the travel consultancy "Discover Madagascar." She is also Attache at the Madagascar Consulate in London. She is passionate about promoting the culture of Madagascar which she believes to be unique and as endangered as the wildlife of the island.

PICO IYER

✶ ✶ ✶

Mondays Are Best

…for one of the most unusual sights
in the holy city of Lhasa.

ONE MORNING IN LHASA, I AWOKE TO FIND SNOW BLANKETING THE
mountains, and a fine rain misting the town. As if in a dream, I made
the long ascent up to the Potala Palace, whose thirteen white and
brown and golden stories preside over the town with silent majesty.
Inside, the secret rooms were heavy with the chanting of holy texts.
The smell of butter lamps was everywhere, and flashes of a sky, now
brilliant blue, outside. Banners fluttered in the wind, prayer bells
sounded. Sunlight and silence and high air.

In some rooms, ruddy-cheeked girls and women in many-
colored aprons bowed before monks who poured blessings of water
in their hands; in others, ancient men placed coins and bank notes
on the altar. And into the empty spaces, the slanted sunlight came
softly, filtered through red or golden curtains. Uplifted by the
chants, the smiles, the holy hush, I felt myself to be a clean and
empty room, thrown open to the breeze.

And then came the golden afternoon. Then lightning over distant purple mountains. Then nightfall, and silence, and the stars.

Yet the greatest of all the sights in the holy city, according to the
wisdom of the Banak Shol, was the sacred rite known as the
Celestial Burial. Each morning, at dawn, on a hillside five miles out

of town, the bodies of the newly dead were placed on a huge, flat rock. There a sturdy local man, dressed in a white apron and armed with a large cleaver, would set about hacking them into small pieces. Assistants would grind the bones. When at last the corpses had been reduced to strips of bloody flesh, they were left on the Promethean stone for the vultures.

For Tibetan Buddhists, the ritual was a sacrament, a way of sending corpses back into the cycle of Nature, of removing all traces of the departed. For the visitors who had begun to congregate in larger and still larger numbers to watch the man they called "the Butcher," the rite was the last word in picturesque exoticism.

Some knowledge of the practices of the Issedones has come through to us: for instance, when a man's father dies, his kinsmen bring sheep to his house as a sacrificial offering; the sheep and the body of the dead man are cut into joints and sliced up, and the two sorts of meat, mixed together, are served and eaten.

—Herodotus, *The Histories, Book IV*

I was no different, and so one morning, I got up at four o'clock and walked for more than an hour through the night, crossing a field full of bones and wading through an icy stream that left my thighs stinging with the cold. By the time I arrived on the sacrificial rock, three Westerners were already seated, cross-legged, around a fire, murmuring Buddhist chants and fingering their rosaries. Twenty others stood around them on the darkened hillside, faces lit up by the flames. As the sky began to change color, three Tibetans picked up a body, wrapped it from head to toe in bandages, and gave it to the flames. Then, as the body burned, they handed some of us sticks of incense to hold, while the chanting, continued. Afterward, with customary good humor, they brought us glasses of butter tea and chunks of bread the color of red meat.

Then they marched back to the rock, where the corpses of two more affluent citizens had been placed. One of the Tibetans tied an apron around his waist, picked up his ax and set about his work. As he did so, a gaggle of onlookers—most of them Chinese tourists from Hong Kong—started to inch closer to the sacred ground, chattering as they went. The man muttered something to himself, but continued about his task. Still, however, the visitors edged closer, giggling, and whispering at the sight. The Tibetan stopped what he was doing, the gossip continued. And then, all of a sudden, with a bloodcurdling shriek, the man whirled around and shouted again and, waving a piece of reddened flesh, he came after the visitors like a demon, slicing the air with his knife and screaming curses at their blasphemy. The tourists turned on their heels, still the Tibetan gave chase, reviling them for their irreverence. Terrified, the Chinese retreated to a safe position. The man stood before them, glowering.

After a long silence, the Tibetan turned around slowly and trudged back to his task. Chastened, we gathered on a hillside above the rock, a safe distance away. Before long, however, we were edging forward again, jostling to get a better glimpse of the dissection, urgently asking one another for binoculars and zoom lenses to get a close-up of the blood.

"Sometimes I think that we are the vultures," said a Yugoslav girl who had come to Tibet in search of an image glimpsed in a dream a decade before.

"Oh no," said a Danish girl. "It's always wild on Mondays. The butcher takes Sundays off, so Monday's always the best day to come here." She turned around with a smile. "On Mondays, it's great: there are always plenty of corpses."

Pico Iyer was born in Oxford in 1957 and was educated at Eton, Oxford, and Harvard. He is an essayist for Time *magazine, a contributing editor at* Condé Nast Traveler, *and the author of* The Lady and the Monk *and* Video Night in Kathmandu, *from which this story is excerpted.*

SUKIE MILLER, Ph.D. with SUZANNE LIPSETT

⋆ ⋆ ⋆

Crossing Borders
Within and Without

*Did this really happen? Is the imagination a frontier
between life and death? You decide.*

ONE DAY AS I WORKED IN MY APARTMENT IN NEW YORK SUR-
rounded by stacks of books on death and the afterdeath, I called my
colleague Edmundo Barbosa. It was a call that would ultimately lead
me to a mystery within myself. This was the vital imagination, the
conduit in the psyche to unseen aspects of reality, of which the afterdeath was perhaps the most compelling.

"Look, I'm bored with my reading again," I told Edmundo on
the phone. "I can't pick this stuff up only off the page, I've got to
experience it. I want to go back to Brazil. It's time to take a trip."

"Journey, not trip," he corrected me, making a distinction he had
made many times before. Then my dependable magic tour guide
half spoke, half sighed. "Ah, Sukie," he said through the international phone wire, followed by a single word: "Candomblé."

I hadn't done all that reading and note-taking for nothing. I
knew what he meant. Besides, we had discussed Candomblé many
times as the ultimate goal of Brazilian research. This was an Afro-
Brazilian religion originating in West Africa that had found a way
to hide itself in the rich folds of the garments of Brazilian
Catholicism. Deep within the skirts and ruffles of the Catholic
Church lived—and I do mean *lived*, with a secret, irrepressible

vitality—a panoply of saints and gods that the pope and his bishops had never heard of.

Even for the most devout Brazilians, the spirit world of Candomblé is not easy to enter. A seven-year initiation precedes the moment when, with shaved head, an initiate yields to the call of an Orisa—a particular, personalized god—and dances into an altered state during which the Orisa climbs onto the person, rides, and directs. It is called incorporation.

A year earlier, Edmundo had taken me to an evening-long Candomblé ritual in Brazil, and I had found myself transported, by the incessant drumming, out of my Western skepticism and natural fear of migraine into a state in which all aspects of life were brightened, lightened, charged with electricity. Xango, the god of thunder and fire, to whom the evening was dedicated, did indeed arrive on the scene, and nobody could have escaped the excitement of his arrival.

But I had never been to the heart of Candomblé, where the dead—the Egun—live. I knew through my research and the strange half-gossipy, half-scholarly trail Edmundo had been guiding me along in Brazil for several years since I'd met him there each September, on a small island off the coast of northern Brazil, that the Egun appeared to the living in a forty-eight-hour ritual of the Return of the Dead. When Edmundo spoke that word "Candomblé" into the phone, I knew he meant it was time for us to travel to the heart of the matter. For years we had been painstakingly following the threads that crossed the boundaries and even wove together the worlds of the living and dead. It seemed that now was the time to plunge from one to another, to meet the Egun on their yearly return.

The journey was hellish. Everything went wrong. My luggage was lost. Lost also were our Candomblé contacts—long cultivated, dearly protected: all had somehow sustained sudden accidents and were unable to accompany us. Things went wrong at our hotel, too. Both Edmundo and I became ill; it rained steadily every day, every hour; and everything conspired against our finding and then reaching the island off the coast where the dead would return to the living.

"But you understand, Sukie," said my urbane colleague, "one does not simply walk into the afterdeath. The journey itself is part of a barrier between worlds. Patience, patience. We will arrive. Or we will not."

Typically Brazilian in his ambiguity: reassuring, and not.

All our plans failed, but by a series of extraordinary coincidences we managed to find transport to the island. Once there we sought the chief as we had been directed. We had been told that it was critical that we find him and introduce ourselves, since he would not know that we, strangers and foreigners, were coming. I was apprehensive, but the chief, a huge man, received us open-armed, saying, "We have been expecting you. They are awaiting you on the *terreiroi*."

"The sacred ground," Edmundo translated for me, whispering, his face showing that he, too, was thinking as I was, that perhaps the chief in his unexpected expansiveness had us confused with someone else.

The chief led us to a cottage without a floor, inner walls, furniture, or bathroom, but clearly a place of honor only twenty feet from the temple itself. "Don't leave," he warned. "The Egun are all around us, as are the Aparca—tall ghosts in limbo who shriek out their misery. Be careful! Careful! Walk only with an initiate. We will come and get you when it is time."

At sundown, in our little house, I wondered at the wisdom of coming here. We were trapped on sacred ground with no floor, no bathroom, and no friends. I chided myself. It was typical of these trips for me to become so engrossed in the strategies of getting to a place that I gave little thought to whether it made more sense to stay home.

This night, still ill and without even the amenities of walls to afford privacy, I didn't have to wonder. Warnings we had received and that I had taken in stride with my New York bravado—"Do not share your water with anyone! They will want your water," and "Avoid all blood sacrifices! They will want *you* to make a blood sacrifice!"—suddenly came back to haunt me. The sheer eeriness of what we were doing in tracking shadowy images of the dead wouldn't leave me. I was sick, tired, far from home, on a mountaintop on an island—and on sacred ground with no discernible exit.

But time to worry was short. The sun set, the stars began to shimmer, and initiates came to sweep us into the hot, crowded, urine-smelling temple, where there were two lime-filled bathrooms—one for men, one for women (the ritual would last forty-eight hours)—and where nonstop drumming was already going on. Babies were passed overhead from hand to hand the moment they fretted—though when they reached me, which they did every so often where I stood on the women's side of the room, they would mortify me by bursting out wailing. The drums changed rhythm as two young men were initiated, covered in the blood and feathers of the live chickens that the chief had waved throughout the room moments before.

Overwhelmed by the sheer lack of anything familiar within the temple—Edmundo was on the men's side and hidden from my view by a pillar—I focused my concern on the children. To be sure, the babies were kept safely in the women's section, but the older children were together, alone, with no parental supervision right up in front where the rituals were taking place. They seemed to be having a grand old time, but I worried: what are the children doing here at the Return of the Dead? The drumming was pounding in my head. The smell of blood mingled with the odor of urine and sweat. The human heat, building fast, made me long for our floorless shelter.

Suddenly the locked double doors at the back of the temple flew open and something magnificent rushed in! A whirling, twirling headlessness in a robe—a robe the many colors of Joseph's, a robe, I was told, that would burn you if you touched it—flew singing and rumbling and chanting through the white-dressed initiates, dodging and pirouetting up to the front.

It was an Egun, an Ancestor, a Dead. And it was glorious!

I stood, mouth open and spontaneous tears streaming down my face, watching the children, who immediately stood up and began singing and clapping out what appeared to be a welcoming song. A thrilling tension built between the Egun and the crowd in the hall as the initiates began to chase the spirit with special sticks, pounding them on the floor to make rhythmic taps and filling the room with a beautiful pandemonium that drowned out the drumming. Chased in a fashion that reminded me somewhat of the Keystone Kops, the Egun disappeared, ran back into the night—magical, colorful, graceful, headless dancing creatures—spun through the hall and elicited the rhythms of people's clapping hands and clacking sticks. My reticence, my nervousness, my resistance to the heat and smells and sounds had all flown away with the appearance of the first Egun. Transported into the afterdeath, I was having as exciting and wonderful a time that night as I ever experienced anywhere.

For years I had been working, reading, traveling, interviewing, collecting, and integrating data. On the night of the Return of the Dead, the dependable boundaries in my mind between the real and unreal, fact and fiction, perception and hallucination disintegrated under the bombardment of sounds, sights, odors, colors, and rhythms. Suddenly, through the force of my own vital imagination—a force I shared with the strangers on that island but had never to such a conscious degree experienced in my life in New York—I was mingling with the living and the dead. Bouncing between wonder and joy, I clapped and laughed with the others, delighting with them at the return of the magnificent, colorful, formidable, incredibly vital, energetic dead.

At dawn, with cracks of light penetrating the tightly shuttered windows and doors of the temple, the crowd moved slowly outside. The sun was beginning to rise as the moon began to set. Both hung in the sky and the air was sweet and cool. Someone told us to wait—something special was about to happen.

What more wonderful things could take place? I wondered, but then I saw. Gathered in the meadow below us were all the Egun together at once. I counted sixteen, but they continued to dance and swirl, so I'm not really sure of the number. Now I noticed that little mirrors were embedded in their twirling robes that caught the light and threw it back to us. The initiates surrounded the Egun at intervals, alert, their sticks pounding, to enforce the line between the living and dead. Then an Egun got away! He was the newest one, someone told me, and still very frisky. (All Egun are male—when women die, they return to nature as do most men. Only some men go on to become ancestors.) Puppylike, the new Egun ran and skipped toward the crowd with the little bells on his robe ringing, obviously very pleased with himself. This Egun ran fast, but so did the initiates, and they cornered him at last before he reached the crowd and escorted him back down the little hill to the meadow to join the others. All the Egun danced and marched away behind the temple. The sun was fully up now and the moon had disappeared.

The ritual went on for another day. A goat we had seen at the entrance to the *terreiroi* was assisted into the afterdeath and cooked and distributed in a grand picnic lunch. Then there was time for talk, rest, and reflection along with digestion before the initiates arrived again, and we entered the temple for another night of reunion.

After forty-eight hours on the island, Edmundo and I, dazed by the experience, returned to the mainland, and then I flew home. For years

---

As a researcher, I can assure you that any type of near-death experience can be life changing.

But as an experiencer, I can positively affirm that being bathed in The Light on the other side of death *is more than life changing*. That light is the very essence…of ecstasy. It is a million suns of compressed love dissolving everything unto itself, annihilating thought and cell, vaporizing humanness and history, into the one great brilliance of all that is and all that ever was and all that ever will be.

You know it's God.

No one has to tell you.

You know.

You can no longer believe in God, for belief implies doubt. There is no more doubt. None. You *know* God. And you know that you know. And you're never the same again.

—P. M. H. Atwater, Lh.D.,
*Beyond the Light: The
Mysteries and Revelations of
Near-Death Experiences*

we tried, unsuccessfully, to go back. But wherever I went I carried with me memories of those two extraordinary days.

Five years later, after much travel, particularly in the East, collecting information and images of the afterdeath, I returned home from a trip with a raging virus. I was miserably ill. I arrived in New York with a 103-degree fever and the whole known array of what I took to be flu symptoms. But the night of comfort in my own bed I had obsessively imagined throughout the long flight home was not to be—at least not quite yet. I returned to discover that my mother was deathly ill and had to be hospitalized. As a doctor's daughter I knew all the right things to do and did them, all the while shaking and trembling with fever. But once my chronically ill eighty-one-year-old mother was admitted into the hospital, she suffered a heart attack. Her immediate future looked very problematic.

My flu prevailed as did my mother's reactivated tuberculosis, so the bedside vigil I intended and wanted very much to keep was not to be. I was infectious and was sent away. I had to go home and go to bed. Finally, I could collapse.

I filled the tub and soaked in my bath. Then I shook and cramped my way into bed. I sank down beneath the covers, each lovely detail of which I had imagined on the plane. Sleep, beautiful sleep, gradually overtook me, and I drifted.

I woke to a drumming. I dragged myself upright and listened.

Drumming. That damn kid next door, I concluded, and roused myself to pound on our shared wall. As my fist was about to meet the wall, I listened more carefully. The drumming was in my living room, and furthermore, I *knew* that drumming. It was the drumming I had heard on the island on the night of the Return of the Dead. It wasn't coming from next door. It was in my living room.

Confused as to who had invaded my apartment, I forced myself out of bed and toward the sound of the drums.

In the living room I found *everyone*, everyone, living *and* dead, who had filled the hall on that faraway island—now dancing and welcoming me in my own home. Everyone had come and everyone smiled—as if we had always met this way and as if each person in the community was very glad to see me. No one spoke, everyone smiled, and the drummers drummed.

Luis was there, a man who had befriended us during our time on the island and spoken of the Aparaca, miserable shrieking ghosts who accompany the arrival of the Egun. He was dressed in the whites of the initiate, his stick in his hand ready to ward off the ghosts that made the eerie sounds and to physically maintain the boundary between the living and the dead.

Christina was in my kitchen cooking for the assembled, just as she had done on the island, and a magnificent odor of I have no idea what came drifting toward me as I stood astonished.

Another familiar face smiled up at me from a chair; still another face gazed from next to my bookcase. Beer was flowing liberally (I don't keep beer), I could hear the toilet flushing, and children played tag around the coffee table. Everywhere were people I remembered. "Everything, it will be all right," said Luciano, who had visited Edmundo and me in our wall-less house and talked with us there for a long time. He had told us that the Egun had appeared at his baptism and run off with him, to the consternation of those gathered in the temple to witness the ceremony. Later, a senior researcher explained to us that Luciano had been a very sick little baby and that the Egun had taken him away to cure him.

Sergio gave me the first of the food prepared in my kitchen, but the crowd, the smoke, the sweet odor filling my living room became too much for me, and suddenly I rushed out. An intense, colorful, headless, muttering figure followed me—an Egun! I was careful not to let his robes touch me. I stopped, deeply honored, overwhelmed with gratitude at his visit.

"Sukie, you're hallucinating," said I, the surgeon's daughter, psychotherapist, and New York skeptic as I bowed to this most magical and foreign entity. "Go back to bed, take some aspirin, and go to sleep."

In the midst of this commotion Edmundo called—it was 6 A.M. in Brazil. His wife had had a miscarriage.

Then the hospital called. My mother had had a second heart attack. Still banished from her bedside, I returned sadly to bed.

Still the drums persisted, and I noticed that, against all odds and for no accountable reason, I was calm—and the feeling of being honored and comforted by the presence of the exotic creatures from the other side of life in my living room would not leave me.

Questions floated through my mind as I lay down and began to drift to the drums:

- Was my mother, who was about to die, also about to disappear? The answer came as concrete as the colorful figures in the crowd on the other side of the wall. Hardly, I thought, she would simply "cross over," and perhaps not so impermanently.

- If I were to take a sudden turn for the worse and begin to court death—such ideas occur to a doctor's daughter when temperatures rise steeply—would that be such a tragedy? Here too my attitude toward death seemed softened and tempered by the rich blend of interacting, interweaving living and dead currently inhabiting my living room while the heat of my fever was burning away the orderly boundaries between life and death.

What on earth happened in my apartment that night? Was I dreaming? Fantasizing? Hallucinating? There is an answer: I was imagining. But not in the way we are used to understanding and using that term to refer to a slightly childish, vaguely useless pursuit akin to daydreaming. Rather, the extreme conditions of my life that night—exhaustion, high fever, unrelenting anxiety regarding my mother—combined into a classic trigger for my vital imagination, the capacity of my psyche not merely to visualize but to experience another realm of reality.

My research had accustomed me to the idea that a large proportion of the world's people can access other realms: reports brought back by shamans, descriptions embedded in the culture, mental maps of the afterdeath geography, and accounts of the inhabitants there—these are all integrated without awe into daily life. For many people of the world, realms after death are as indisputably there as San Francisco is to New Yorkers, as Africa is to Brazilians. It is a case of living within the whole of reality, not just the parts one can see.

Many in the West have written of such realms, and a growing body of literature not only poses the existence of other aspects of reality but minutely studies the rare but powerful capacity to apprehend them. "The voyage of discovery lies not in seeking new vistas but in having new eyes," wrote Marcel Proust, emphasizing the focus on *how* we reach exotic realms rather than the realms themselves.

At the center of these investigations lies the work of French Islamic mystic and scholar Henry Corbin. Corbin made the now classic distinction between an imagined realm and what he called an *imaginal* one. The former might be the Egun as you, the reader, apprehended them in your mind in response to my description of them. The imaginal realm is a real world, apprehended not by the five usual senses alone but by a highly sensitized, transformed imagination that functions in and of itself as an organ of perception. In other words, not fantasy, not dreaming, not hallucination, but the perception of an aspect of a greater reality not ordinarily seen.

Many have responded to Corbin's ideas, developed them further, and related them to their own innovative work. Most suggest that this capacity to apprehend the hidden is identical to the powers of the shamans of tribal cultures—after intense training—to cross the borders limiting ordinary experience. Some, in particular Kenneth Ring, also link this crossing over into another aspect of existence to the experiences reported by those who have had near-death experiences. That is, the apprehension of a great light, the tunnel, and the reunion with loved ones is to these writers the same kind of experience as that of shamans who transcend the ordinary and enter the invisible—although the content they find there is not necessarily the same at all.

The hard sciences have shown equal interest in the imaginal world, at least along their more radical borders. Physicist Michael Talbot speaks to the work of Corbin in his book *The Holographic Universe*, calling it the land of nowhere, and physicist Fred Alan Wolf uses the concept of the imaginal as well in his book *The Dreaming Universe*.

Other links in Western writing, too, identify visionary experience with this extraordinary capacity for perception. Samuel Taylor Coleridge and William Blake are two poets who have contributed to our Western canon of literature detailed images from other worlds, worlds hidden by reality as we ordinarily perceive it. In contexts both spiritual and adventurous, certain psychedelic drug experiences suggest an identical breakthrough: Terence McKenna, describes psychopharmacological episodes as findings from the afterdeath.

All these disparate descriptions describe ways into—or over, or behind, or through—ordinary reality. Most significant, though, is not where the extraordinary realm lies but *that* it lies: it is real, it has form and dimension, and above all it is inhabited.

Those I encountered in the imaginal realm on the night my mother was dying were the Egun. Both my ability to see them and their presence itself were aspects of the vital imagination.

For many tribal peoples of the world, hidden realms are as real and ultimately reachable as a destination on an airline schedule. They may be invisible but they are nevertheless a known part of the whole and taken for granted as such. This tells us that it is not necessary to be a shaman, a Near Death Experiencer, or a particularly gifted individual to experience the vital imagination. I want to suggest that such a capacity to apprehend the extraordinary exists universally in all human beings. The vital imagination is both tool and goal. We draw on this capacity both within ourselves and to reach into other realms. This most difficult and elusive of concepts jumps boundaries. It is neither this nor that, it is both: the vessel and its contents; the airplane and the destination; the hammer, the nails, and the house. Its effects, both in us and around us, are incredibly powerful.

So what *was* going on in my living room that night?

I have no doubt: my vital imagination had been triggered, and I had broken through the normal bonds of perception. Most accounts of such breakthroughs describe them as resulting from extreme conditions that serve as stimuli. For shamans and mystics, and those seeking mystical experiences, such conditions are often rituals designed to provide extraordinary perceptions. For other kinds of seekers the triggers can be psychedelic drugs. For those who cross the borders involuntarily, near-death or other traumas evoke the perceptions. For me, that night, it was the combustible combination of exhaustion, illness, and anxiety that induced my vital imagination. But there was more as well that contributed to its accessibility: I had a longing to know, a yearning to experience the unknown, the ambiguous, the mysterious. These yearnings sharpened my ability to approach the border.

The experiences that the vital imagination yields need not be so dramatic and extreme as my midnight visitation. There are moments of breakthrough as subtle and penetrating as a dance, as natural as the wind. The effects of these moments are immeasurable, but to brush them aside without appreciating their essence is to lose the touch of the extraordinary that they lend to everyday life.

Sukie Miller, Ph.D., a psychotherapist, is one of the first researchers to study the cross-cultural dimensions of the afterdeath. She was an early director of the Esalen Institute and has been a member of the Jung Institute of San Francisco and the Board of Medical Quality Assurance for the state of California. In 1972 she founded and directed the pioneering Institute for the Study of Humanistic Medicine. She is currently founder and director of the Institute for the Study of the Afterdeath. Suzanne Lipsett was a member of the publishing community for over twenty years. Her writing career followed the birth of her two sons. Her books include Coming Back Up, Out of Danger, Remeber Me *(which was nominated for a Pen West Award), and* Surviving a Writer's Life. *Suzanne lost a long battle with breast cancer in 1996. This story was excerpted from their book,* After Death: How People Around the World Map the Journey After Life.

✦ ✦ ✦

Benares

To the ghats let us go.

BENARES IS THE OLDEST INHABITED CITY ON EARTH AND CONSID-
ered to be among the holiest as well. In particular, Benares is famous
as a pilgrimage site for the dying. For nearly 10,000 years, Hindus
have gone there to live and wait out their last days, and afterward
to be cremated along the banks of the River Ganges. It is said that
to die in Benares promises a happy rebirth, and some 35,000 bodies are disposed of every year at the two crematoria along the river.
To make my own pilgrimage to Benares now seemed urgent. I
sensed that there was something I needed to learn there, watching
the corpses go up in flame—some teaching that might help me
cope with what lay ahead.

I landed in Bombay and was greeted again by that unmistakable
flower-and-bones smell that had struck me on my arrival in India
five years before. After taking a flight to Benares, I made my way
to the Harishehandra ghat, where the cremations were performed,
and was wandering in a narrow street when a man in a Michael
Jackson t-shirt pulled me aside.

"Lodging, sir?"

His name was Bhose, and he ran a squalid little pension, the Yogi
Lodge, just a few steps away. In its tiny, smoky office, he took my

passport, and when he saw from my visa that I was a writer, the floodgates opened.

"I know what you want in Benares," Bhose said. "You want to find God. Everyone comes here to find God, but God's not here, God's not anywhere. I don't believe in God. I've met so many great people. I've met Mother Teresa, Anandamayi Ma, the Daily Dilemma."

"Who?"

"The Dalai Lama. I've met all these people, but they don't do nothing for me." This obnoxious little man lit a cigarette and offered me a beer, though it was only 7 A.M. "This is the '90s man, wake up and smell the coffee. I mean Benares is shit."

"I thought it was supposed to be holy," I said.

"That's just tourist stuff. There's no such thing as holy. Not India, not now. They're all a bunch of crooks."

Bhose depressed me, and I left him as soon as I could dump my backpack, and wound my way down past the *chai* stalls, cattle, dogs, and beggars clogging the street. A bus careened by me streaming cellophane flags, garish cartoon versions of the goddess Durga riding her tiger painted on the front. Children ran after the sacred cows, scooped up their turds, and carried them to the gutter, where they squatted, laughing and patting the dung into burger-shaped lumps to sell as fuel for fires. The place looked surreal through my jet-lagged haze—even more so when I reached the river.

A man stood half naked in the brown Ganges, brushing his teeth and spitting, while the bloated corpse of a cow floated by belly up. A group of old women in white—who I assumed had come from the widows' ashram up the hill—walked by me on the way to their morning ablutions. Holy men in *lungi* skirts stood waist deep, dipping themselves, chanting prayers, cupping the water in their hands, and holding it up in offering, while a boat of Japanese tourists slid by, cameras poised and clicking. Everywhere were the *doms*, the caste below the untouchables, who preside over the cremation grounds. Groups of *doms* were asleep under their carts, while their children surrounded me in swarms, filthy, with strangely ancient faces, holding out their hands for rupees. A little girl sat in the dust next to a scrawny dog turned on her side, covered with a litter of puppies, next to a smoking pit. A group of teenage boys were playing stickball with bones—human or other, I couldn't tell.

A short distance down the river, I saw a family sitting on the ground by a corpse bound in white and strapped to a bamboo litter, and headed toward them for a closer look. When I ventured too close, however, a member of the family—a handsome young man in a spotless white outfit—shooed me away. I took a seat at a polite distance from the proceedings and observed.

Once the body had been immersed for a last time in the river, a Brahmin priest anointed it and prayed; when he gave the signal, the corpse was hoisted onto the pyre and covered with saffron and flowers. The young man in white (whom I took to be the eldest son) circled the body, then took a lit stick from a priest and touched it to the woodpile. I watched as the kindling slowly began to catch fire, then the logs, and finally the fabric enshrouding the corpse, which fell away gradually to reveal the body underneath: its charred face, the nose hooked and narrow like a mummy's. The deceased was a woman, I saw now, watching with fascination as this extraordinary process took place in full public view, without sentimentality or wailing (considered bad luck for the dead). I watched for a long time as the

> The most desirable pilgrimage for each male Hindu is to carry the ashes of his dead father to the Ganges. In the big riverside shrine cities, Brahmin priests keep palm-leaf ledgers of the deposition of ashes, family by family, some going back centuries. Census of the living is relatively new in India. For centuries in that land, one came into being officially only when one died.
>
> —Eleanor Munro, *On Glory Roads: A Pilgrim's Book About Pilgrimage*

flames rose to consume this woman and her family watched her disappear. When finally nothing was left but bones and cinder, the young man threw a clay pot of water over his shoulder onto the smoldering pyre and walked away from the cremation site, followed by the rest of the family. No one looked back.

I sat there mesmerized by what I'd just seen, wondering whether I could ever be this matter-of-fact about the death of someone I loved. Staring at the river, I remembered a story about a saint named Ramakrishna who lived close to this spot at the turn of the century. Sitting by the Ganges one day, gazing at the river as I was doing now, Ramakrishna had seen a beautiful woman emerge from the water and come toward him, radiant and naked. As she approached, her body swelled to the point of bursting, and a child appeared between her legs. As Ramakrishna looked on, the woman of the river took the infant up to her breast and suckled it; then, just as simply, she broke the child's neck with her bare hands and, transformed into Kali—the dark mother—she consumed the child before his eyes. When the infant's blood and bones were gone, the goddess turned and walked back into the river.

I was strangely comforted by this story and by the raw extremity of what I'd just seen in real life. There was relief in the naked truth—shock, but revelation, too, in the face of it. Mortality was just a word, but this heap of smoking dust was more. If I could accept *this*, I thought, turning from the cremation site back toward the Yogi Lodge—if I could pass through the incomprehensibility of this process and stand on the other side—nothing could scare me anymore. I would be free.

When I returned, Bhose interrogated me as to where I'd been. "To the barbecue?" he asked with a cynical wink.

Three days later, having watched half a dozen more cremations, I left Benares for the south, in no way suspecting how much further this initiation had to go.

Mark Matousek also contributed "The Survivor" in Part One.

★ ★ ★

A Party at the Cemetery

*We are all dancing in the dark. Some, however,
have better night vision than others.*

I HAD NEVER BEEN TO A PARTY AT A CEMETERY BEFORE, BUT LUPE said it would be fun. She wanted me to help her with the preparations and accompany her there. I wasn't sure what this entailed since Day of the Dead in America is essentially Halloween, so I asked if she wanted me to help her make costumes for the children. But she said no, it wasn't like that at all; if we could work in my kitchen, she would teach me.

Lupe brought over a giant cauldron, and we began baking breads and small cakes. We shopped for cinnamon, pecans, brown sugar, flour, eggs, food coloring, colored sugars. In the cauldron, we put a kilo of sifted flour, ten eggs. We put in the grated cinnamon, the sugars, pecans. Then she made small cups and in the cups she put food coloring and she dyed the dough. Then she hand shaped the dough. She made little lambs and elephants, reindeer and skulls, coffins and flowers. I watched as she carved skulls, shaped coffins, wove funereal wreaths with her colored dough.

Death was everywhere for days. In town all the stores were selling the little cakes and cookies, sugar candy, and funereal wreaths, and everyone was laughing and happy and having a wonderful time. The night before we went to the cemetery, we stayed up, making

181

another batch of breads. I asked Lupe how she had learned to be such a good cook and she told me she had carefully watched the *patrones* she had worked for and remembered what they did. Even though she could not read recipes, she could remember.

"I remember everything," she told me. And suddenly she began to cry. She broke down and sobbed into her apron. Another one of José Luis's women was pregnant, and Lupe was pregnant, and she remembered everything, all the good and all the bad, and it was all rolled into one. "I am sick of all these men," she said. "If I didn't have so many children, if it weren't for this"—she patted her belly—"I'd get away from them all." She said José Luis had told her that afternoon that if she went to the movies alone—or went out anywhere alone—it meant only one thing. That she was looking for a man. He said that if she did that, he would kidnap Pollo and take her to one of his other señoras. "How can I look for a man like this? He doesn't even want me anymore," she said, "but he threatens me."

Lupe said she was a slave to that man and she'd been a slave to the man before him. "Don't ever be a slave," she told me. "Be free. Always be free." Then she apologized for crying, and we went back to shaping our skulls, our tiny coffins.

Mexico is the land in which Xochipilli, the young god of beauty, love, and youth, was depicted with a death's head contorted into the most hideous of smiles. Life to the Aztecs came only from death. One flowed naturally into the other. The people who worshipped Xipe Totec, god of vegetation, watched as their priests flayed victims alive and walked around in their warm skins. Children still play with puppets called Dead Mariachi or Dead Peasant or even Dead Dead Man. To be Mexican means to be well acquainted with birth and death.

The cemetery in San Miguel is about an hour's walk outside of town and I'd never been there before that day. We left early in the morning, Lupe, me, and all of the children except María Elena, who was pregnant and not feeling well. We carried our flowers and baskets of food. Lupe had a dear friend, she told me, who had died the year before, and she also had a child who had been born dead. We would go to their graves.

The cemetery was alive with people, flowers, and streamers. Families gardened around graves, pulling up weeds, planting flowers. Everyone was eating cookies and cakes, drinking coffee or tequila, passing food around. The festivities were everywhere except for in a small enclosed area near the middle of the cemetery. I asked Lupe what it was. She said she didn't know, so I went over. It was the American part, all fenced in, well gardened and kept up, but with no visitors, no one bringing flowers. It seemed lonely and sad. "Lupe," I said, "if I die here, will you be sure I am buried in the Mexican part of the cemetery?"

She laughed. "It is sad over there, isn't it?"

Suddenly it became very important to me that she make this promise. "Promise me," I said. "I won't be buried in the American part."

She squeezed my arm. "I promise, but you won't die in Mexico."

We reached the grave of Lupe's friend. Two of Lupe's other friends, sisters named Carmen and Consuela, were clearing a nearby grave, scrubbing the tombstone. They had a large picnic basket with them and offered us some slices of chicken and a beer. I wasn't hungry, but I understood that it would offend them if I refused. They seemed very content. Both had strange, witchlike faces. Carmen had clear green eyes, unusual for a Mexican, and silver hair down to her waist. After a while she began to talk about the grave she was clearing. "It is my son's," she said. "And my mother." She looked at Consuela. "Our mother." Consuela nodded.

"Oh, your son," I mumbled.

"And our mother," Consuela said, as if she were proud of this fact.

"Yes, my son was killed last year. With an ice pick in his head." She said this as if she were telling me about a new movie she's seen.

"And our mother died of grief, six weeks later," Consuela said. It was like a routine the two of them had worked up together.

"So we buried them together. We have just put the tombstone in. It is very nice, I think, don't you?"

Lupe said she thought it was very nice and for a while we all admired the tombstone. They insisted that we touch the cool reddish-gray stone, run our fingers over the carved letters, look at our reflections in its polished surface. Then they offered us some little cakes and Lupe offered them some of ours. They admired the basket Lupe had brought. "These are beautiful." And they took a coffin and skull and offered them to their dead.

"You don't eat them?" I said.

"Some do. I prefer to offer them," Carmen replied. "So"—she grinned at me— "if you die in Mexico, you will be buried there." She pointed to the American enclave.

Lupe laughed, knowing I was being teased. "Oh, no," Lupe said as if on cue. "She will be here with us."

Then Lupe wanted to find the grave of her stillborn child. She had an idea of where it was, but as we walked to the children's part of the cemetery, she became confused. The grave was unmarked and more graves had appeared since she'd last been there, and she couldn't find it.

Instead we cleared away the weeds on the grave of an unknown child. We planted the pansies and a small rose sprig, we had brought with us. We knew that the rose sprig would not live without care, but we planted it anyway. Then we sat beside the grave and ate avocado sandwiches. A priest came by and blessed the grave with holy water from a pill bottle.

In the far corner of the cemetery a bonfire burned, but Lupe didn't want to get near the fire. I asked her what it was. "They are burning the coffins of those who could no longer pay to stay there." She asked if I would help her make a bank account. She said she never wanted them to burn her coffin. "All right," I said. "I won't let them burn your coffin if you don't let them bury me where the Americans are." We shook hands, sealing our pact, both laughing at the thought of our impending doom.

Toward the end of the day some people began to leave while others dragged out more beer and bottles of tequila; for them the festivities would continue into the night. Lupe was ready to leave so we said good-bye to Carmen and Consuela. They asked if she'd be back that night, but she said no.

As we walked back across the fields, I asked her why she wouldn't return that night, but she shook her head. "It is one thing to go in the day." she mumbled. "It's another to go at night."

That night I returned and found the cemetery transformed. It was a blaze of fires and strange dances, of drunk men staggering and women incanting. Candles burned on tombstones. Odd shadows illumined the faces of the living. I passed Consuela and Carmen, their faces even more witchlike now, glowing red in the flames. I waved, but they did not see me. I stopped beside them, but they did not recognize me. Carmen rocked back and forth, her silver hair glistening as if on fire. Death masks abounded and skeletons marched. The ghosts were on parade.

I journey among the dead, wandering from grave to grave. Flames dance in the shine of tombstones. Dancers try to pull me into their dance. A young man appears before me, thrusting a bottle into my hand. He insists that I drink. I drink as if from a well. When I go to hand him the bottle, the boy is gone and an old woman is there. Her hair is pure white, her eyes flashes of silver. She breathes on me and my body is warmed. She looks at me through an eye of glass. She tells me my name and where I am from. She whispers the name of the person I last loved. "Who are you?" I say.

But she says nothing. Instead she leads me somewhere and I follow. Around us the dancers dance. I feel the heat of the flames. The drunk get drunker. We pass the American part of the cemetery

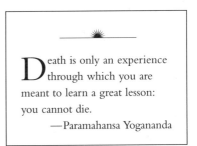

Death is only an experience through which you are meant to learn a great lesson: you cannot die.
—Paramahansa Yogananda

and it is quiet and still. I walk quickly, following the old woman, her hair like a trail of moonlight on water. I do not know where we are going but she beckons to me. Then she stops. She extends her arms, opens her skirts. She covers the ground. I am the mother you never had, she tells me. I am the daughter you will one day be. I can make nothing of her gibberish. Instead I curl into her arms.

I wake to find myself lying on a small grave, a rose sprig above my head, about to blossom.

Mary Morris is the author of four novels, two collections of short stories, and two travel memoirs, Wall to Wall: From Beijing to Berlin by Rail *and* Nothing to Declare: Memoirs of a Woman Traveling Alone, *from which this story is excerpted. She has also coedited* Maiden Voyages, *an anthology of travel writings by women. She lives with her husband, Larry O'Connor, and daughter, Kate, in Brooklyn, New York.*

✶ ✶ ✶

A Grandfather's Farewell

What is gravity?

WHEN I WOKE UP IN THE MORNING, I WAS NOT BESIDE GRAND-father, but in one of the corners of the tiny cement room. I stretched my legs, rubbed my eyes, and looked around me. The sun had already risen. Its penetrating rays were already biting my skin through the corrugated iron roof of the building. Grandfather was still lying where I had seen him last night, and he seemed to be in a deep sleep. I got up and walked to him. Picking up one of his hands, I called him aloud. He did not answer. When I called again, he remained quiet. My father was not around, and I didn't know any of the many villagers in the room. I sensed, however, that they must be the leaders of other compounds. I looked at them for help to find out why Grandfather was still sleeping.

"You will never hear him speak again," one of the strangers said.

"He has become a spirit," another one said.

I still didn't understand, but I hesitated to ask for further expla-nation. Confused, I sat quietly. It was a long time before my father returned with the doctor who had examined Grandfather the night before. The doctor did the same ritual and left. Then my father stood in front of Grandfather's bed and put on a grave air. He held up something that looked like a tail mounted with two handles decorated with cowrie shells, stretched it out, and put it in Grandfather's hand.

As soon as the tail touched his hand, Grandfather opened his eyes and sat up, all in slow motion. His behavior seemed strange. Because he wouldn't let go of the tail my father had given him, he could not use his other hand to support himself while maneuvering to sit up. This seemed very odd to me. Ordinarily, Grandfather took an endless time to get up from his couch. He would begin by grinning and groaning while he turned himself over. Then he would grip the mat with his hands, and one by one bend his legs. From then on, every movement upward would force a yell out of his mouth, until he was on his feet. But this time nothing of this sort happened.

Grandfather's torso sat up as if moved by an invisible hand, then became immobile. Following the same impulse, his legs bent over the side of the bed, although they were cracking like dry leaves. Fascinated and speechless, I watched. Everybody seemed captivated. Then he began to rise, as if under a slow and steady impulse, his body resembling one of the village spirit statues. I was not only fascinated, but also afraid that he might lose control and break his back. No one could possibly get up this way without using one or both of their hands to balance their weight. But Grandfather's only contact with the ground was with his bare feet, and one could see the muscles of the lower part of his legs compressed and straining under the thin dark skin. Presently, he was standing straight up.

This miracle completed, I rushed to him and grabbed his right hand, the one that was free. My father made a movement to stop me, but decided against it.

Keeping his authoritative tone, my father spoke to my grandfather in secret primal language. Grandfather said nothing in response, he just walked out of the room preceded by my father and followed by the delegation. I walked at his right side, still holding his hand. He moved strangely—too straight, too rigid, unnatural, yet very conscious of any obstacle. Once outside, the crowd joined to make a circle around us. Although I was too young to understand the significance of this ritual, or why all these people were not speaking with one another, I was glad to return home with Grandfather—even if he did not seem to want to speak to me.

The four-mile walk took an equal amount of hours. Dead people don't walk very fast. They are not in a hurry. We must have reached home around noontime, for upon our arrival we were each walking on his own shadow. People we encountered along our way stopped, left the road, and assumed a somber mood. At home men and women were everywhere, having come from all directions to wait for Grandfather. Those who had arrived earliest were sitting under the shadows of the trees surrounding the compound, others stood under the biting sun. Many more were still arriving. When we reached the yard outside the main gate, our delegation stopped. Five old men came out of the compound and saluted us in mystical terms, each one kneeling down with a grave air. I felt proud to be at the center of so much attention. They murmured something to Grandfather. He continued to be unresponsive, but they did not seem to mind his silence at all.

I'm going to stop here for a moment to make a point. Different cultures have different relationships with their dead, and I know very well that in a culture of skyscrapers and high technology, dead people don't walk. Instead, they are placed in nice expensive caskets and driven to the cemetery in elegant black cars. They are put quickly out of sight so that life can go on.

Why do the dead walk where I come from? They walk because they are still as important to the living as they were before. They are even more meaningful, as the breadth and depth of our funeral ritual shows. We do not hide their bodies away—because we want to see those bodies to help us remember the person's life and all the good they did for us. We need to remember that they are well on their way to becoming an ancestor. We must see our dead so that we can truly mourn them, all the way through, without restraint, to release the grief from our hearts once and for all. True, every dead person is not asked to walk. My grandfather died on the mission hill, thus in a foreign land. He was an elder and a leader of great power, and should have died at home. The only way to correct a death of such an important person when it occurs in the wrong place is to walk the dead home. Once the funeral ritual is at an end, his body would be carried to the burial ground.

Grandfather's eyes were peering at something beyond them, his face and body expressionless. Of all of us, he was the least concerned about what was going on. Presently, the people were cleared away from the gate and he walked into the compound. Looking behind me, I noticed that the crowd under the trees had stood up and were reverently taking part in everything that was going on. Beyond them the whole millet field was colored with men and women in blue, white, yellow, red, and black clothing, still arriving.

As I marveled at this colorful panorama, I was dragged into the present by a pull from Grandfather, who had begun walking again. We walked into his room. There a kerosene lamp cast a faint yellow light, disturbed now and then by the wind penetrating from the skylight in the roof. As Grandfather moved toward his mud bed, he looked both comic and dramatic. His stiff movements and his almost ghastly air gave him a look that was both authoritative and indifferent. He leaned forward, just as he was about to reach the low elevation of his bed. He lifted his left foot and put it hesitantly upon the platform, as if doubting the propriety of his actions. Then he stepped straight up until he was standing on the bed. Once his equilibrium was established, he turned around and faced the entrance door as if to contemplate the small crowd that had followed him into the room. There was no real eye contact, however,

> In Tibetan Buddhist literature there are also the *das-lok* or returned from the dead writings. There are hundreds of accounts of people who have come back to life before being cremated or buried. Usually the dead person meets with deceased relatives and friends or famous people of old, and is asked to take messages back to the living. Thereafter the person is often transformed into a wandering prophet or teacher, warning people to avoid evil and cultivate goodness.
>
> —Susan Blackmore, *Dying to Live: Near-Death Experiences*

because Grandfather was now existing in a space that was beyond the living. Although he was physically present with us, he was only really alive in the world of the spirits.

My father came to Grandfather and took the hyena tail out of his hand while two robust men supported Grandfather from the back. Grandfather let himself fall into their hands and, with due ceremony, he was laid out on his couch. Once again he looked as if he were deeply asleep. Disoriented by his sudden immobility, I looked around me in search of an explanation.

The crowd outside was growing rapidly and I could tell something was very wrong. A little more than twenty-four hours ago I had been transported into the future by Grandfather's speech. Now he was sleeping, peaceably, as if indifferent to what was going on around him.

The five or six men who had accompanied us into Grandfather's room were now busy. Some were rearranging the order of the gourds and cans in the room, others were preparing medicine or lighting aromatic plants.

My father had once again disappeared, but I could hear him speaking to a group of old women who were standing at the entrance of Grandfather's room. "Get the material ready for the meal, and warm up the water. Make haste. Everything must be finished before the sun cools down."

He came back to Grandfather and proceeded to strip him of the remnant of clothing he wore. Then he massaged his body slowly and carefully. One of the men brought a clay pot containing some foaming liquid, inside of which was a double-edged knife. My father lifted Grandfather's head while another man proceeded to shave his white hair. He wetted a portion of the snowy skull, then cleaned away whatever hair was there. Then he collected the fallen hair and handed it up to another man near him, who passed it to another, and so on until I lost track of it. The shaving went very slowly. When there was nothing left, the hairdresser put the knife back into the pot, then pronounced some lugubrious words. The gourds and cans in the room responded by knocking against one another.

At that moment the women entered the room. They put down an enormous clay jar full of warm water and three other medium-sized pots. One contained more water, another some seasoning ingredients, and the third one some millet flour. The women left without a word. The men rushed to the potful of warm water and carried it to Grandfather's deathbed. They mixed the water with three different roots and two liquid substances that they picked out of some of the surrounding gourds and washed his body carefully. Grandfather's last toilet, took an interminable time. Those who labored on him were singing solemnly in harmony, a sort of genealogical recital. I can still recall some of the names, and later I understood that they referred to my very ancient ancestors.

After that the men recited the prayer of the dead. Other men who had not entered into the earlier singing now sang the canticle to the spirits, who know no death. These spirits live in the underworld, in the air, in the water, and in the fire. The awesome voices of the men, tremulously mounting in the air like a mournful complaint, were seconded by other voices outside, at the entrance. The women's song was the most thrilling. Men who heard it groaned a brief *sanwéi*, which means in our language, "Oh, Father," The women's shrill voices rose sharply like daggers and penetrated every heart, blocking our throats, sending chills all through our bodies, and causing tears to well up from our eyes. I was crying not because Grandfather was dead—for up till now I had but a faint idea of what death meant—but because these female singers made such a miserable lament that I was beginning to suspect some sort of tragedy had occurred.

The room was suddenly overtaken by a blanket of darkness, thick and heavy, punctuated here and there by something that resembled a yellow glitter, a mild lightning. Behind the singing voices, there was a continuous murmur, an unfailingly monotonous buzzing sound that was coming out of the surrounding gourds and cans. They were hitting against one another as if moved by the ropes that held them in place. Next, I heard the sound of marching feet, pounding the ground everywhere in the tiny room. The darkness became deeper and more terrifying. Footsteps also sounded on the roof of the house, and little bits of dirt falling from the ceiling seemed to indicate that the roof was groaning under their weight. Inside, the invisible marching people shouted at each other cacophonously and stomped loudly in every direction, bumping into invisible objects that fell catastrophically on the ground. The noise was getting to be unbearable.

Then everything began to revolve in a circle around me. I had the feeling that I was on a raft that kept turning and turning and not going anywhere. On the raft were half a dozen elderly people, each one my grandfather, and each one making fun of me. They were laughing loudly, mindless of whatever I wanted to ask them. I kept trying to speak to them, but my mouth wouldn't form the questions that my eyes kept asking over and over. The raft finally took off into the air. In an ultimate movement, it dived into the void like a spaceship. Overtaken by fear, I yelled. Everything ceased instantaneously, and I saw my father bending over me with an anxious face asking, "Are you all right?" I realized I was lying next to Grandfather on his bed. They had dressed him up the way they dress everyone who dies. I wondered what had happened to me.

Singers, washers, and hairdressers had finished their cabalistic activities and were now all interested in another no less mysterious one. They had transformed Grandfather's room into a kitchen where everything was happening upside down. A clay pot full of water was boiling quietly on the ceiling, its bottom sitting against the roof. Beneath it was a fire dancing inside a triangular fireplace, its boundaries marked off by medium-sized stones, each of which could easily have weighed ten kilos. The whole—fireplace, fire, stones, clay pot, and water—were suspended as if by enchantment on the wooden ceiling. Beneath this vertiginous fireplace, men were busy readying the many condiments necessary for the preparation of a meal outside the force of gravity.

I was fascinated by this upside-down boiling pot of water. The whole thing appeared to me like a joke. I had never seen anything like this before, and Grandfather had surely never mentioned it.

One of the men poured some flour into a basket of water yellowed by a mixture of herbs, stirred it carefully, and tossed its contents toward the boiling pot. Instead of falling down onto the floor, the contents obeyed another law. They landed in the boiling water, which splashed upward onto the wood of the ceiling. Everybody went about their tasks as if unmindful of how strange their activities appeared. It was as if they were operating in a circle that defied natural laws, involved in a strange conspiracy to challenge the Great Master of the Universe.

Soon, the clay pot was filled with a gelatinous mass which roared like a volcano in action. Cooking vapors filled the entire room. The man who had poured the flour into the boiling water grabbed a flat wooden stick called a *vuul* and plunged it into the roaring, sticky porridge in the upside-down pot. He began stirring clockwise, then counterclockwise. Meanwhile, another man standing next to him poured dry flour from a basket he was holding into the pot at regular intervals. The millet cake in the clay pot was slowly increasing in size, thickening, hardening, and making the stirring movements harder and harder. The first man was perspiring, his muscles contracting with each movement; he and the cakes were now growling in unison.

When the first man was finished, he put his *vuul* down on the floor next to the second man, grabbed two pieces of cloth to protect himself from the heat, took hold of the clay pot and its contents, and pulled very strongly, holding his breath. The clay pot resisted for a while, then gave up and rushed toward the ground. The man quickly executed a rolling gesture, turning the clay pot upright, to avoid pouring any of its contents onto the ground. That way, container and contents were deposited safely on the floor of the room, unspoiled. Almost immediately another man performed the same rolling movement backward with another clay pot half filled with water. The new pot rose in the air, made a U-turn in the middle between the ground and the ceiling, and backed up onto the fireplace. Before the water began to boil, the man had already put some okra flour in it, along with some condiments.

He added some dry monkey meat and a huge number of other medicinal products. In the meantime other people were serving out the millet cake. One portion of the cake was put near Grandfather's deathbed. The other portions were placed in smaller pots and distributed to the women who were waiting outside at the entrance. When the sauce in the second pot was cooked, the men took it down just as they had taken down the previous pot. The sauce was also served into clay pots and distributed, and a portion placed near Grandfather's deathbed.

At that time the cooks and my father approached Grandfather and sat around the still-smoking meal. My father pulled out the terrible hyena tail once again and put it into Grandfather's left hand. Grandfather had been sleeping all this time, indifferent to what was going on in his own room. Now he jerked as if bitten or shaken by an electrical shock. He opened his eyes and fixed them on the ceiling.

My father said, "Father, get up. The last meal has arrived. Eat with us this food that strengthens the body and keeps the mind in a state of wakefulness. You cannot begin the trip to the ancestors on an empty belly. It is a long trip, a difficult journey. Eat with us that which, while living, you never wanted to miss."

Grandfather did not answer. He stretched slowly upward until he was sitting. He gazed inquiringly from left to right, and from right to left, as if to inspect his own room, then brought his lifeless eyes down to the dish in front of him. Everybody was silent and fascinated. There was a calabash full of warm water near Grandfather, and he plunged his right hand into it and washed, while his left hand continued to hold the hyena tail. Then he picked up a piece of the millet cake, plunged it into the sauce, and carried the whole toward his mouth.

Five pairs of eyes vigilantly watched his every gesture. I noticed that the food disappeared before reaching the interior of his mouth. An invisible force simply absorbed it before it reached his lips. Nobody said anything or seemed surprised by any of this, so I stopped watching. Following the example of the other guests, I began eating. I was hungry enough to swallow an entire roasted monkey and a few gallons of its gravy. We ate without a word as Dagara customs command: "The mouth that eats cannot be the mouth that talks."

Grandfather was the first to stop eating. He let his hand fall onto his upper leg for a short time, then lifted it toward the calabash and again washed his fingers. That activity took a comparatively long time. He did not seem to be in a hurry at all. When he finished, the other men followed his lead; all washed their hands, and I was left alone to eat the leftovers. I pulled the two clay pots and their contents nearer to me. Everybody was looking at me, and without a word I understood that I better eat fast.

Years later, when I was older, I would come to understand what I had seen that day. The out-of-gravity culinary art was a secret practice performed only when a leader of exceptional standing died. The day of my grandfather's death was the first and last time I ever saw it. For, as things changed in our tribe, the practice passed away, perhaps along with the secret. Today it has become a tale. But for those who had direct contact with the reality of *satulmo*, as it is called, it is a sad thing to realize how much my people have lost and how much yet of our reality is to be buried in the pit of oblivion.

The food preparation within the precinct of reverse gravity was a symbolic enactment of the realm that the great ones enter through death. By leaving his body, Grandfather had escaped the laws of physicality; therefore, only food cooked according to the laws of the new realm he now inhabited could be eaten and digested effectively. There are secret plants in nature that are very powerful. By using some of these plants, known only by healers and men and women in touch with the great medicine of Mother Earth, our cooks were able to produce, for a short time, an area free of gravity.

Malidoma Patrice Somé, born in Upper Volta (now Burkina Faso), West Africa, is initiated in the ancestral traditions of his tribe, and is a medicine man and diviner in the Dagara culture. He holds three master's degrees and two doctorates from the Sorbonne and Brandeis University, and has taught at the University of Michigan. He is the author of Ritual: Power, Healing and Community, The Healing Wisdom of Africa, *and* Of Water and Spirit: Ritual Magic and Initiation in the Life of an African Shaman, *from which this story was excerpted. He currently devotes himself to speaking and, with his wife, Sobonfu, conducting intensive workshops throughout the United States. They live in Oakland, California.*

$\star$ $\overset{\star}{}$ $\star$

Last Rites

That was one small step for a priest,
one great leap for his parishioner.

I REMEMBER WHEN I WAS IN GRADUATE SCHOOL, I WAS LIVING IN A rectory. I was just supposed to be in residence there, but they often were able to prevail upon me to do various assignments.

The first night I was there—I had just been ordained a couple of weeks—the priest in charge wanted to get a night's rest without the pressure of a late call, so he left me with the beeper for the hospital.

Now he assured me that he had gone up there the day before and "oiled everybody in sight," and that there would be no occasion for me to be called. But just in case there was an untimely emergency, there was a beeper.

So I took the beeper to bed. And sure enough, at three o'clock in the morning, it went off.

So I slapped water on my face and got dressed, drove up to the hospital, put myself on "automatic priest," and went into the room.

The nurse showed me a little woman who had been brought to die in the hospital. She was a tiny Irish woman in her nineties; she had even a little brogue. And she asked to be given the Sacrament of the Sick—she called it "Extreme Unction." She asked to receive Communion, to be absolved, and to be given the final blessing. So, sure enough, I heard her confession, gave her Communion, and anointed her to die.

And in the midst of giving her a final blessing, she grabbed hold of my hand midway through the sign of the cross, and pulled it to herself and wouldn't let go.

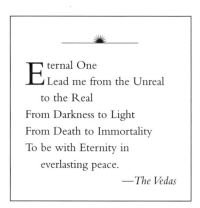

Eternal One
Lead me from the Unreal
  to the Real
From Darkness to Light
From Death to Immortality
To be with Eternity in
  everlasting peace.
                    —*The Vedas*

And she said to me—in the eloquent way the Irish speak—she said, "Father, linger with me awhile." Actually I had no choice; she had a very strong grip!

So I said, "Surely I'll stay with you." And I lingered with her.

We prayed a few prayers. A few songs I remembered by heart, I recited to her. And she seemed to fall asleep—but she didn't let go.

A couple of hours passed, and through the window the light began shining, it became nearly dawn. She began to relax her grip and she woke up. And she said to me as she let go, "Thank you, Father, for coming to visit. I hope you didn't mind me calling you out of bed. I know I wasn't taking you away from anyone." (It's the best argument for clerical celibacy I've ever heard!)

And she said, "And thank you for coming to bless me. They weren't your hands, you know. For me, tonight, they were God's hands, and I am going escorted."

And those were her last words. She closed her eyes and went to sleep.

Father Mark Gruber, a Benedictine monk of St. Vincent Archabbey in Latrobe, Pennsylvania, is currently teaching classes in anthropology at St. Vincent College. To fulfill part of the requirements for his doctorate, he spent a year in Egypt studying desert life and spirituality in Coptic monasteries.

PART FOUR

SHADOWS

DIRK BOGARDE

✳ ✳ ✳

In Normandy

Caen fell, and the Germans began
their terrible retreat to the east.

THE SKY WAS ALWAYS BLUE, THAT STRANGE INTENSE BLUE OF
northern France, sea-washed, wind-cleansed, limitless, crisscrossed
with lazy scrawls of vapour trails like the idle scribbles of a child in
a crayoning-book.

In the orchards the shade lay heavy beneath the trees, spiked here
and there with emerald blades of grass and clumps of campion.

But everywhere the land was still. There was no birdsong.

Sometimes a bee would drone up and away, or a grasshopper
scissor in the crushed weeds of the chalky soil, and then fall silent as
if the effort had been too much, in the still heat, or as if, perhaps,
reproved that there was no response in the ominous quiet.

No rabbits scuttled in the hedgerows, the corn stood high, ripe,
heavy in the ear, unharvested, and in the meadows cows lay on their
sides, stiff-legged, like milking stools, bellies bloated with gas.

Sometimes one of them would explode with a sound like a
heavy sigh, dispersing memories of a lost childhood in the sickly
stench of decay.

Death was monarch of that summer landscape: only the bee and
the grasshopper gave a signal of life, or suggested that it existed. The
familiar had become unfamiliar and frightening. A world had

stopped, and one waited uneasily to see if it would start again: a clock to be rewound in an empty room.

But that comforting tick-tock of normality, of the life pulse, had been provisionally arrested. In some cases it had been stopped for good, for a little farther back, toward the beaches, they were burying those who would remain forever in silence.

There was plenty of noise back there: of gears grinding, engines roaring, tracks rattling, metal groaning.

At the edge of an elm-fringed meadow, I stood against a tree watching, curiously unmoved, the extraordinary ballet between machines and corpses, which proved conclusively that the human body was nothing but a fragile, useless container without the life force.

For some reason it had never fully occurred to me before: I had seen a good number of dead men and had, as a normal reaction, felt a stab of pity, a creep of fear that perhaps it could be me next time, but I had become accustomed to them and got on with my own living.

But that afternoon in the shade of the elms I stood watching the bulldozers (a new toy to us then) shovelling up the piles of dead very much as spoiled fruit is swept into heaps after a market day, and with as little care. Shuddering, wrenching, jerking, stinking of hot oil in the high sun, they swivelled slowly about with open jaws ripping at the earth to form deep pits, and then, nudging and grabbing at the shreds and pieces, rotting, bloody, unidentifiable, which heavy trucks had let slither from raised tailboards in tumbled heaps of arms and legs, they tossed them into the pits.

Back and forth they droned and crunched, swinging about with casual ease, manoeuvred by cheerful young men, masked against the stench and flies, arms burned black by the August sun.

"Tidying up," said someone with me. "One day they will turn this meadow into a war cemetery. Rows and rows of crosses and neat little walks; perhaps they'll erect a fine granite monument, a flagstaff will carry a proud flag to be lowered at the Last Post, they'll plant those bloody yew trees, and relatives will walk in silence through the toy-town precision and order, looking for their dead."

I remember what he said, because I wrote it all down later, but I can't remember who he was.

Fairly typical of me, I fear.

The words stayed with me for the simple reason that they moved me more than the things which I was observing. The dead lying there in putrid heaps among the sorrel and buttercups didn't move me at all: they were no more than torn, tattered, bloody bundles. The soul had sped; there could only be regret for those who had loved the individual bodies in this seeping mass: for everyone there had once belonged to someone. That was the sadness.

The absolute anonymity of mass death had dulled grief.

The silence didn't last long—silence in war never does. One gets to discover that very early on.

The ominous stillness which had reproved both grasshopper and bee simply preceded a gigantic storm: Caen fell, the Germans began their terrible retreat to the east. The battle for Normandy was over.

I use the word "terrible" advisedly, for the retreat, estimated at that time to be composed of at least 300,000 men plus vehicles and arms, crammed the dusty high-hedged roads and lanes, even the cart tracks through fields and orchards, in a desperate attempt to reach the ferries across the river Seine: the Allied armies surrounded them on three sides. We knew that all the main bridges had been blown, so it appeared evident to us that we contained the entire German fighting force in one enormous killing ground. Tanks and trucks, horse-drawn limbers, staff cars, private cars, farm carts, and all kinds of tracked vehicles, anything in fact which could move, inched along the jammed lanes and roads in slow convoys of death.

Unable to turn back, to turn left or right, they had no alternative but to go ahead to the river, providing undefended, easy targets for Allied aircraft which homed down on them as they crawled along and blasted them to destruction: ravening wolves with cornered prey.

By 21 August it was over.

Across the shattered farms, the smouldering cornfields, the smoking ruins in the twisting lanes, smoke drifted lazily in the heat and once again the frightening silence came down over a landscape of shattering carnage.

Those of us in the middle of things really thought that a colossal victory had been achieved. The Germans had been destroyed along with their weapons. There could be nothing left of them to fight, the Russians were about to invade their homeland, surely now victory was ours, and war would finish before the end of the summer?

We were wrong. The people who are in the middle are nearly always wrong. The canvas of war is far too great to comprehend as one single picture. We only knew a very limited part—and even that part was not as it seemed. Gradually we began to realize that the war was not over, that it was going to go on, that the Germans were still fighting, still highly armed, stubborn and tougher than they had been before. Slowly "a colossal victory" faded from our minds, and we accepted the fact that something must have gone a little bit wrong in our jubilant assessment of an early peace.

It had indeed gone wrong. But it was only some years later, when the generals who had squabbled, quarreled, and bickered all the way through the campaign began to write their autobiographies, all one learned that, far from a victory, the retreat had been a catastrophe.

By that time it was far too late for thousands of men to worry.

They were laid out in neat rows under white crosses.

What had happened, quite simply, is that the Allied generals, by disagreeing among themselves, had left the back door open to the killing ground permitting thousands of Germans, and their arms, to escape and live to fight another day.

But we didn't know it, fortunately, at the time.

Standing in the aftermath of violent death is a numbing experience: the air about one feels torn, ripped, and stretched. The cries of panic and pain, of rending metal, though long since dispersed into the atmosphere, still seem to echo in the stillness which drums in one's ears.

On the main road from Falaise to Trun, one of the main escape routes which we did manage to block, among the charred and twisted remains of exploded steel, dead horses indescribably chunked by flying shrapnel, eyes wide in terror, yellow teeth bared in frozen fear, still-smouldering tanks, the torn, bullet-ripped cars and the charred corpses huddled in the burned grass, it was perfectly clear that all that I had been taught in the past about hell and damnation had been absolutely wrong.

Hell and damnation were not some hellfire alive with dancing horned devils armed with toasting forks. Nothing which Sister Veronica or Sister Marie Joseph had told me was true. Clearly they had got it all wrong in those early, happy Twickenham days. Hell and damnation were here, on this once peaceful country road, and I was right in the middle of it all.

My boots were loud on the gravel, oily smoke meandered slowly from smouldering tyres. Blackened bodies, caught when the petrol tanks of the trucks and cars had exploded, grinned up at me from crisped faces with startling white teeth, fists clenched in charcoaled agony.

Down the road in a haze of smoke stood a small boy of about seven; in his hand a tin can with a twisted wire handle.

I walked toward him, and he turned quickly, then scrambled up the bank where a woman was bending over a body in the black grass, a hammer and chisel in her hand.

The boy tugged at her skirts, she stood upright, stared at me, shading her eyes with the flat of her hand, then she shrugged, cuffed the boy gently, and bent again to her task.

Hammering gold teeth from the grinning dead.

The boy raised the tin for me to see. It was almost a third full of bloody nuggets and bits of bridge-work.

Waste not, want not.

In the ditch below us a staff car lay tilted on its side, the body-work riddled with bullet holes in a precise line as if a riveter had been at work rather than a machine gun from a low-flying plane.

A woman was slumped in the back seat, a silver fox fur at her feet, her silk dress blood-soaked, a flowered turban drunkenly squint on her red head. A faceless man in the uniform of the SS lay across her thighs.

I kicked one of her shoes lying in the road, a wedge-heeled, cork-soled scrap of coloured cloth.

The woman with the hammer shouted down, *"Sale Boche! Eh? Collaboratrice…c'est plein des femmes comme ça! Sale Boche!"*

I walked back to my jeep. My driver was sitting in his seat smoking.
"Where do they all come from?"

"Who?"

"Those blokes…wandering about having a good old loot. They just go through the pockets, get the wallets, pinch the bits of jewellery. There's a squad of women civilians in all this lot. Gives you a bit of a turn seeing dead women in this sort of set-up."

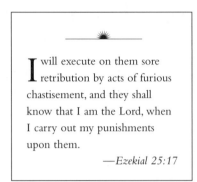

I will execute on them sore retribution by acts of furious chastisement, and they shall know that I am the Lord, when I carry out my punishments upon them.

—*Ezekial 25:17*

Here and there, pulling at the blackened corpses, wrenching open the doors of the bullet-riddled cars, a few elderly peasants clambered about the wreckage collecting anything of value. God knew where they had come from—every building nearby was destroyed, but like the women on the bank with the boy, they had come to scavenge what they could.

As we drove away, the first bulldozers began to arrive to clear the road. I didn't speak: the sight of the dead girl with the red hair had distressed me profoundly.

I was prepared for people to be dead in uniform, but my simple mind would not come to terms with the sight of a dead woman in a silk dress on a battlefield. That didn't seem to be right. They hadn't warned us about *that* on the assault course in Kent.

We had to pull aside to let a bulldozer grind past; I looked back and saw an old man dancing a little jig. In a fox fur cape.

Dirk Bogarde, poet, autobiographer, and novelist, began his acting career on the stage. He is the author of a number of books, including Short Walk from Harrods, A Gentle Occupation, Jericho, *and* Backcloth, *from which this story is excerpted. He died in 1999.*

$\star$ $\star$ $\star$

Taken for a Ride

Cultivate your instincts.

I WAS ON MY DREAM VACATION. THE SIGHTS WERE NEW AND EXCITING. I was busy taking it all in. But I had a foreboding that we shouldn't be with Joel.

It was summer. I had joined a friend, Vicki, and her friend, Sarah, in London, for what we'd planned to be our college education grand tour. When Vicki said they'd met a guy named Joel in the bookstore at Oxford University, accompanied him to Stratford-on-Avon, and accepted his invitation to drive to Paris, I immediately responded, "No, I don't want to go by car."

Several people had cautioned, "European drivers are crazy. Roads are circuitous. It's better to take the train."

Vicki overrode my objection. "It's so much fun to be able to stop whenever you want." The trip was supposed to be fun. No one expected to have to make a life or death decision. So I didn't say any more.

They'd bought concert tickets with Joel for the evening; but, exhausted from being up all night on the flight from New York, I begged off.

Joel picked them up; he was a slight young man who slouched and shrugged nervously, and he repelled me. His eyes avoided mine. I shrank back. An alarm went off in my brain: don't drive with him! However, jet-lagged, I ignored my inner voice, crawled into bed and slept.

We didn't see him the next day; I was glad. Arrangements were made by phone to try to link up the day after in Dover. I assumed Dover would be a large city, we'd never meet, and I dismissed him from thought.

Late the following afternoon, we arrived in Dover. We exited the train station, and right at the bottom of the steps was a red MG. My companions exclaimed, "It must be Joel's." I stiffened. Dread filled me while they hurried over, peered inside. They scribbled a note, shoved it under a wiper blade. My impulse was to snatch the note and destroy it.

It *was* his car and we joined him for dinner. When he took us back to our hostel, he drove much too quickly down a steep hill. As he tried to steer on the unfamiliar left side of the road, his hands shook. He knew none of the curves, or where streets intersected. After he'd dropped us at the hostel, I spoke up, "He's a lousy driver. I don't want to drive with him."

"He hasn't been driving long. I'm sure he'll be fine," said Vicki. How come she didn't feel the concern I did? He gave me the creeps. I had to keep shoving my feelings aside.

We took the morning ferry across the English Channel to Calais, France. In a field outside the town, we shared a picnic lunch of bread, pâté, and wine.

I asked Joel to teach me to drive his car. I had never driven a car with a shift. Every time I stepped on the clutch, the engine stalled. On an empty country road, stalling wasn't hazardous. But I was scared to get into traffic, so I relinquished the wheel to Joel. I sat in the front passenger seat that afternoon.

Used to driving a much larger car, I didn't like so little distance between me and the car ahead. The following day I made sure to sit in back.

We left Rouen after breakfast. We chose a road that wound through beautiful meadows and woods. It was being resurfaced. If it was too torn up, we all agreed we'd go back and take the highway.

After a few minutes, we'd passed the face-lifted area, and then continued on the scenic route.

Soon Joel was tailgating the car ahead. In the lane to the right, a second car rode neck and neck beside it. Joel swerved into the oncoming traffic's lane to pass. The car in the right lane sped up and changed lanes into the spot Joel was aiming for. Now he had two cars to pass. Suddenly, the oncoming cars loomed threateningly close.

Sarah, sitting beside Joel, sobbed hysterically.

"Cover your face, Sarah," I shouted.

Joel floored the gas, and, through a miracle, passed both cars and squeezed back onto our side of the road just in time.

"Please slow down," Sarah pleaded.

"We're in no hurry," Vicki yelled.

"Shut up, I know what I'm doing," he said through clenched teeth.

In the distance, a train sped across the fields. I wished we were on it.

A couple of hours into the journey we passed a roadside fruit stand; doubled back for a snack. Since Sarah spoke French, she and Joel went to buy the produce.

I said to Vicki, "I don't like the way he drives; I won't go with him after we get to Paris." She finally agreed.

While we ate peaches, Joel reached under the driver's seat, and pulled out the bottle of wine we'd all shared the previous day during our picnic lunch. He gulped down the wine. I was on the verge of asking him not to drink, but the bottle was empty.

Back on the road, Joel drove faster. The little car rattled. His hands shook on the steering wheel. A nervous chill raced through me. Trying to calm myself I rationalized, nothing will happen; we'll be in Paris soon. I started to read a Paris travel brochure.

In the middle of my prayers to slow down, Sarah's voice shrieked, "Why are you passing on the right? You can't see. There's construction ahead."

Screams ripped the air. The brochure dropped from my hand. We were about to crash into a wooden barricade. It happened so fast, I froze. Joel spun the steering wheel hard. Too hard. We shot across the road, out of control.

Facing us was an approaching gasoline truck. Suspended in shock, my thoughts raced. Drop to the floor? If the seat jumps back, I'll be crushed. How will we get to Paris now? Dear Mom and Dad, We had a little accident...

I woke up four weeks later, and they were by my bed. They told me what had happened. Sarah died instantly. Joel lost an arm and a leg. Vicki's legs were broken; one will never bend. My right arm and hip broke in so many places I'm constantly in pain.

My inner voice is a part of me now, and when it speaks, I listen.

Ronnie Golden has written television documentaries as well as travel articles. She has traveled extensively and has lived in Florence and Prague. She is presently writing the book and lyrics for a musical, and resides in Studio City, California.

* * *

When It's Your Turn

*We're all booked on this journey—we just
don't know the departure date.*

WHAT WOULD YOU DO IF YOU HAD FOUR MONTHS TO LIVE? OVER
the years, I've met several people facing that plight, and they've asked
me to share my best fishing spot, the most beautiful hidden waterfall,
the most pristine meadow, the prettiest drive, the most secluded, untouched beach. A few explained that they wanted to venture to a very
special place, a place where they could best take in the natural powers of the earth and try to come to terms with their predicaments.

I never figured I'd be doing the same thing myself any time soon.
But I was.

I went down to this little brook next to a meadow, the place
where I remember feeling the happiest in my entire life, a place I'd
discovered with my sweetheart, and just sat there, watched the
water go by, and wondered, "How did I ever get in this situation?"

Four months to live. That was the worst-case scenario.

In mid-August, on a trip to the Sierra foothills, I woke up one
morning with this deep soreness under my ear, on the side of my
neck. On instinct, while still mostly asleep, I touched it, and to my
surprise, there was significant swelling. Now I was fully awake. The
swelling stretched from just below the right ear, under the cleft of
the jaw, nearly to my throat.

I know what this is, I thought, a swollen lymph node.

Later that day, I went swimming to cool off, and my right ear seemed to plug up. For days, it wouldn't clear. And the swelling kept getting bigger. The doctor said, yes, I had an ear infection all right, and as for the lymph node, "We'll put you on antibiotics for an infection." But three weeks later, after continuous doses of different antibiotics, the node was bigger than ever.

At times, it felt like a railroad spike was hammered through my neck. At one campsite on a warm night, I woke up at midnight, covered in sweat, freezing cold. The next day, I was hiking across a meadow to the foot of a mountain with my sweetheart fiancée, Stephani Cruickshank, and kids, Jeremy and Kris, scouting out a deer trail. My legs, back, and arms became so sore that I had to sit down on a log for twenty minutes. Then on a fishing trip in my canoe with my brother, Rambob, I suddenly became so exhausted that I almost went to sleep while paddling.

My doctor squared his shoulders to mine and explained that the antibiotics should have worked, but they didn't, so I might be dealing with lymphoma, Hodgkin's disease, maybe leukemia, and with luck, maybe a deranged lymph gland out of control. All the symptoms, he noted, were present, and now more doctors would be brought in.

The lymph system is your body's immune system, the doctor explained, with a network of nodes throughout your body that makes every person capable of fighting infections and purging toxins. When it goes haywire or is corrupted by cancer, such as with lymphoma, it can spread quickly and render you defenseless. So doctors started an extensive series of blood tests, X-rays, biopsies, and scheduled surgery.

At this point, I flew my little airplane around California for a day, across hundreds of miles, first all around the Bay Area, then far beyond as well, scanning the land and reminiscing over the experiences I have had with the people I care for, and the lakes, rivers, forests, wetlands, deserts, bays, and coast that I love so much.

At midday, I landed in Dunsmuir to fill up with gas before heading south along the Cascades and Sierra, and looked for my old friend, Carl Hutchins, the airport manager. Instead I was told he "was gone," that "lymphoma got him," diagnosed in early summer, gone by September. Four months.

That night, I found another small lump, this one in my groin, the location of another lymph node, and felt fear extend through every cell in my body. Then I felt the lump on my neck. God, it was huge now. On Monday, the doctors said the node was twenty times its normal size, and by Thursday, the morning of surgery, it was twenty-five times its normal size.

On Wednesday, in my canoe with my brother on a hidden lake, I showed him where I wanted my ashes scattered. On a walk across an untouched meadow, I finally admitted to my fiancée that I was scared. Then alone, sitting on a log near that little brook, watching the water go by, I thought about how it didn't seem fair.

Hey, I'm only forty-four years old. Always in perfect health, and as a pilot, checked

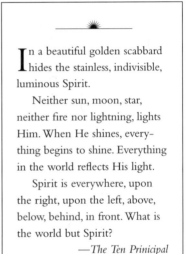

In a beautiful golden scabbard hides the stainless, indivisible, luminous Spirit.

Neither sun, moon, star, neither fire nor lightning, lights Him. When He shines, everything begins to shine. Everything in the world reflects His light.

Spirit is everywhere, upon the right, upon the left, above, below, behind, in front. What is the world but Spirit?

—*The Ten Prinicipal Upanishads*

by a doctor every year. Climbed all the highest mountains, hiked 20,000 miles. Don't smoke, hardly drink at all, never did drugs, don't even drink coffee, and yet here I was, watching that water go by. I couldn't understand how it could be that twenty-two years after meeting Stephani in college I had found her again, become engaged, had bonded with her two boys, Jeremy, ten, and Kris, seven, and how ecstatic I was about facing future adventures and new challenges. And now this?

I started remembering each of the people I've talked with who had terminal illnesses, how they asked me about the most beautiful places and how they wished they had spent more time in the outdoors, especially exploring.

As they wheeled me into the operating room, the air filled with the scent of antiseptics, I realized that the most special places are always brought to life by sharing them with the people you love and care for, and I'd rather just sit by that little brook with Stephani, Jeremy, and Kris, than head off around the world and catch a world-record fish or climb a mountain by myself.

"So where is this thing?" asked a surgeon's assistant.

"Over here, under the right ear," answered the surgeon.

"Yikes! The thing is huge."

That's all I remember. Then I blacked out.

The next thing I remember was waking up in the recovery room, almost incoherent, and there Stephani was, holding my arm and hand and then whispering to me, "You're O.K., you don't have cancer, I talked to the doctor and he said you're going to be fine."

Surgeons went in on my neck, starting with an incision below the ear and extending down toward the vocal cords, and they found evidence of two infections, an old one with dead tissue that apparently had blocked the node and a new one that was an offspring from the summer ear infection. With the block in place, the node could not purge or cleanse itself, and thus it started swelling. From the lab, the biopsy was clean: no cancer.

Meanwhile, the lump in my groin turned out to be a very small hernia, not a lymph infection, and stands to barely slow me down.

This past month has been very difficult, and I realize that the cost of living is dying, and some day we're all going to have to pay up. But I also realize that by knowing so, there can be magic in every breath, especially by sharing special places with the people you care for most.

The great outdoors is truly grand. But love, my friends, is all that matters in the end.

Tom Stienstra is an avid adventurer who searches for incredible experiences and secret spots that involve camping, backpacking, and fishing. As a nationally acclaimed outdoors writer, he has a column in the San Francisco Examiner *and has published eight books, including* Epic Trips of the West.

* * *

Why the Dogs of Rwanda
Are Overfed

Even in Hell on Earth, the spirit lives.

"WELCOME TO THE HOTEL MILLE COLLINES," READ THE brochure, a faded relic from the 1970s that I'd picked up while idling in line at the reception desk. Under an illustration of the obligatory mountain gorillas and flowering trees, it went on, "Enjoy Eternal Springtime In This Peaceful, Central African Paradise." The reservations clerk interrupted the march of silverbacks up the side of the volcano to ask for my passport.

"Welcome to Rwanda," he said, in heavily accented English. As a result of the rebel takeover, Rwanda was quickly becoming a bilingual country. Without looking up, he handed me my key. So far, the atmosphere wasn't exactly friendly. These days, the hotel was hardly a tourist destination. I thanked him and smiled, "By the way, can you tell me where the bar is?"

"Oh yes, Madame, seventh floor." A big, toothy African smile flashed across his face. "It opens at 5 P.M....go early before it gets too crowded."

A lopsided sign reading "TEMPORARILY OUT OF ORDER" hung on a chain across the elevator door. I glanced at the porter who looked worn and way past retirement—he'd probably climbed the equivalent of Mount Kili that day—and decided to pitch up my own bags. I followed him toward the stairs.

The room held no surprises. It looked like any other second-class hotel room in this part of the world, which is to say, adequate and utterly plain. I had no complaints. Besides, with the workload ahead, I knew I wouldn't be spending much time there.

Like many consultants, I'd come to Rwanda in the wake of the 1994 genocide to lend a hand to the new government. In my case, I'd been hired to help organize a conference that would gather together hundreds of experts from around the world to explore the roots of this particular genocide and offer suggestions for pulling the country together again. A Humpty Dumpty situation if ever there was one. I'd accepted the assignment reluctantly, not at all sure I'd be up to the task. Now that I was here I needed to gather a lot of information in a very short time. The bar seemed like a good place to start.

I threw my bags on the bed and hurried to the 7th floor. A journalist friend had tipped me off to the Mille Collines. He had described it as a classic watering hole—a place where "*le tout*" Kigali [the capital], everyone from news hounds and politicians to guer-rillas and bush pilots, gathered to gossip and take bets on the next political moves. Among other things, it seemed like a good place to scout for a driver—someone well-educated, who knew his way around. The fact that jobs were scarce around here would work in my favor.

I arrived shortly after five, and pushed my way through the crowd to the bar. A high-decibel din, a mixture of friendly chatter and clinking glass filled in for the band that hadn't shown up yet. I ordered a beer and found a spot against the far wall where I could survey the room without being noticed. For women, there's a cer-tain etiquette for entering a bar alone. I had to be careful not to send the wrong message.

It wasn't long before I spotted my guy. Short and nearly bald, he was working the room like a pro. His green and brown soccer jersey wound its way through the crowd like a grass snake, pausing now and then just long enough to refill his glass or shake a hand. He seemed to be everywhere at once. Not everyone was dressed as casually. Some of the men wore big-shouldered suits, and crisp, white shirts—even in this humidity. The women—there were only a handful—were dressed modestly, in surprisingly dull colors for Africa. This was a church-going country, and it showed. Some of the younger men wore army fatigues and heavy black boots.

I decided to circulate, and automatically gravitated toward the green and brown jersey. Social behavior was governed by a different set of rules here, and approaching a stranger was perfectly acceptable. His name was Maneno, and we quickly fell into an easy conversation. Strikingly handsome, he looked like a miniature Mario Peeples with eyes like little bonfires that burned with intelligence and subtlety. If anything was going to happen, he would know it first. We struck a deal. He'd be at the hotel with a car first thing in the morning.

Back in my room, night had fallen. I flipped a switch and took a look around. The carpeting was a cheap Motel 6 olive green, covered with dark, blotchy stains. From my vantage point five and a half feet up, it looked like camouflage—a popular pattern in this country. On the far side of the room, half-hidden behind a set of tattered,

---

Decimation means the killing of every tenth person in a population, and in the spring and early summer of 1994 a program of massacres decimated the Republic of Rwanda. Although the killing was low tech—performed largely by machete—it was carried out at dazzling speed: of an original population of about seven and a half million, at least eight hundred thousand people were killed in just a hundred days. Rwandans often speak of a million deaths, and they may be right. The dead of Rwanda accumulated at nearly three times the rate of Jewish dead during the Holocaust. It was the most efficient mass killings since the atomic bombings of Hiroshima and Nagasaki.

—Philip Gourevitch, *We Wish to Inform You that Tomorrow We Will Be Killed with Our Families: Stories from Rwanda*

yellowed curtains that hung like a pair of high-water pants, was a poorly mounted sliding glass door. A hefty shove exposed a small balcony.

Here, finally, was a glimpse of the "Eternal Springtime" the brochure had touted. The garden below was magnificent, crowned at one end with a seventy-foot tree with a leafy canopy that fanned out and over a broad expanse of faultlessly groomed lawn. I wanted to pitch a tent right there. The songbirds were rehearsing at full volume, and I wondered if they quieted down at night. Through the branches I spotted a handful of diners enjoying an early dinner. Off to the right, a lone swimmer, arms churning rhythmically, broke the placid surface of a turquoise-tiled swimming pool. For a moment I forgot where I was.

It was way too early to sleep, but I fell into bed anyway, bone-tired from two days of travel. Loose springs and close, stale air would keep me on this side of dreamland for a long, long time. I thought of opening a window, then remembered it was rainy season, and anything in the neighborhood with wings would be gunning for me. Halfway through the night, a tropical downpour pounded the windows like a thousand tiny jackhammers, joining the low animal groans of ancient plumbing pipes coming from the bathroom. Together, they provided the perfect sound track for a horror movie. Before long I became aware of an eerie restlessness in the room. I felt surrounded by dozens of bodies moving in a kind of slow-motion dance. The air was charged with a heaviness I could not name.

Africans are superstitious. The president of the Republic consults a shaman before taking a trip, and taxi-men wear amulets around their necks to ward off evil. Stones speak, rivers house demons, and ancestors prowl the earth, especially at night. You'll rarely see an African far from his compound after dark. In this environment, the presence of spirits in my room should not have surprised me. But this was different. It felt more like a gathering of clans re-enacting some kind of ritual. Out in the bush, with the drums going and the griots lobbing hexes around, I would have felt threatened. Here I felt more like an intruder or a voyeur. What they were up to had nothing to do with me.

I was happy to see the sunrise, and even happier to hear Maneno's warm, relaxed voice calling from the lobby. He greeted me with an eager handshake, African-style, sliding his fingers across my palm and snapping my ring finger just before letting go. He was even shorter than I remembered. I knew very little about him…only that he was a Tutsi survivor, and Tutsis, if you believed the colonial literature, were supposed to be tall and thin…"lords" to the short and stocky Hutu "serfs." Maneno's wiry, muscular frame fell into neither category.

Dwarfed behind the wheel of a colonial-era Land Rover, he maneuvered us out of the parking lot and onto the nearly deserted streets. A year and a half had elapsed since the end of the war, and Kigali was still a ghost town. Most of the cars we passed were big, lumbering four-wheel drive vehicles, that bore the worn logos of voluntary agencies—WHO, UNDP, RED CROSS—stenciled on their doors. Many had been painted over with the bright orange initials of the Rwandan Patriotic Front, the current revolutionary rulers.

Right away I was struck by the sight of thousands upon thousands of sandbags, stacked up in uneven piles on both sides of the road, as if a rain of biblical proportions had coursed through these quiet streets in search of a riverbed or canal. They were all that remained of the dreaded Hutu checkpoints and bunkers which served as execution sites for the fleeing Tutsis.

The wreckage from countless street battles scarred the landscape. Toy-sized goats and chickens rooted around in the burnt-out chassis of rusted army tanks and once-proud colonial homes stood abandoned, their doors and windows wide open and vulnerable, crying out silently for their long-gone occupants. The shadowy figures of squatters shuffled about aimlessly in their overgrown, debris-strewn gardens. On the Boulevard Habyarimana, ragged curtains hung out of the broken windows of vacant office buildings, like wispy flags of surrender. There is nothing so forlorn as a battle-scarred, deserted city. It looked like a stage set someone had forgotten to strike.

I let out a low whistle. "What a nightmare!"

"You must understand," Maneno was choosing his words carefully, "in this pathetic country, there is not even money to bury the dead. Last week I drove the American ambassador to a meeting. He announced to me that now we are the poorest country in the world...he made it sound like some kind of achievement!"

He adjusted the rearview mirror. An ambulance with two flashing blue lights rotating on its roof was following us. "That's the vice president." He pulled over and ran to the passenger side, where I could see him shaking hands with Colonel Kagame, who in addition to being vice president, was also minister of defense.

Back in the car, he stated matter-of-factly: "There are so many threats...he wanted to know your mission here. The city looks quiet, but don't be fooled." He paused. "So you think this city is a mess? This is nothing! You should see the countryside. My father was a farmer. In our prefecture, he was the spokesman. Everyone looked up to him. Agriculture was his life. Before the war, farming was the backbone of this country. There were farms on every hill. Now, the new minister of agriculture said in an interview the other day, 'agriculture? *Ça n'existe pas!*' The same for health...for culture. We have nothing."

I persisted. "But what about the international community? The U.N.?"

He snapped, unexpectedly. "Don't talk to me about the U.N. As for the others...don't you see? We are like lepers! No one will touch us. To them we are *all* killers, murderers."

He didn't sound bitter. It was more like a recitation of facts.

"There are many fine distinctions to be made, like anywhere else. But because we are black and poor, they see only one thing— animals, savages!"

It was true. I had read dozens of accounts of the genocide in foreign newspapers. Few reporters provided a true analysis of the problems in Rwanda. It was too complicated. And besides, sensational headlines, like "Tribal Warfare," sell more papers.

I rephrased my question: "Well then, how do people live?...make a living?"

"What people?" He laughed. "They are all dead. In Kigali, they are all dead. Only a few like me are living." He laughed again. A short, hard laugh.

"Most of the Tutsis you see here are exiles. They are part of the diaspora. Now, since the war, they are coming home, from Uganda, from Belgium, even from the United States. Some of them have money, but most, like me, just survive."

"What about your family? Did they survive?"

"Maybe some are alive. I don't know. Everyone tries to get news, any news, about their families. But it is impossible. We are scattered like chickens. My own family is very large. For poor people, our children are a great pleasure." He grinned. "They help with the crops."

"How many were you?"

"Twelve. I am the oldest, can't you tell?" He cocked his head. Here, as elsewhere, it was an honor to be the eldest.

"Most of my brothers and sisters left Rwanda some years ago…for Tanzania, Zaire… you name it. We Tutsis are the gypsies of Africa…always on the move…so many massacres."

He was referring to the thirty or forty massacres that had occurred since colonization.

"I myself went to Zaire, to study medicine. In a year, I was broke. I managed two more years, on scholarships, but that was all. Back then, Kinshasa…it was a nice place…but it, too, became hell for us Tutsis. In some ways worse than here. Their own people had no jobs, no food. At the same time, at home, the massacres were increasing. No one felt safe."

"What finally brought you home?"

"My parents. They were growing old and couldn't keep up the

The Genocide Convention, adopted by the United Nations on December 9, 1948, requires the countries that signed it to intervene in cases of genocide. For this reason, the Clinton administration in 1994 carefully avoided using the word "genocide" in connection with the Rwanda slaughter, instead citing only "acts of genocide." This inaction was legally defensible, and the killings proceeded with the full kowledge of Western governments.

—JO'R, SO'R, & RS

farm. Like I said, at that time Zaire [now the Democratic Republic of the Congo] was becoming worse than Rwanda, so, really, I had nothing to lose. Of course, there was no work. I used to go out to the *"colline"*—that's what we call our homesteads. It means 'little hill' in English—there, on weekends, I would help them. Now, like the farm, they too are gone."

I didn't know if I should pursue this subject, but before I could say anything he'd begun again,

"After the war, the last one...or should I say, the *worst* one, I returned to my *colline*. No one knew what had happened in the countryside—we had no newspapers or radios, and no one wanted to believe the rumors. They were too bleak. People were saying that the countryside was abandoned...churches, schools, homes...all vacant...fruit rotting on the trees...cattle loose—well, when I arrived home, I found my mother, she was an old woman, almost eighty...they had chopped off her legs and left her to die, to bleed to death, in our family house. My father died with his heart broken. He, too, suffered terrible wounds, but they couldn't heal...his heart was too weak. That is what I came home to. Nothing! The others? I don't know. Some may still be alive in refugee camps across the border."

"Have you looked for them? Are you hopeful?"

He gripped the steering wheel hard with both hands.

"Mademoiselle, that is not a word I use."

We drove in stony silence for a while. Exploring the limits of acceptable conversation posed certain risks. I hoped I hadn't overstepped them. Within a few minutes he had regained his composure and was once again pointing out the sites of executions and massacres, like a tourist guide in another city might draw your attention to monuments or historical buildings.

As we rounded a corner, a mangy, overfed mongrel sauntered out from between two parked cars and crossed in front of us. Maneno, ever alert, anticipated my question:

"You are wondering about the dogs, no? Why they are so fat...have you noticed? They are everywhere. If we had the bullets, we would shoot them! Everyone asks about the dogs. You know, in Africa, dogs are usually skinny and timid. Are you sure you want to know the answer?"

"Why not?" I said, unsure of what he was getting at.

"Well, O.K. then. We call them Tutsi dogs…'*les tou-tous Tutsis.*' You speak French!"

He smiled at his private joke. I was still missing something here..

"Why Tutsi dogs?" I asked lamely.

"Because, *ma chere*," he paused theatrically, to make sure I got the point. "They ate our dead. It's true. Who could stop them? There were bodies everywhere."

I swallowed hard and must have let out a groan, for he quickly took my hand and patted it gently before continuing.

"Don't think badly of us. We are just trying to cope. They are still finding bodies. Right here, downtown. Now, there are not too many left, after two rainy seasons…but, as you can see"—he pointed to the sky—"the birds are still optimistic. In fact, they may be the only optimists left in this country!"

I looked up and caught the sight of hundreds of vultures circling overhead. It looked like the ghats of India.

Kigali had been the epicenter of the genocide. I imagined Chernobyl must have felt like this after the explosion—eerily quiet and lifeless. We passed a few pedestrians shuffling along like zombies, eyes vacant and fixed on the ground in front of them.

"What are you thinking?" Maneno broke in. I shared some of my thoughts, and he added, "At least in Chernobyl, you could blame it on a technical error, whereas here, it was the work of twisted, demented minds. What happened here, believe me, was premeditated and thorough—an 'ethnic cleansing,' to use a popular term. Compared to this, radiation seems benign. Don't you agree?"

We came to a sudden stop in front of the municipal hospital. It was much smaller than I had imagined, and deserted, like everything else. Two lone Tutsis, wearing bright yellow and purple socks outside their pants, stood guard at the door, rifles in hand. Maneno must have understood the surprise in my face. Looking genuinely amused, he said, "It is strange, no?…You see, the rebels…they had very little…very few supplies. Especially in the bush. For clothes, they took whatever they could find. For example the socks…some had no mates. When the peasants saw mismatched socks they were reassured. It became a symbol of the rebel army. Now, even here in the city, all the soldiers wear them."

With a broad sweep of his hand, he drew my attention to the gutters surrounding the building.

"Only two weeks ago, they dug up 6,000 bodies, right here in front of the hospital. Even here, while the brave doctors tended to the thousands of wounded—many without arms or legs—some even came with machetes still stuck in their heads, or their backs—of course, there were not enough doctors, even with the Hutu doctors helping, and many did, even here, even in the operating rooms, the murderers forced their way in to finish off the half-dead!"

"Are you saying there was no neutrality…no safe zones?"

With eyebrows slightly raised, he looked over at me, and responded in calm, even tones: "That's right…hospitals, churches, embassies…ha! My cousin Emmanuel, he worked at the French Embassy—for twelve years. He and all the others, they begged the ambassador to take them with him on the plane. You know what he did instead? He burned all the cables, the 'paper trail' I think you say…padlocked the embassy and left for the airport in a bullet-proof car with the French staff. There are many similar stories of betrayal. Too many!"

We were heading for the Église Sainte Famille, the largest church in downtown Kigali, which I had seen that morning from my hotel room. Without setting the brake, Maneno jumped out ahead of me and greeted the pastor, who was chatting with a group of young people out front. From the looks of their shabby clothes, I guessed they were street urchins, or, more likely, war orphans. He introduced me, and in the same breath, picked up where he had left off…

"Here, the brutal Father Winslaw *offered* his people to the killers."

The pastor, a man in his late fifties, nodded solemnly. He had the same sad, tired look I had seen on other faces that day…only his seemed to be a mixture of shame and grief.

"You see…the hospitals, the churches, they were like traps. Naturally, the people thought they would be safe here. This is a

Christian country...90 percent Catholic! But the fear and panic made Judases of many...even some of the good men—men of the cloth and the oath. Yes, many collaborated to escape death, and maybe receive some favors. After all, they are human, too. *Merde!* What am I saying? They are *not* human! If they were, I could forgive them.

"Two of my sisters, the youngest, came here, to this church. Father Winslaw—he was the devil—he took them to his private rooms and raped them. Then he handed them over to the Hutus, who raped them again...in front of the altar."

I noticed the children listening with expressionless faces. "I am so sorry! My poor Maneno. Where are they now, your sisters?"

"Dead from machete wounds. They bled to death in front of the church. The butchers said they were not good enough for bullets. My uncle saw them. He could do nothing, the poor man. No one could. The oldest would be sixteen years old now, if she had lived."

Genocide, after all, is an exercise in community building. A vigorous totalitarian order requires that the people be invested in the leaders' scheme, and while genocide may be the most perverse and ambitious means to this end, it is also the most comprehensive. In 1994, Rwanda was regarded...as the exemplary instance of the chaos and anarchy associated with collapsed states. In fact, the genocide was the product of order, authoritarianism, decades of political theorizing and indoctrination, and one of the most meticulously administered states in history. And strange as it may sound, the ideology — or what Rwandans call "the logic"—of genocide was promoted as a way not to create suffering but to alleviate it. The specter of an absolute menace that requires absolute eradication binds leader and people in a hermetic utopian embrace, and the individual—always an annoyance to totality—ceases to exist.

—Philip Gourevitch, *We Wish to Inform You that Tomorrow We Will Be Killed with Our Famlies*

"And Father Winslaw?"

"The *pig*!" Maneno nearly spit the word out. "Last week, my friends in the government brought me pictures from a French newspaper. There he was! Saying Mass in some village…living there, out in the open. *In France! A civilized country! A*nd still wearing his collar! He should be wearing a noose!"

The betrayal of the clergy struck me as even more egregious than what had happened at the hospital, or the embassy.

"Are you saying there was no safe haven anywhere? What about the women?…the pregnant women?…the little children?…the old people?"

"No. I'm telling you. The killers had no heart. Many were drinking and laughing while they did their 'work.' To them it made no difference who they killed or raped, as long as it was a Tutsi."

Before we left the little group, one of the children approached me, and with an innocence only a child is capable of, she asked, shyly, "Madam, do you know Michael Jackson?"

Her question caught me completely off guard.

"Well, I know who he *is.*"

"Well, when you see him, will you tell him to come to Rwanda and teach us dancing…the moon walk, no? He will come, no? He loves the children. That's what the American soldiers told us."

There was such irony in the child's request. Of course I couldn't tell her about the lawsuit he was embroiled in at the time. She wouldn't understand. Anyway, I'm sure he *does* love children in his own way. I said I'd do what I could, then shook her bony little hand—it felt so frail and delicate—and followed Maneno to the car. As we drove away, I looked back to wave, but they had already regrouped around the pastor. I wondered what he could be telling them. With so few adults to turn to, the surviving priests like this one had an impossible burden.

It was way past lunchtime and my stomach was beginning to growl. I asked Maneno to find us a café.

"Oh, that's easy! There is only one. Lebanese…they are always the first to return after the massacres. I'm not complaining. In a way, they provide the only continuity we have here."

We parked in front, alongside a dozen other four-wheel drive vehicles. This is the country of *mille collines*—a thousand hills—most of them unpaved. The little dirt roads that give off the main arteries are one of Kigali's few charms. Without the traction of four-wheel drive, circulation would be impossible.

The café's terrace was crowded, mostly with disheveled aid-workers and U.N. personnel. You could spot the latter by their neat, freshly pressed business suits. I eyed a few Africans here and there. Most were accompanied by whites. As we took a seat in the shade, three of Maneno's friends appeared, and eagerly accepted my invitation to join us. The two women worked in the newly formed Ministry of Justice. The third, a rather nervous-looking young man, whose glasses sat precariously close to the end of his nose, chose not to respond to my inquiries about his work. They struck me as an odd threesome. The waiter arrived shortly, and we ordered sandwiches.

The women were serious as judges, and very very beautiful. Long-limbed, with delicate, aquiline features, in another city they could have been fashion models. I guessed they were in their mid-thirties. Before the war they had been professors at the University of Butare, where they had earned their law degrees. Butare had been the center of Tutsi intellectual life. Sadly, these days the university was no longer functioning, having lost most of its students, and nearly all its faculty in the genocide.

I admired their poise and fought hard to overcome my initial intimidation. Looking in their general direction, I asked, "What is happening with the legal system? I know it must be difficult. You must be working from scratch."

Rachel, the taller of the two women, responded coolly, "It will take a long time to reconstitute it. And we are under tremendous pressure. Right now, among other things, we are working on a new constitution. We want to model many things after yours. Rwanda will have a true democracy, you will see!"

Her confidence impressed me. Her friend, Monique, was less sanguine.

"First we must solve our biggest problem—accountability. There are thousands of Hutus in prisons all over the country. The conditions, as you must know—all the major international news-papers seem obsessed with it—are terrible. But what can we do? We have no courts, no lawyers. Tell me, how can we bring them to trial? Believe me, it is not to our advantage to keep them there! The longer they stay, in the prisons that is, the more sympathy the world showers on them. That is not where the attention should be! They do not deserve sympathy. People forget that they are murderers. That is the plain and simple truth! They deserve punishment. Fair punishment, yes. But who is to decide what is fair?"

It seemed a strange word to use in these circumstances. I admired her for maintaining a certain objectivity. Among many Tutsis, par-ticularly the less educated, Old Testament attitudes seemed to prevail.

What she said next surprised me.

"You know, not all Hutus are equally guilty. In the countryside, the people are poor and ignorant. They are like children. Under colonialism, we could not grow up. And so, when the authorities told them to kill, they killed...their wives, their neighbors...even their own children. For many, it was kill or be killed. I don't say that to exonerate them. They are deformed...from the propaganda, the schools, the government. This should not be overlooked."

That was a brave and compassionate statement coming from someone who, I was to learn later, had seen her entire family slaughtered, while she hid in the roof of her family's home.

The sandwiches arrived, and the conversation drifted. The young man with the odd spectacles seemed anxious to talk to Maneno about the troubles in the refugee camps in Eastern Zaire. It seemed that several Hutus had been killed in recent clashes with Tutsis.

Maneno cut him off curtly. "This is not the time to spread rumors of retaliation! Wait until the facts are verified. Then we will talk."

Duly chastised, the young man pushed his chair back from the table and lowered his eyes.

Now seemed like an appropriate time to get the answer to a question that had plagued me for weeks. I knew I'd have to ease my way into it, even with this group of highly educated people. The subject of race, especially in these fractious countries caught up in the throes of civil wars, was never an easy topic. Like the skilled diplomat that I'm not, I began, tentatively.

"Race is a taboo word here, isn't it? What I mean is tribal identity, that sort of thing."

Maneno took the bait. "Well, how do you Americans say… it is 'politically incorrect'… yes…but go ahead. It is too obvious to play games with."

I had something specific in mind. I looked at the others for any signs of discomfort. They looked back at me, poker-faced, so I continued.

"O.K. Look around here, Maneno. Can you tell who is Hutu and who is Tutsi?"

I indicated a table with four or five Africans close by. He smiled patiently, suppressing a giggle. The others tried to look disinterested, but I could feel their distress. They weren't at all sure how he would respond. He was known to shoot from the hip.

"Well, can you?" I persisted.

A look of mock helplessness came over his face, and he shrugged his shoulders playfully. "The truth is, Lord!, I do not know. Really! I would

> The healing of evil—scientifically or otherwise—can be accomplished only by the love of individuals…. As C.S. Lewis wrote: "When a willing victim who had committed no treachery was killed in a traitor's stead, the Table would crack and Death itself would start working backwards."
>
> I do not know how this occurs. But I know that it does. I know that good people can deliberately allow themselves to be pierced by the evil of others—to be broken thereby yet somehow not broken—to even be killed in some sense and yet still survive and not succumb. Whenever this happens there is a slight shift in the balance of power in the world.
>
> —M. Scott Peck, M.D., *People of the Lie: The Hope for Healing Human Evil*

have to talk with them. Even then, I may guess wrong. At any rate, there is no way to tell by looks alone. Take *me,* for example!"

The others looked down at their hands, or their feet—anywhere but at me.

What *weren't* they saying? I certainly didn't believe in racial stereotypes. At least, not in *this* population. They had lived together so closely, for hundreds of years. But there must be *cultural* distinctions? What did it *mean* to be a Hutu, or a Tutsi?

Casting his eyes around the table, Maneno readied himself for the explanation he was about to deliver. He pulled at an imaginary beard, then began, "In Rwanda, we take our tribal identification from our mothers. Many marriages, as you know, are mixed. What's more, we don't even have family names in this country. Every child is given her own name."

"First *and* last?" I asked.

"Yes. And another thing, everyone's native tongue is Banyarwanda. I admit, it can be very confusing. We are one culture here. I know, it is hard for foreigners to understand all this. The world insists that Tutsis and Hutus are two distinct tribes. As you can see, that is patently untrue! Just look at me! I am the living proof."

He was obviously alluding to his own mixed heritage.

"And it gets even more complicated. Listen to this! Until the 1960s, we did not make such a distinction. The Belgians changed all that. They made us carry cards denoting our tribal identity. We became the pawns in a political power game—divide and conquer! The Belgians backed the Hutus; Tutsis with money bought Hutu identity cards. It was all very simple. Everything's for sale at the right price. Even one's identity! So Tutsis became Hutus. We are all dogs, aren't we! But better a living dog, than a dead one!"

My head was spinning. Everything was illusion. Maneno seemed bemused by my reaction. Obviously, he'd encountered it before.

From the doorway, a big booming voice caused everybody in the restaurant to turn and stare.

"Neno, Neno, my old friend!"

He strode across the café like a Goliath.

"How are you, my friend? Can I join you? Ah, I see you are with the lady from the hotel. How are you, madam? Hello, my friends—oo-la-la! the beautiful jurists. Has the court adjourned? Lucky me!"

All I saw was a bright, shiny-red sport coat hanging from a

seven-foot frame, and a full, gleaming set of the whitest, most perfect teeth I had ever seen this side of a toothpaste ad. A yellow-flowered tie swung from side to side like the pendulum on a grandfather's clock, providing rhythmic accompaniment as he strode toward our table.

Once he'd taken a seat, I recognized him from the bar that first night. On that occasion, he'd worn an iridescent purple silk shirt over starched white duck pants. In a place as conservative as Rwanda, he stuck out like a Harlem pimp!

"May I ask what you are discussing? I know it must be interesting. Ah…my Neno! He knows everything, eh? We used to debate in high school. He always won! We called him the hyena—he was so tricky!"

In addition to his appointment as chef de protocol in the new government, Gideon was the president's speechwriter and general front man. Born to the role, and bigger than life, his nickname was, appropriately enough, "The Bible." People loved to quote him, and then, to underscore the veracity of what he'd said they would add "but it's from 'The Bible!'"…as if that made it true. After just a few minutes in his company, I was convinced he could sell Hutu souvenirs to the Tutsis!

At this point in history, Rwanda needed a good PR man. I remembered a story he had told me in the bar. How he had accompanied a team of Tutsi basketball players to the States—to Detroit, to be exact. Nobody cared about the game, he said. They all just wanted to stand next to a Tutsi and have their picture taken. He himself was nearly seven feet tall!

"Americans love anything big." He slapped himself on the chest, in case we'd missed the point. "I love Americans!"

There was more to Gideon than simple affability. Behind the big personality, I sensed an even bigger heart. Unlike some of the government ideologues I'd met, he had no particular turf to defend…no party line. On the contrary, his entire essence seemed fed by spontaneity and soul—rare commodities in these parts. To be fair, he was probably coping like everyone else, but he was doing it with just a little more style.

He was eager to talk, and I was anxious to hear his views on a subject which, in some ways, was even more sensitive than race. For years, Central Africa had been experiencing a raging epidemic of AIDS. Now, after all the bloodletting and rape, I figured the virus must be completely out of control. The silence surrounding the subject had only heightened my curiosity. I was struggling with an opener, when Gideon suddenly announced, "I have just come from a conference on AIDS, at the president's office."

In addition to everything else, he was telepathic! I relaxed and sat back in my chair, prepared to listen.

"We are facing the worst crisis now," he began.

"You mean, since the war?" I ventured.

"Exactly."

He adjusted the flowering pendulum of his tie, fluffing it out in front of him, then tucking it into his belt. He paused, took a sip of his coffee, then continued. "There were so many pregnant women, as a result of all the rapes. Just today I learned that every second baby born now, is seropositive. No one knows what to do. And think of the poor women! Many of them were still girls…children! They were the most vulnerable. I have two young daughters. Happily they were with their mother in Uganda. I don't know what I would have done!…But these women, think of it…they have been twice-cursed! First the rapes, then this dreadful disease. It is especially terrible to see a child die from slims."

"Slims" was the name they gave to AIDS in this part of the world, long before the virus had been officially identified.

"And that is only a part of the problem." Maneno slammed both hands down on the table, like a judge about to deliver a verdict. The glasses jumped. "Remember, the war, for the most part, was fought *by hand,* with machetes. There were no Scud missiles, none of those smart bombs like you Americans used in Iraq. Here it was labor intensive. *Think how many machete blows it takes to kill one million people!*"

I shifted in my chair, pretending to look for something in my purse, all the while imagining the butchery, hundreds of thousands of machetes hacking through bone and gristle—a killing frenzy.

When I tuned back in, Maneno was still talking—something about the machete and the spread of AIDS. What he said shocked me into a new awareness.

"Many people received blows from the same bloody machete. *The machete became a vector!* A thousand times more lethal than a gun. Think of it! "

I didn't need to. It was too graphic.

Gideon's head was jerking up and down excitedly, like an over-full bucket yanked up too quickly from the bottom of a well. This was obviously a subject of critical interest to him.

"Maneno is right. You know, he was studying to be a medical doctor. He understands these things better than most of us. Here, the doctors are afraid of the wounded. Many, especially the foreign ones, won't touch them. In a way, you cannot blame them. We do not have…how do you say?…the proper prophylactics—the gloves and the masks."

I thought this might be a good time to lighten things up. Monique must have read my thoughts. She fixed me with her big, round eyes and, in a quiet voice stripped of emotion, said, "Mademoiselle, for us, there is nothing else to talk about. We must somehow come to terms with our memories. Like children, they need to be let outside from time to time."

Rachel continued in the same solemn tone. "For us it is not a choice. We *must* tell our stories, until people are sick and tired of hearing them. And even then, we must keep telling them. What do you think, Gideon?"

"*It is the only way we will heal—that's what I think!* We have all been poisoned. The ones who don't talk become even sicker. With the little children…many cannot speak…the fear has frozen their tongues. We make them draw pictures. It is amazing the things they draw! They have seen everything, even more than us adults."

I remembered Isabelle, from Belgium, a mixed-parentage Tutsi, gathering ravaged orphans who were roaming the countryside like starving wolves, wild children, traumatized beyond song, no longer even able to dream.

At this point two young men dressed in the unmistakable camouflage of the Freedom Fighters pulled up chairs and arranged their long legs under the table. They seemed to know everyone there. Neat and clean-shaven, they represented the elite corps of the rebels, hand-picked by Kagame. Everyone knew Kagame ran a tight ship. As a young man in exile in Uganda, the defense minister had learned the art of guerrilla warfare from President Museveni himself, one of Africa's most revered and courageous leaders. Their arrival provided an excuse to steer the conversation in a new direction. I took advantage of it.

"Do you mind if I ask you about yourselves?" I addressed the question to no one in particular. "Tell me your stories. Who were your angels? Surely you had some, or you wouldn't be here!"

Maneno took a bite of his sandwich, which had turned crusty in the heat, and began chewing thoughtfully, like he'd just discovered a new and interesting flavor. "I will tell you, if you promise to stop me when you've had enough."

He gave Gideon a jab in the ribs. "You go first!"

Gideon begged off. "Neno, *you* have the most incredible story. Have you told her about the hotel?"

"Not yet."

"You mean the Mille Collines?" I asked.

"Yes," Maneno replied. "But what I went through is nothing, compared to Monique! She hid in the roof of her parents' house, for ten days, with nothing to eat or drink. She had to listen to the thugs below, planning the next attacks."

Monique needed very little encouragement. "In Butare, the situation was very tense. People were disappearing...friends, professors. I was targeted, like everyone else on the faculty. Many of my colleagues' families had been harassed. I worried constantly for the safety of my family. Since they lived very close to the university, I made a point to come home every day for lunch.

"We were all at the table together, finishing up our meal, when they came to the door. My older brother, sensing danger, grabbed me and pushed me out the back door and up a ladder that led to the roof. There was so little time. He shoved a liter of water at me and pulled the ladder away, leaving me up there alone in the dark with the rats and spiders. It all happened so fast…the thuds and shouts. I heard my father moaning. They were hitting him with something hard. He was gasping for air. And then I heard my mother…she was whimpering. I heard her say 'Don't touch my children,' then more thuds and loud laughing. They were drunk. I recognized the voice of our neighbor. He was yelling at my brother, telling him to drag the bodies outside. All this time my little sister was screaming. It was a scream of terror, not pain. I'm sure along with everything else, she was being raped.

"Then it was quiet for a long time. A door slammed and I could hear their drunken voices again. There were more this time, eight or ten at least. They were falling down, knocking things over, roaring drunk, every one of them. I heard dishes crashing, furniture breaking. I don't know how long this went on. It was so hot in the roof, and I was so afraid they would discover me. In the dark like that, you have no way of telling the passage of time. I slept a little…but mostly I listened. I was prepared to die. Time passed. Occasionally I would hear their voices…then it grew quiet…for a long time.

"Finally, I could take it no longer, I was so thirsty and my bones were stiff and cramped from not moving. I looked for the hole and let myself fall to the ground below. It was a long drop. All my bones ached. I remember lying there all curled up. The rest all seems like a dream. Somehow I managed to crawl out to the road. The city was empty and silent— like the end of the world. I lay by the side of the road, thinking that now, finally, I would die. After that, I don't remember much. When

> In much of the world, infant mortality remains extremely high. International agencies keep a sort of top twenty of such figures as a general measure of relative "deprivation." An African tax form I once filled in asked matter-of-factly:
> 1. Do you have any children?
> 2. Are any of them still alive?
> —Nigel Barley, *Grave Matters: A Lively History of Death Around the World*

I woke up I was in a jeep on a rough road. It was dark, and some-one kept telling me it would be all right, I should sleep, that every-thing would be all right. He was giving me water from his canteen and cradling me like a baby."

One of the Freedom Fighters suddenly spoke up. "She was skin and bones, and weak, like a baby goat. We took her with us to head-quarters in Kigali."

"This beautiful man saved my life." Monique gestured toward the taller of the two rebels.

"We had passed so many of the dead on the road, but this one," he pointed at Monique, "I could see she was still breathing."

He and Monique smiled shyly at each other.

"She lost all of her family, but now we will make her one of our own."

I was moved nearly to tears by this unexpected revelation.

All this time Rachel had been listening intently. Her eyes had a haunted look, like they were holding back a story too unbearable to be told. Maneno urged her to speak. "Rachel, you, too, were in Butare. Tell us what happened to you."

She glanced vacantly around the table like she was searching for a way to begin. Then, lifting her chin, she directed her gaze at me.

"My story is not special, at least, not for Rwanda." The others shook their heads, making it clear they didn't agree.

"Rachel is very understated, in case you haven't noticed," said Gideon. "She teaches the theory of law, not, like some others in her profession, the calisthenics of the courtroom."

"When I say my story is not special," she continued. "I simply mean that many others survived much worse."

A silence closed in around her. She seemed to disappear into a hidden, interior space. She picked up a stray napkin on the table and began to fold it methodically. "I was with my lover at the university, in his room. They broke down the door and pulled off the blankets. Two of the men raped me. Then one man raised a machete and brought it down on my lover's head, severing it with one blow. They placed it on my chest at eye level. The whole time they were holding me down. Some students in the building next door must have heard my screams and fought their way into our room. The killers hacked them to pieces in front of me. Their bodies fell on me....they were so heavy. I could hardly breathe. I lay there for a long time—hours, maybe days—I don't know. Like Monique, eventually the rebels found me, and here I am."

Her eyes fixed on something outside of our circle. No one spoke. Nothing in my life had prepared me for this. I would never look at these two young women in the same way again. One of the soldiers was drumming the table with his fingers. Finally, Gideon broke the silence.

"Maneno, tell the story of the Mille Collines." I wasn't sure if I could handle any more. Then again, maybe Maneno's story would shed some light on the strange goings-on in my hotel room.

"I am reluctant to begin. Compared to my sisters here, my plight was not so difficult."

Even though they'd heard it before, the others leaned forward in their chairs. A real storyteller like Maneno always had a new twist—a fresh detail, an overlooked moral. Africans never tired of a good story. He wiped his lips with a napkin, and cleared his throat.

"It all began with the plane crash. I was here, in the capital, working on some old cars down at the garage, and heard about it on my friend's radio. It was like a nightmare—the worst kind you can imagine. The plane crashed, and within minutes the city became a killing field...years and years of pent-up hate broke loose, igniting like a grass fire. I expected the worst.

Like everyone else, I began to run. I ran for my life. I knew exactly what was going to happen. It was like being caught in a stampede...if you stood still, you were dead. You can't imagine—it was complete chaos... people screaming and shouting...running in every direction. But it was no use. The killers were everywhere. And they were ruthless."

Gideon broke in. "The worst part is, you recognized them! They were your children's teachers, the merchants who sold you rice, the taxi men. Believe me, not all the killers were soldiers."

"Yes," Maneno picked up. "Wherever we ran, they were there, waiting for us!"

This much I knew: the presidents of Burundi and Rwanda were returning from a summit in Arusha, where a first attempt at power-sharing between Tutsis and Hutus had just been brokered. Despite the protests of the extremists, the president had made certain concessions, to move the process forward. For the first time in years, there was hope in the air. And then came the plane crash—some say the French, who backed the extremists, brought it down. Others claim it was the Hutu presidential guards. We may never know the truth.

"I don't care what they say. It was a genocide. Every move was orchestrated and deliberate. *They had machetes and guns. Thousands of them.* Where did they get them? They threw up roadblocks. The commandos took charge. *They knew just what to do, like they'd been rehearsing it.*"

Up until now, the Freedom Fighters had been attentive, but quiet. Now they were leaning their heads forward, and seemed to be hanging on every word. Maneno had taken on the role of village elder, and in Africa, that was all you needed to get respect.

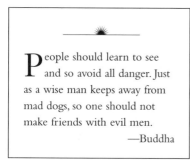

People should learn to see and so avoid all danger. Just as a wise man keeps away from mad dogs, so one should not make friends with evil men.
—Buddha

"But weren't the Tutsis expecting reprisals? Weren't at least *some* of you armed?"

Maneno's voice took on an unfamiliar urgency. He sat forward in his chair, eyes alert. "We knew the situation was getting worse. The hate campaigns had intensified, especially in the last few months. The Hutus had saturated the countryside with cheap transistor radios. The peasants, with a hoe in one hand and a radio in the other, were dupes of a finely calculated propaganda. Day and night the radio vomited out slogans—'Kill the Tutsi snakes and cockroaches'…'The graves are only half-full, go to work,' and so on. But, at the same time, our rebel army was making progress in the Northwest."

Here, the young men straightened their backs. Their corps had been heroes in the Northwest.

"The Arusha meetings were producing results. Maybe, when I look back on it…yes,…*maybe* we were naïve. No one spoke openly of genocide, but there was a feeling in the air, a heaviness, like just before the rainy season begins. And then the plane crash…there was no way of predicting such a thing. It caught us completely by surprise."

Maneno hailed the waiter and ordered a round of Cokes. He excused himself, and joined a friend standing by the entrance who had been waving him over, unsuccessfully, for several minutes. Soon after he returned with a package under his arm which, from where I was sitting looked like hospital supplies.

Impatient to get back to the story, I prompted him. "So you ran…tell me, Maneno, what was it like? Where did you go?"

"Where was I?…oh yes…I was running for my life. In those situations you don't have time to think. Automatically, I headed for the Hotel Mille Collines. I could find it with my eyes closed, through the bushes, like a rabbit. The roadblocks were active now, and people were being attacked by machetes as they ran. The militia were firing automatics, randomly, in every direction. I kept my head low and just kept running. You see, I had worked at the hotel as a busboy for five years, when I was a schoolboy. I knew it would be full of white people. We all believed—at least, we wanted to— that the killers would not hurt whites."

To Maneno's surprise, the only white people left at the hotel were the manager, a brave and dedicated Belgian, and his assistant. The others, international guests and nonnative hotel personnel, were already en route to the airport for the last emergency flights out.

Meanwhile, a frantic crowd of Africans, growing larger by the minute, had gathered at the doors to the hotel, which, at that time, were heavily guarded by U.N. officers. One by one, the officers, mostly Europeans, were screening people, allowing only the elite to enter—high government officials, professionals, intellectuals, the inner circle of the wealthy. Almost everyone who had managed to get to the hotel, had had access to a high-frequency radio, which gave them a good hour's jump on the rest of the population.

"You obviously weren't a member of the elite. How did you make it past the screening?" I inquired.

"They knew me there. The manager, he remembered me. He's a good man, very brave. Braver than many Tutsis. He sent me to the kitchen. I was happy to go to work. It was better to stay busy, to have something to do."

So this was how it came to pass that this quiet little oasis, this "Central African Paradise," this ever-so-ordinary little hotel in the heart of downtown Kigali, where "Springtime is Eternal," became, by a quirk of fate, the only safe-haven in all of Rwanda.

I remembered at one time reading about the Hotel Dorchester in London during the Blitz. They called it "the gilded refuge." Reporters filed stories from its lobby, while the rich drank the hotel's wine cellars dry. Despite its location in the heart of London, not one bomb fell on it. Similarly, the Hotel Mille Collines seemed impermeable to the enemy, as if a steel curtain hung around it. Unlike the Dorchester, however, there were no stories being filed, no wine being drunk. It was hard to believe that just outside its doors, millions of Tutsis, and a small number of Hutu moderates, from one end of Rwanda to the other, were systematically being hunted down and slaughtered like animals.

"Tell me more about this manager. Like Schindler, or Wollenberg, he must have been a saint! What could he do under such circumstances?"

Many people had likened Rwanda to the Holocaust. It had been the third largest genocide of the century. There were, in fact, many similarities.

Maneno looked thoughtful.

"Less than an hour after the butchery had begun, the hotel was already at full capacity. But the people kept coming. Fewer, it is true, as now the roadblocks were functioning efficiently. We could hear the gunshots and screams in the neighboring streets. It made you want to cry, thinking of all that death, so close. About then, the pleading and bargaining began in earnest.

"Just one more, please. She's my sister. She will sleep with me in my bed" or "In the name of God, I beg you, my mother is old

and weak. She cannot return to her home. It has been ransacked."
"This man, he is my brother. He can sleep with me and my wife"...and so on. The manager, he was under tremendous stress, as you can imagine, but he stayed calm. He doubled the room occupancy, then tripled it. After that, no one kept count. He knew better than any of us the fate that awaited those he turned away."

Maneno told us how he recalled seeing thirty to forty people crowded into those small, underfurnished rooms.

"For my part, I was busy tending to practical things. For example, when the water ran out, and that happened the very first night, I found some buckets in the basement. Me and several others, we formed a brigade and began scooping up water from the swimming pool, for cooking and drinking. Food was strictly rationed. Soon there was only rice and canned goods...not much, but we Africans know how to stretch food. The Hutu militia guarded the hotel doors now. They had automatic rifles. Yes, the U.N. troops were there too, but they could do nothing. At least, in the beginning, their presence kept the militia from storming the hotel."

It is now well documented that the U.N. forces were powerless to act during the worst of the conflict. In the case of the Mille Collines, the militia quickly usurped the U.N. troops' position, relegating them to the shadows, where they could only look on helplessly.

Maneno continued, "It is not all their fault. In some ways their hands were tied. Their mandate was to keep the peace, but, under no circumstances, enforce it. All those guns, an internationally sanctioned force, and they could do nothing!"

I began to understand why the Tutsis had such contempt for them. Maneno picked up his narrative,

"Days and weeks of terror followed. Every evening at sunset the militia presented a 'most wanted' list to the hotel's manager, the brave Belgian who had chosen to remain behind, alone among ex-patriots, despite his family's pleas to return to Belgium.

For the first few days, thanks to private generators, he was able to communicate to the outside world using the hotel's fax. With the world as witness, the militia held back. Soon, however, even *that* was cut off. He then appealed to human decency, international laws, whatever he could pull out of his hat to keep the militia at bay.

But he was no match for them. They took things into their own hands, the thugs! Forcing their way into the hotel and fingering the most visible 'enemies.' It was inhuman, how they dragged their victims out at gunpoint, some in their underwear—they had no time to dress—and executed them before the horrified eyes of their family members and friends. You can imagine the terror this instilled in those still inside. We gathered together to pray, to vigil, to comfort each other. Two Catholic priests took turns saying Mass—a perpetual Mass. I can still hear the drone of the Latin in my ears. It was a comfort."

He was coming to the end of his story. I didn't want it to end. None of us did. I was involved in this drama in a way I had never been before.

"By now, the hotel was a holding tank. We were all going to die. It was just a matter of time. No longer did we feel so lucky. Every day our numbers shrank. No one knew who would be next. There was such fear everywhere. And yet, it was as quiet as a church. Even the cries of the surviving babies had frozen in their tiny throats."

Until now, I hadn't even thought about the babies. "How did you cope? The days must have seemed endless!"

"We Tutsis, everyone says we are stoics. Maybe. But we have experience with this kind of thing. Maybe we feel God has forgotten us. Anyway, we took care of each other."

The killings continued over the next four months, and as time went by a hopeless resignation settled over the hotel. The swimming pool was dry. Food supplies were nearly spent. Then, miraculously, the RPF took the city in a series of prolonged gun and mortar battles. Following the victory, 1,500 lucky survivors were escorted to safety by U.N. Peace Keepers. Maneno was among them.

By now the café was nearly empty. The busboys were sweeping up as we headed for the door. At Maneno's insistence, we made a few stops on the way home for drinking water and candles. Though no one spoke of it, the city was still vulnerable. In the refugee camps near the borders, only a few hours' drive from the capital, the Hutus were rearming, and the possibility of a surprise attack kept everybody on edge.

I arrived back at the hotel exhausted, like I'd been gone for days. I fumbled for my key at the door. Everything looked strange and different, as if I were entering the room for the first time. I stood in the semidarkness and took it all in...the stained carpet, the sad, little threadbare towels, the lumpy beds, the soiled curtains and bedspread, the fingerprints on the walls. I singled out each object and studied it, as if each one held the key to a great mystery. One by one they sprang to life, offering themselves up as silent witnesses to a human tragedy played out behind closed doors—one of millions duplicated in countless homes and villages throughout this desperate country.

I imagined the families huddled together around pots of rice on the floor, anxious mothers, cradling their listless babies, old people, eyes vacant, propped against the walls waiting for death, I saw the outlines of frail, frightened bodies clinging to one another under blankets stretched thin across crowded beds. The room took on the sanctity of a chapel, and suddenly there, in that absolute stillness, I came face to face with The Others. I wanted to take them, one by one, into my arms and let them know that I, too, would bear witness, and though it was too late for them, I would tell their story over and over again, for the rest of my life, to all who would listen.

I stepped out onto the balcony. The swimming pool had turned a dark, inky blue in the evening light. It looked so tranquil, like a reflecting pond. I thought of its unlikely role in this drama; of the many lives it had sustained. There was the great tree—I thought of all the misery it had witnessed. Even the shrubbery seemed to speak, reciting the names, like a litany, of those it had sheltered and protected, even if only for a few hours.

Standing there, in the quiet of the African dusk, with the vultures still circling overhead, and a few fat dogs growling somewhere out of sight, the memory of this unspeakable brutality, this unimaginable violence, this wholesale destruction of thousands upon thousands of innocent lives hung heavily in the air. I breathed it all in, deeper and deeper, until, bent over from its weight, I was clutching the railing and sobbing uncontrollably.

That night Maneno joined me for dinner. As we took our seats at the edge of the hotel's rooftop terrace, I noticed for the first time bonfires in the distance, their light reflecting off the walls of the central courtyard of the prison, a half mile away. It was easy enough to see—there were so few lights here at night. I'd been told that there were over 16,000 Hutu murderers being held there, awaiting trials that would, most likely, never take place.

I'd read somewhere that in the old days, that is to say, before the massacres and the pogroms, Rwandans relied on *Gachacha*, or bush justice, to maintain order. The guilty might be assigned a communal chore, like weeding the fields, or repairing fences. In the case of a more serious offense, he might be banished to another *colline*, until he had repented, or his people invited him back.

In these times, because of the scale of the atrocities, and the sheer number of murderers—one million? two million?—international tribunals had replaced the traditional *Gachacha* and were now deliberating on the fate of the perpetrators. Like at Nuremberg, justice here will deliver too little, and come too late.

Eyes full of mischief, Maneno raised his glass in the direction of the prison, and with a slight nod of his head, said, "Bon appetit." Glancing in my direction, he added impishly, "And you say we're not civilized?"

A laugh escaped me, signaling, at least to me, my initiation into the subterranean territory of black humor, which I'd always considered the last stop before despair.

The waiter appeared, ready to take our order. As I inquired about the fish on the menu, Maneno interrupted, and without a trace of emotion in his voice, cautioned, "Please, anything but the fish. They come from the lake. They have been eating human flesh for the last year. The dogs, the crows, the fish, they are all fattened on human flesh."

The waiter stood there, nonplussed. Then, with the first trace of cynicism I had yet detected (or was it simply more of the survivors' black humor?), he added, "We must honor the dead wherever they appear. Besides, who knows, it could give you heartburn!"

He and Maneno both chuckled conspiratorially.

Meanwhile, I had reconsidered. "I'll have the pasta primavera."

Pasta primavera? Was that actually on the menu, or did I make it up?

I drank a toast to Kigali's "Eternal Spring" and winked at Maneno, who was winking at me from across the table.

Dorothy Leroux is a happy survivor of twenty-five years of Third World bush travel, where she works with local people to help them implement their very own (and often surprisingly effective) solutions to endemic poverty. She attributes her longevity in the field to "intestinal fortitude," the miracle of antibiotics, and, most importantly, a persistent, grail-like quest for the source of the inexplicable humor and simple joy that distinguishes these populations from our own.

$*\ ^*\ *$

Blademaster

*Tell yourself, "Today I will
bleed a little."*

UNDER THE DARKENED BOWER OF MY INTEREST IN ALL THAT crawls, limps, or runs in screaming terror, I had found myself in the stunningly mild presence of the man who had elected to teach me the ten best ways that he knew of to kill someone with a knife.

Johnnie—he insisted on being called by the all-American variant of his given name—was a fellow traveler with a singular interest in sunny places for shady people, and we had met because the ragtag community of his very respectful peers and shadowy street boulevardiers had wanted to introduce him to the American fighter (I've manifested a more than abiding interest in martial arts), and more importantly, American writer. He was a star in their world, and from fighting in Thailand, to training the Sri Lankan national police how to best extract confessions in their struggles against the Tamil Tigers, to mainland China mayhem, and eventually to London's Indian community, the man had made his way teaching people what he was offering to teach me—call it blood politics. And though the entrance fee to any secret society is, of course, secrecy, talking to a writer from California held as much reality for them as the $1,500 suits advertised in the pages of GQ magazine. What did I want to know?

Whatever. Knives placed in the throat from the front, from the side, through the foreman magnum, under the ribs at the shirt's third button from the top, into the kidneys, and into where most people didn't have the "inside strongness" to get to, the eyes. At 5' 9" and weighing in at about 150 pounds, Johnnie was what heavyweights like me would describe as a "slip of a man," and in a cinderblock garage in the southwest of London where my tutorial took place, his sleeves slipped down his raised arms, revealing a cicatrix of angry lines crisscrossing both forearms. He caught me looking and smiled.

"When you use a knife on a man who also has a knife, the first thing you must tell yourself is that 'Today I will bleed a little.' It will relax you and allow you to focus."

Focus.

"But I am not teaching you fighting tricks. I'm showing you how to use a knife, you see?"

Facing me, he holds up his right arm to show me where he's cupped the black-handled, five-inch blade. Used to the more pedestrian martial arts classes, I had been ready for a rubber blade, and said so.

"Those are for play," he shakes his head vigorously, "we can play later." I want to question the advisability of using real steel, but I'm wary of seeming like what I am: a tourist in his world. I had learned about him from some semi-spook friends of mine and had been informally tracking him, hoping that time and circumstance would conspire to have us in the same place at the same time. He had been in Southeast Asia, while I was trying to get to Southeast Asia. He was in the Balkans when I was in eastern Italy across the Adriatic. I was in Amsterdam when he was in Berlin. A history of near misses, or near hits, but I had been lucky enough to be in London for some other business and making a round of phone calls found out that we'd finally get to meet before he headed off to Chile, and I headed back to California. So I didn't want to blow it even if it seemed that would mean an edge weapon wound of some sort.

"Okay," I say.

He holds the blade in his hand like he's fingering a violin bow.

The butt of the knife is against his forearm and the sleeve of his shirt on his now straight arm makes it almost invisible to my eye. He begins walking toward me and just as quickly he's standing behind me now, walking casually away and my shirt is cut and my chest is stinging from a small cut.

He smiles and says, "I show you again." And this time, moving more slowly he steps toward me and in one move when his body is parallel to mine, he bends his arm up at the elbow, slides the butt into his hand, and the no-reflect blade (he derides "shiny steel" as only good for robbers who want the knife to be seen) is sticking into my sternum where he jerks it sharply to his right, my left, before swinging his arm in a graceful arc, back in pace with his walk, the knife, once again, invisible. Looking at my chest I notice I have two semi-circular scratch wounds, little red half-moons that do a little more than sting now.

"See? No fighting is involved." And he's right, and it dawns on me that I must make an adjustment. I will not be learning defensive maneuvers. What I will be learning are offensive maneuvers of the most crucial kind. "You don't want to stand and fight. You just want him to die."

He smiles at me genially, and I find myself wondering about this altogether pleasant man's whys and wherefores. Though his personal take on his start might be semiapocryphal—after having been beaten and thrown out by an abusive father, he fought in the alleys of Thailand for fun, profit, room and board, whatever—these scars are very real. As real as he is when he explodes, this time from a standstill, into a flash of knife blade and just as quickly returns to his almost lazy, slightly bent knee stance. I wonder aloud if Western technology, impersonal and less messy feeling, might be better. I mean you might just be better off with a gun.

"Me? No. Because of tendon problems," he rubs his forearms, "I can't handle a large-caliber gun. But you are American, and it seems guns are like Americans. Loud. And easy to use. You turn on a light switch, you start a car, you pull a trigger. It's like they say: 'Guns kill people, people don't kill people.'" It's the other way around, and I correct him. "Yes, but knives are quiet, and sometimes not very expensive. Let me tell you a story," and standing under the gently humming florescent bulbs I hear what I had been smirkingly assured by his handlers I would want to hear: stories of unusual heroism. Emphasis on unusual.

"When I was in China, in Shanghai, I had been in a restaurant. After I get on my bike and start to ride out of the alley, I run into a young couple. The man was about twenty-six and so was his woman and they were on their way to a party and had two bottles of wine that fell to the ground. I say that I am sorry. The woman starts to complain about who will pay for the broken bottles. I have no money so I say I am sorry again and she tells her man, 'Kick his ass.' I say something like that I'm sorry again but only because my Mandarin is not so good and I don't know how to say more. So he starts

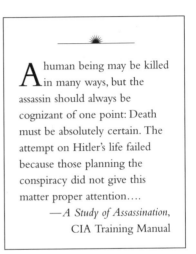

A human being may be killed in many ways, but the assassin should always be cognizant of one point: Death must be absolutely certain. The attempt on Hitler's life failed because those planning the conspiracy did not give this matter proper attention....
— *A Study of Assassination,* CIA Training Manual

shoving me," and Johnnie starts mimicking the wild flail of a non-fighter. "I had knives. Two. And I put them here and here," he points to spots on either side of my neck, "and he fell down and his woman kept screaming and I waited and then I ran and that was the first man I had killed. I think. I say I think because I did not stay. He was not moving when I ran." He is not sobered by the story as I am. He seems distracted by the randomness of it and displeased with his lack of closure. And there seems to be, I hesitate to use the word since it seems at once not enough and then again too much to describe him, a distinct amorality about his concerns. In fact he and his handlers all seem to be not only amoral but apolitical about what they do. I'm not saying that they were without passions, but there was not a pie-eyed fanatic in the bunch. They could have been CPAs. CPAs with knives, but CPAs nonetheless.

"In Sri Lanka, though, I had a job for the police. There was a big, what, party?"

"Festival?" I offer.

"Yes. I walk behind the job and," his bladed hand moves like a piston, out and back again, "put the knife here on the back of his neck and drop it and keep walking. He falls down on his bottom…"

"In a sitting position?"

"Almost. But plenty of people had been falling because they were drinking and so they did not notice at first. But that was the first time I knew. I knew because they paid me, and they don't pay for bad jobs. I then began to train the police and left only after the rebels had taken a job out on me and the police would not help my safety."

And he recites a brief litany of his police interrogation tactics: glass rods into urethras (in the rare instance when the interrogation went beyond this, the inserted rods were broken with the authoritative snap of a stick); abrasion and the creative use of sandpaper; joint manipulation; and, what he deceptively calls, "water play."

"Water play?"

"Suffocations," he quietly explains.

We continue to drill with the knife until the handlers return, and they smile as they watch me move through the paces of what Johnnie knows as casually as most Americans know how to throw a Frisbee. Later, as we step into the cooling night and they walk me over to the Underground to catch the Northern line at Stockwell, they inquire after my silence. Did I enjoy myself?

"Well, yeah." My head was spinning with what I had learned and my impending return to California and beyond, what would be the passage of my life.

"Good, heh?" They ask nodding their heads and smiling in agreement.

"I'm not sure about that."

"You will be sure when you need to be."

Eugene Robinson is a lifetime adherent to whatever martial arts he can get his hands on from Shotokan karate and Shaolin kung fu to Muay Thai (Thai boxing), grappling, and most recently, submission fighting, also known as Ultimate Fighting. A singer in a band called Oxbow (http://www.theoxbow.com), his touring has carried him into shadowy nooks and crannies worldwide.

PETER HOLT

✦ ✳ ✦

Reading the Leaves

Do you really want to know the future?

I HAD ONE FINAL MISSION BEFORE I RETURNED TO MADRAS. Ramesh suggested that if I wanted to discover more of the secrets of India—and, indeed, myself—I should go to a Nadi reading.

The Nadi is the world's most mysterious system of astrological prediction. Here you find Indian mysticism at its deepest.

The Nadi dates from around 2,000 years ago when a *rishi* called Brighu produced a vast series of personal horoscopes on palm leaves called *saraswathi*, after the goddess of knowledge. He dictated his predictions to a team of scribes, who wrote them down in Mundu Tamil, the ancient form of Tamil.

Rishi Brighu is said to have had the power of divine insight, and he was able to write down the past, present, and future lives of individuals, who would make their stay on this planet in years to come.

It seems difficult to believe, but the Nadi readers claim there is a palm leaf for nearly everyone in the world. It seems mathematically impossible that Brighu would have had the time to write down the past, present, and future of billions of people. But the Nadi readers counter this argument by saying that many people share the same palm leaves. Therefore, on that basis there are perhaps thousands of people out there with the same past, present, and future as yourself. Likewise, Brighu based his philosophy on the fact that when a person died his or her spirit would pass to another person.

The Nadi differs from other horoscopes in that it uses no intuitive, instinctive skills of clairvoyance. First you provide your date of birth and an impression of your thumbprint—the right thumb for males, the left for females. Then you are asked a few questions as a sort of index: Are your parents still alive? Do you have brothers and sisters? Then the reader looks for the palm leaf corresponding to you. All the Nadi reader does is relate exactly what is written on the palm leaf. Nothing else. Ramesh was able to read the ancient Mundu Tamil script. When his Nadi was read a few years ago, he asked to look at the palm leaf afterwards. "What the man had just told me was exactly the same as what was written down," he said. "Just from my thumbprint, the palm leaf got my whole family history absolutely accurate as well as my life to that point. As to whether the future was accurate, I have yet to find out."

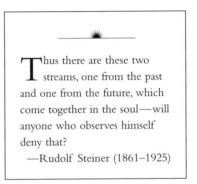

Thus there are these two streams, one from the past and one from the future, which come together in the soul—will anyone who observes himself deny that?

—Rudolf Steiner (1861–1925)

If you don't believe in horoscopes, then all this will sound like nonsense. But it must be said that the Nadi is one of the great mysteries of India. And Indians take their readings very seriously indeed.

The Brighu Samhita, or collection, was duplicated 150 years ago. And one of the sets of inscriptions had ended up in the little town of Vaithishwaran Koil, thirty miles south of Pondicherry. The palm leaves were kept in a small terraced house in the centre of town.

When I turned up, a minibusload of rich Indians from Madras were crowded on the verandah waiting to have their leaves read. A man in the office seemed amazed that an Englishman had heard about the place. He arranged for me to see a reader immediately. The problem was that no one spoke much English. Help appeared in the form of a well-to-do tea-planter and his wife from Ootacamund, the hill station on the western boundary of Tamil Nadu. They had travelled 250 miles specially to have their fortunes read. They spoke good English, and they agreed to sit in on my reading and translate what the reader told me.

We sat down on the floor in a large room with shuttered windows. It was dark and gloomy and lit by a single candle. The Nadi reader was called Mr. Chellian. He sat on a cushion behind a low lectern. He took my thumbprint and asked a few questions about my family. Then he disappeared into a backroom and returned with a set of palm leaves. They were long strips, measured about one inch by a foot, and tied together with leather thongs. They were covered in the neat, tiny script of Mundu Tamil.

Mr. Chellian flicked through the leaves and came to the one that corresponded to me. He began reading it. I have to admit that although he was not entirely accurate about my childhood and immediate past, he got most of it right. It galled me to be reminded, for example, of my lack of academic study at school. He also correctly identified my father's occupation—farmer—and informed me, correctly again, that my sister was an actress.

Mr. Chellian moved to my future...and then to the end of my future. And this was the bit I had not wanted to hear.

He lowered his voice. My interpreter, the tea-planter, did the same. Suddenly everything had become very solemn. I had a nasty feeling about what was going to happen next. The Nadi reader continued. The tea-planter translated: "At the age of...you will leave this life. It will be in a hospital on the...of...and you will go peacefully." That was enough for me. I stood up, thanked everyone for their time and handed Mr. Chellian his fee. He looked puzzled. Why was I in such a rush to go? I muttered something about needing a breath of fresh air. Not for a moment had he thought there was anything wrong in telling a person when and where he was going to die.

And that put an end to my metaphysical meanderings. It was time to return to Madras and get stuck back into Clive's trail. Bala was preparing to leave his yoga studies to fly back to Australia and

I promised Ramesh that I would look him up again before I left India. I was sad to leave Pondicherry. The place had given me an insight into what India could offer the world. That nothing should be clear-cut; that we should take nothing for granted; that it is too easy to explain events as mere coincidence; that the forces of destiny are guiding us all.

Peter Holt is the great-great-great-great-great-grandson of Robert Clive, who defeated Sirāj-ud-Dawlah, the nawab of Bengal, along with his French supporters at the Battle of Plassey in 1757. Clive's victory ushered in almost 200 years of British rule, and Peter Holt's book, In Clive's Footsteps, *from which this story is excerpted, is a journey in search of his ancestor. He lives in London.*

PART FIVE

BLESSINGS

JACQUES LUSSEYRAN

✦ ✦ ✦

Second Sight

What happens when "seeing" is a function
not of the optic nerve, but of the soul?

THE INVALIDS' BLOCK WAS A BARRACKS LIKE THE OTHERS. THE ONLY difference was that they had crowded in 1,500 men instead of 300— 300 was the average for the other blocks—and they had cut the food ration in half. At the Invalids' you had the one-legged, the one-armed, the trepanned, the deaf, the deaf-mute, the blind, the legless—even they were there, I knew three of them—the aphasic, the ataxic, the epileptic, the gangrenous, the scrofulous, the tubercular, the cancerous, the syphilitic, the old men over seventy, the boys under sixteen, the kleptomaniacs, the tramps, the perverts, and last of all the flock of madmen. They were the only ones who didn't seem unhappy.

No one at the Invalids' was whole, since that was the condition of entrance. As a result people were dying there at a pace which made it impossible to make any count of the block. It was a greater surprise to fall over the living than the dead. And it was from the living that danger came.

The stench was so terrible that only the smell of the crematory, which sent up smoke around the clock, managed to cover it up on days when the wind drove the smoke our way. For days and nights on end, I didn't walk around, I crawled. I made an opening for myself in the mass of flesh. My hands traveled from the stump of a leg to a dead body, from a body to a wound. I could no longer hear anything for the groaning around me.

Toward the end of the month all of a sudden it became too much for me and I grew sick, very sick. I think it was pleurisy. They said several doctors, prisoners like me, and friends of mine, came to listen to my chest. It seems they gave me up. What else could they do? There was no medicine at all at Buchenwald, not even aspirin.

Very soon dysentery was added to pleurisy, then an infection in both ears which made me completely deaf for two weeks, then erysipelas, turning my face into a swollen pulp, with complications which threatened to bring on blood poisoning. More than fifty fellow prisoners told me all this later. I don't remember any of it myself. I had taken advantage of the first days of sickness to leave Buchenwald.

Two young boys I was very fond of, a Frenchman with one leg, and a Russian with one arm, told me that one morning in April they carried me to the hospital on a stretcher. The hospital was not a place where they took care of people, but simply a place to lay them down until they died or got well. My friends, Pavel and Louis, didn't understand what happened. Later they kept telling me that I was a "case." A year afterwards Louis was still amazed: "The day we carried you, you had a fever of 104 or more, but you were not delirious. You looked quite serene, and every now and then you would tell us not to put ourselves out on your account." I would gladly have explained to Louis and Pavel, but the whole affair was beyond words and still is.

Sickness had rescued me from fear, it had even rescued me from death. Let me say to you simply that without it I never would have survived. From the first moments of sickness I had gone off into another world, quite consciously. I was not delirious. Louis was right, I still had the look of tranquillity, more so than ever. That was the miracle.

I watched the stages of my own illness quite clearly. I saw the organs of my body blocked up losing control one after the other, first my lungs, then my intestines, then my ears, all my muscles, and last of all my heart, which was functioning badly and filled me with a vast, unusual sound. I knew exactly what it was, this thing I was watching: my body in the act of leaving this world, not wanting to leave it right away, not even wanting to leave it at all. I could tell by the pain my body was causing me, twisting and turning in every direction like snakes that have been cut in pieces.

Have I said that death was already there? If I have I was wrong. Sickness and pain, yes, but not death. Quite the opposite, life, and that was the unbelievable thing that had taken possession of me. I had never lived so fully before.

Life had become a substance within me. It broke into my cage, pushed by a force a thousand times stronger than I. It was certainly not made of flesh and blood, not even of ideas. It came towards me like a shimmering wave, like the caress of light. I could see it beyond my eyes and my forehead and above my head. It touched me and filled me to overflowing. I let myself float upon it.

There were names which I mumbled from the depths of my astonishment. No doubt my lips did not speak them, but they had their own song: "Providence, the Guardian Angel, Jesus Christ, God." I didn't try to turn it over in my mind. It was not just the time for metaphysics. I drew my strength from the spring. I kept on drinking and drinking still more. I was not going to leave that celestial stream. For that matter it was not strange to me, having come to me right after my old accident when I found I was blind. Here was the same thing all over again, the Life which sustained the life in me.

The Lord took pity on the poor mortal who was so helpless before him. It is true I was quite unable to help myself. All of us are incapable of helping ourselves. Now I knew it, and knew that it was true of the SS among the first. That was something to make one smile.

But there was one thing left I could do: not refuse God's help, the breath he was blowing upon me. That was the one battle I had to fight, hard and wonderful all at once: not to let my body be taken by the fear. For fear kills, and joy maintains life.

Slowly I came back from the dead, and when, one morning, one of my neighbors—I found out later he was an atheist and thought he was doing the right thing—shouted in my ear that I didn't have a chance in the world of getting through it, so I had better prepare myself, he got my answer full in the face, a burst of laughter. He didn't understand that laugh, but he never forgot it.

On May 8, I left the hospital on my two feet. I was nothing but skin and bones, but I had recovered. The fact was I was so happy that now Buchenwald seemed to me a place which if not welcome was at least possible. If they didn't give me any bread to eat, I would feed on hope.

It was the truth. I still had eleven months ahead of me in the camp. But today I have not a single evil memory of those 330 days of extreme wretchedness. I was carried by a hand. I was covered by a wing. One doesn't call such living emotions by their names. I hardly needed to look out for myself, and such concern would have seemed to me ridiculous. I knew it was dangerous and it was forbidden. I was free now to help the others; not always, not much, but in my own way I could help.

I could try to show other people how to go about holding on to life. I could turn towards them the flow of light and joy which had grown so abundant in me. From that time on they stopped stealing my bread or my soup. It never happened again. Often my comrades would wake me up in the night and take me to comfort someone, sometimes a long way off in another block.

Almost everyone forgot I was a student. I became "the blind Frenchman." For many, I was just "the man who didn't die." Hundreds of people confided in me. The men were determined to talk to me. They spoke in French, in Russian, in German, in Polish. I did the best I could to understand them all. That is how I lived, how I survived. The rest I cannot describe.

Jacques Lusseyran was blinded at the age of eight. He has learned to see the world from within. Although he was prevented for years from gaining his professorship due to the Vichy government barring "invalids" from public employment, he finally prevailed. He taught in France and then later in the United States. He died at the age of forty-six in a car accident, with his wife Marie, while visiting France. This story is excerpted from his book, And There Was Light, *which chronicles Jacques's role as a student leader in the French Resistance during WWII and as a survivor of Buchenwald.*

SISTER HELEN P. MROSLA

$\star \: {}^{\star} \: \star$

Lists

Life is short. Don't waste
it with negativity.

HE WAS IN THE FIRST THIRD-GRADE CLASS I TAUGHT AT SAINT Mary's School in Morris, Minnesota. All thirty-four of my students were dear to me, but Mark Eklund was one in a million. Very neat in appearance but had that happy-to-be-alive attitude that made even his occasional mischieviousness delightful.

Mark talked incessantly. I had to remind him again and again that talking without permission was not acceptable. What impressed me so much, though, was his sincere response every time I had to correct him for misbehaving—"Thank you for correcting me, Sister!" I didn't know what to make of it at first, but before long I became accustomed to hearing it many times a day.

One morning my patience was growing thin when Mark talked once too often, and then I made a novice-teacher's mistake. I looked at him and said, "If you say one more word, I am going to tape your mouth shut!"

It wasn't ten seconds later when Chuck blurted out, "Mark is talking again." I hadn't asked any of the students to help me watch Mark, but since I had stated the punishment in front of the class, I had to act on it.

I remember the scene as if it had occurred this morning. I

walked to my desk, very deliberately opened my drawer, and took out a roll of masking tape. Without saying a word, I proceeded to Mark's desk, tore off two pieces of tape, and made a big **X** with them over his mouth. I then returned to the front of the room. As I glanced at Mark to see how he was doing, he winked at me. That did it! I started laughing. The class cheered as I walked back to Mark's desk, removed the tape, and shrugged my shoulders. His first words were, "Thank you for correcting me, Sister."

At the end of the year I was asked to teach junior-high math. The years flew by, and before I knew it Mark was in my classroom again. He was more handsome than ever and just as polite. Since he had to listen carefully to my instructions in the "new math," he did not talk as much in ninth grade as he had in the third.

One Friday, things just didn't feel right. We had worked hard on a new concept all week, and I sensed that the students were frowning, frustrated with themselves—and edgy with one another. I had to stop this crankiness before it got out of hand. So I asked them to list the names of the other students in the room on two sheets of paper, leaving a space between each name. Then I told them to think of the nicest thing they could say about each of their classmates and write it down.

It took the remainder of the class period to finish the assignment, and as the students left the room, each one handed me the papers. Charlie smiled.

Mark said, "Thank you for teaching me, Sister. Have a good weekend." That Saturday, I wrote down the name of each student on a separate sheet of paper, and I listed what everyone else had said about that individual.

On Monday I gave each student his or her list. Before long, the entire class was smiling. "Really?" I heard whispered. "I never knew that meant anything to anyone!" "I didn't know others liked me so much!"

No one ever mentioned those papers in class again. I never knew if they discussed them after class or with their parents, but it didn't matter. The exercise had accomplished its purpose. The students were happy with themselves and one another again.

That group of students moved on. Several years later, after I returned from vacation, my parents met me at the airport. As we were driving home, Mother asked me the usual questions about the trip—the weather, my experiences in general. There was a light lull in the conversation. Mother gave Dad a sideways glance and simply said "Dad?" My father cleared his throat as he usually did before something important.

"The Eklunds called last night," he began.

"Really?" I said. "I haven't heard from them in years. I wonder how Mark is."

Dad responded quietly. "Mark was killed in Vietnam," he said. "The funeral is tomorrow, and his parents would like it if you could attend." To this day I can still point to the exact spot on I-494 where Dad told me about Mark.

I had never seen a serviceman in a military coffin before. Mark looked so handsome, so mature. All I could think at that moment was, Mark, I would give all the masking tape in the world if only you would talk to me. The church was packed with Mark's friends. Chuck's sister sang "The Battle Hymn of the Republic." Why did it have to rain on the day of the funeral?

It was difficult enough at the graveside. The pastor said the usual prayers, and the bugler played taps. One by one those who loved Mark took a last walk by the coffin and sprinkled it with holy water.

I was the last one to bless the coffin. As I stood there, one of the soldiers who had acted as pallbearer came up to me. "Were you Mark's math teacher?" he asked. I nodded as I continued to stare at the coffin.

"Mark talked about you a lot," he said.

After the funeral, most of Mark's former classmates headed to Chuck's farmhouse for lunch. Mark's mother and father were there, obviously waiting for me. "We want to show you something," his father said, taking a wallet out of his pocket. "They found this on Mark when he was killed. We thought you might recognize it."

Opening the billfold, he carefully removed two worn pieces of notebook paper that had obviously been taped, folded and refolded many times.

I knew without looking that the papers were the ones on which I had listed all the good things each of Mark's classmates had said about him. "Thank you so much for doing that," Mark's mother said. "As you can see, Mark treasured it."

Mark's classmates started to gather around us. Charlie smiled rather sheepishly and said, "I still have my list. It's in the top drawer of my desk at home." Chuck's wife said, "Chuck asked me to put his in our wedding album." "I have mine too," Marilyn said. "It's in my diary." Then Vicki, another classmate, reached into her pocketbook, took out her wallet and showed her worn and frazzled list to the group. "I carry this with me at all times," Vicki said without batting an eyelash. "I think we all saved our lists."

That's when I finally sat down and cried. I cried for Mark and for all his friends who would never see him again.

Sister Helen Mrosla is a member of the Roman Catholic religious order known as Franciscan Sisters of Little Falls, Minnesota. She received her Doctorate in Instruction from the University of North Texas and has taught in Saint Paul, Kentucky, and Seattle.

FENTON JOHNSON

✦

The Weight of Memory

…in a handful of gravel.

I AM IN FRANCE, DRIVING LARRY ROSE SOUTH AND WEST FROM Tours, along the banks of the Loire. Two days later he will be dead, impossible to believe then or now, but in this moment we are driving, we are fleeing south and west, to Nantes, the Atlantic, the Gironde, Bordeaux, the Pyrenees, Spain, Morocco. We will run as far as we can, as far as it takes.

The Loire flows on our left, a broad, silvered mirror reflecting the towering pastels of this Fragonard sky. On our right, yellowing poplars shiver behind limestone-walled villages and ornate châteaus.

I drive until I am blinded by tears—my lover is so quiet, so ill. Under the crenellated medieval towers of Langeais I stop the car and turn to him. "Are you in pain?"

"No."

"We could turn back."

He presses his finger to my lips. "I'm happy being quiet here with you." (This is what I have learned, the gift grief has given me: the sufficiency and necessity of being quiet here with you.)

But we have no choice. We cross that river, we turn and head back. Life takes the shape of an hourglass, focusing down, past and future falling away until there is nothing but this moment, this present place, the two of us amid this ancient, pastoral, autumnal countryside. Surely this is as close as I will get—surely it is as close as anyone could bear—to love pure as sunlight; to our reason for being alive.

And the sun sinks lower in the sky, the light fails, time is running out; a day, a life is racing to its end. The sunlight slants across the reed-choked Indre, shining white on the raked and graveled paths of Azay-le-Rideau, this fantasy castle. A swan sinks on extended wings to meet his double, rising in the lake's emerald mirror. He lands— the château's slate-sheathed towers shatter, ripple, then reassemble their inverted perfection. Stark sharp shadows of osiers, black rapiers against green water, my lover and I set out to walk the symmetrical paths except that he cannot lift his feet, shoes scrape gravel, and so he turns back to the car. I turn to follow, but instead crouch to take up a handful of pebbles, to lodge in memory the feel of this place that I will surely never touch again in the presence of this man, this friend of my youth. The rough and raked stoniness grates against my palms, the gravel runs through my fingers but it is the ash of the burned and blackened Oakland hills, and before me lies the long, cantilevered bridge, the dark mass of Yerba Buena Island rising from the black mirror of San Francisco Bay. The city glitters beyond.

I am in California, not in France. It is almost two years later, I am here and he is not, but this is the lesson that I take, for a comfort that must and will suffice: in his absence, in my grief, there is continuity—not in life, but in love.

> After Bruce Chatwin died for the first time, to be brought back to life by the doctors only to die definitively a little later, he told me that to die was finally to penetrate behind that great Renaissance painting which lies at the back of the minds of all of us as a symbol for this world and the next.
> —Matthew Spender,
> *Within Tuscany*

Fenton Johnson is the youngest of nine children born to a devoutly Catholic rural Kentucky family. He is the author of Scissors, Paper, Rock, Song of the Soil, Crossing the River, *and the memoir,* Geography of the Heart, *which chronicles the death and the life of his partner.*

* * *

The Light

In silence, many things
can be learned.

As an adolescent, I had a summer job working as a volunteer companion in a nursing home for the aged. The job began with a two-week intensive training about communicating with the elderly. There seemed to be a great deal to remember, and what had begun as a rather heartfelt way to spend a teenage summer quickly became a regimented set of techniques and skills for which I would be evaluated by the nursing staff. By the first day of actual patient contact, I was very anxious.

My first assignment was to visit with a ninety-six-year-old woman who had not spoken for more than a year. A psychiatrist had diagnosed her as having senile dementia, but she had not responded to medication. The nurses doubted that she would talk to me, but hoped I could engage her in a mutual activity. I was given a large basket filled with glass beads of every imaginable size and color. We would string beads together. I was to report back to the nursing station in an hour.

I did not want to see this patient. Her great age frightened me, and the words "senile dementia" suggested that not only was she older by far than anyone I had ever met, she was crazy, too. Filled with foreboding, I knocked on the closed door of her room. There

Silence was absolute

was no answer. Opening the door, I found myself in a small room lit by a single window which faced the morning sun. Two chairs had been placed in front of the window; in one sat a very old lady, looking out. The other was empty. I stood just inside the door for a time, but she did not acknowledge my presence in any way. Uncertain of what to do next, I went to the empty chair and sat down, the basket of beads on my lap. She did not seem to notice that I had come.

For a while I tried to find some way to open a conversation. I was painfully shy at this time, which was one of the reasons my parents had suggested I take this job, and I would have had a hard time even in less difficult circumstances. The silence in the room was absolute. Somehow it almost seemed rude to speak, yet I desperately wanted to succeed in my task. I considered and discarded all the ways of making conversation suggested in the training. None of them seemed possible. The old woman continued to look toward the window, her face half hidden from me, barely breathing. Finally I simply gave up and sat with the basket of glass beads in my lap for the full hour. It was quite peaceful.

The silence was broken at last by the little bell which signified the end of the morning activity. Taking hold of the basket again, I prepared to leave. But I was only fourteen and curiosity overcame me. Turning to the old woman, I asked, "What are you looking at?" I immediately flushed. Prying into the lives of the residents was strictly forbidden. Perhaps she had not heard. But she had. Slowly she turned toward me and I could see her face for the first time.

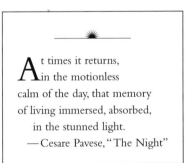

At times it returns,
in the motionless
calm of the day, that memory
of living immersed, absorbed,
in the stunned light.
— Cesare Pavese, "The Night"

It was radiant. In a voice filled with joy she said, "Why, child, I am looking at the Light."

Many years later, as a pediatrician, I would watch newborns look at light with that same rapt expression, almost as if they were listening for something. Fortunately, I had not been able to find a way to interrupt.

A ninety-six-year-old woman may stop speaking because arteriosclerosis has damaged her brain, or she has become psychotic and she is no longer able to speak. But she may also have withdrawn into a space between the worlds, to contemplate what is next, to spread her sails and patiently wait to catch the light.

I had found her by accident, or perhaps by grace. I have often wondered what would have happened had I been the highly trained technical physician I would shortly become. At that time I would not have known how to find her and sit with her. How to learn from her about silence and trusting life. Now, many years later, I hope that I do.

Rachel Naomi Remen, M.D., is a physician, therapist, and professor of medicine who is active in the mind-body health movement. She is the author of Final Wisdom: What Dying Can Teach Us About Living, The Roots of Healing, *and* Kitchen Table Wisdom: Stories That Heal, *from which this story was excerpted.*

ALLEGRA TAYLOR

$\star$ $\overset{\star}{}$ $\star$

Last Wish

A father and mother accompany their beloved
daughter on her final journey.

THE MOST MOVING TALE OF TRANSITION AND TRANSFORMATION I ever heard was told by Robert White, an American factory worker from North Carolina.

The story had begun when Robert and his wife went to visit their daughter Lee in hospital as they did every evening.

"It's not easy to die when you are fifteen, but Lee had already accepted her fate," said Robert. As he spoke, his eyes were full of tears, and he could barely keep his voice steady. "She knew she had an illness that would not spare her. She knew that in spite of their finest efforts the doctors couldn't save her. She suffered a lot but never complained. This particular evening she seemed tranquil and composed but suddenly she said, 'Mama, daddy—I think I'm going to die soon and I'm afraid. I know I'm going to a better world than this one, and I'm longing for some peace at last but it's hard to accept the idea that I'm going to die at only fifteen.'"

"We could have lied, telling her of course she wasn't going to die, but we didn't have the heart. Somehow her courage was worth more than our pretence. We just cuddled her and cried together. Then she said, 'I always dreamed of falling in love, getting married, having kids...but above all I would have liked to work in a big marine park with dolphins. I've loved them and wanted to know more about them since I was little. I still dream of swimming with them free and happy in the open sea.' She'd never asked for anything, but now she said with all the strength she could muster, 'Daddy, I want to swim in the open sea among the dolphins just once. Maybe then I wouldn't be so scared of dying.'"

"It seemed like an absurd, impossible dream but she, who had given up just about everything else, hung on to it.

"My wife and I talked it over and decided to do everything we could. We had heard of a research centre in the Florida Keys and we phoned them. 'Come at once,' they said. But that was easier said than done. Lee's illness had used up all our savings, and we had no idea how we would be able to afford air tickets to Florida. Then our six-year-old, Emily, mentioned that she'd seen something on television about a foundation that grants the wishes of very sick children. She'd actually written down the telephone number in her diary because it seemed like magic to her.

"I didn't want to listen. I thought it sounded like a fairy tale or a very sick joke, and I gave in only when Emily started crying and accusing me of not really wanting to help Lee. So I phoned the number and three days later we were all on our way. Emily felt a bit like a fairy godmother who had solved all our problems with a wave of her magic wand.

"When we arrived at Grass Key, Lee was pale and terribly thin. The chemotherapy she'd been having had made all her hair fall out and she looked ghastly, but she didn't want to rest for a minute and begged us to take her straightaway to the dolphins. It was an unforgettable scene. When she got into the water, Lee was already so weak she hardly had the strength to move. We had put her in a wet suit so she wouldn't get cold and a life preserver to keep her afloat.

"I towed her out toward the dolphins, Nat and Tursi, who were frolicking around about thirty feet away from us. At first they seemed distracted and uninterested but when Lee called them softly by name they responded without hesitation. Nat came over first, raised his head and gave her a kiss on the end of her nose. Then Tursi came over and greeted her with a flurry of little high-pitched squeaks of joy. A second later they picked her up with their mighty fins and carried her out to sea with them."

"'It feels like I'm flying!' cried Lee, laughing with delight. I hadn't heard her laugh like that since before she became ill. I could hardly believe it was true, but there she was gripping Nat's fin and challenging the wind and the immensity of the ocean. The dolphins stayed with Lee for more than an hour, always tender, always attentive, never using any unnecessary force, always responsive to her wishes.

"Maybe it's true that they are more intelligent and sensitive creatures than man. I know for certain that those marvelous dolphins understood that Lee was dying and wanted to console her as she faced her great journey into the unknown. From the moment they took her in hand they never left her alone for a second. They got her to play and obeyed her commands with a sweetness that was magical. In their company Lee found for one last time the enthusiasm and the will to live. She was strong and happy like she used to be. At one point she shouted, 'The dolphins have healed me, daddy!'"

"There are no words to describe the effect that swim had on her. When she got out of the water it was as if she had been reborn.

"The next day she was too weak to get out of bed. She didn't even want to talk, but when I took her hand she squeezed it and whispered, 'Daddy, don't be sad for me. I'll never be afraid again. The dolphins have made me understand that I have nothing to fear.' Then she said, 'I

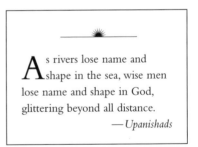

As rivers lose name and shape in the sea, wise men lose name and shape in God, glittering beyond all distance.

— *Upanishads*

know I'm going to die tonight. Promise me that you'll cremate my body and scatter my ashes in the sea where all dolphins swim. They gave me the most beautiful moments of my life. They have left me with a great feeling of peace in my heart and I know they will be with me on the long journey that lies ahead.' Just before dawn she woke and said, 'Hold me, Daddy, I'm so cold.' And she died like that in my arms a few minutes later—passing from sleep to death without a ripple. I only realized her suffering was over because her body became colder and heavier.

"We cremated her as she wanted and went out the next day to scatter her ashes in the ocean amongst the dolphins. We were all crying, I'm not ashamed to say; not just my wife and I and our three other children, but even the sailors on the boat that had taken us out into the bay. Suddenly, through our tears, we saw the great arching silver shapes of Nat and Tursi leaping out of the water ahead of us. They had come to take our daughter home."

Allegra Taylor is a practicing healer, dreamer, and author. Her books include A Kibbutz in Israel, Healing Hands, Ladder to the Moon, *and* Acquainted with the Night: A Year on the Frontiers of Death, *from which this story was excerpted.*

✦ ✦ ✦

In the Mirror of Death

He learned the art of dying
at an early age.

My own first experience of death came when I was about seven. We were preparing to leave the eastern highlands to travel to central Tibet. Samten, one of the personal attendants of my master, was a wonderful monk who was kind to me during my childhood. He had a bright, round, chubby face, always ready to break into a smile. He was everyone's favorite in the monastery because he was so good-natured. Every day my master would give teachings and initiations and lead practices and rituals. Toward the end of the day, I would gather together my friends and act out a little theatrical performance, reenacting the morning's events. It was Samten who would always lend me the costumes my master had worn in the morning. He never refused me.

Then suddenly Samten fell ill, and it was clear he was not going to live. We had to postpone our departure. I will never forget the two weeks that followed. The rank smell of death hung like a cloud over everything, and whenever I think of that time, that smell comes back to me. The monastery was saturated with an intense awareness of death. This was not at all morbid or frightening, however; in the presence of my master, Samten's death took on a special significance. It became a teaching for us all.

277

Samten lay on a bed by the window in a small temple in my master's residence. I knew he was dying. From time to time I would go in and sit by him. He could not talk, and I was shocked by the change in his face, which was now so haggard and drawn. I realized that he was going to leave us and we would never see him again. I felt intensely sad and lonely.

Samten's death was not an easy one. The sound of his labored breathing followed us everywhere, and we could smell his body decaying. The monastery was overwhelmingly silent except for this breathing. Everything focused on Samten. Yet although there was so much suffering in Samten's prolonged dying, we could all see that deep down he had a peace and inner confidence about him. At first I could not explain this, but then I realized what it came from: his faith and his training, and the presence of our master. And though I felt sad, I knew then that if our master was there, everything would turn out all right, because he would be able to help Samten toward liberation. Later I came to know that it is the dream of any practitioner to die before his master and have the good fortune to be guided by him through death.

As Jamyang Khyentse guided Samten calmly through his dying, he introduced him to all the stages of the process he was going through, one by one. I was astonished by the precision of my master's knowledge, and by his confidence and peace. When my master was there, his peaceful confidence would reassure even the most anxious person. Now Jamyang Khyentse was revealing to us his fearlessness of death. Not that he ever treated death lightly: he often told us that he was afraid of it, and warned us against taking it naïvely or complacently. Yet what was it that allowed my master to face death in a way that was at once so sober and so lighthearted, so practical yet so mysteriously carefree? That question fascinated and absorbed me.

Samten's death shook me. At the age of seven, I had my first glimpse of the vast power of the tradition I was being made part of, and I began to understand the purpose of spiritual practice. Practice had given Samten an acceptance of death, as well as a clear understanding that suffering and pain can be part of a deep, natural

process of purification. Practice had given my master a complete knowledge of what death is, and a precise technology for guiding individuals through it.

After Samten died we set off for Lhasa, the capital of Tibet, a tortuous three-month journey on horseback. From there we continued our pilgrimage to the sacred sites of central and southern Tibet. These are the holy places of the saints, kings, and scholars who brought Buddhism to Tibet from the seventh century onward. My master was the emanation of many masters of all traditions, and because of his reputation he was given a tumultuous reception everywhere we went.

For me that journey was extremely exciting and has remained full of beautiful memories. Tibetans rise early, in order to make use of all the natural light. We would go to bed at dusk and rise before daybreak, and by first light the yaks carrying the baggage would be moving out. The tents would be struck, and the last ones to come down were the kitchen and my master's tent. A scout would go ahead to choose a good camping place, and we would stop and camp around noon for the rest of the day. I used to love to camp by a river and listen to the sound of the water, or to sit in the tent and hear the rain pattering on the roof.

We were a small party with about thirty tents in all. During the day I rode on a golden-colored horse next to my master. While we rode he gave teachings, told stories, practiced, and composed a number of practices specially for me. One day, as we drew near the sacred lake of Yamdrok Tso, and caught sight of the turquoise radiance of its waters, another lama in our party, Lama Tseten, began to die.

The death of Lama Tseten proved another strong teaching for me. He was the tutor to my master's spiritual wife, Khandro Tsering Chödrön, who is still alive today. She is regarded by many as Tibet's foremost woman practitioner, a hidden master who for me is an embodiment of devotion, teaching through the simplicity of her loving presence. Lama Tseten was an immensely human and grandfatherly character. He was over sixty, quite tall and with gray hair, and exuded an effortless gentleness. He was also a highly accomplished practitioner of meditation, and just to be near him used to give me a sense of peace and serenity. Sometimes he would scold me, and I would be afraid of him; but for all his occasional stern-ness, he never lost his warmth.

Lama Tseten died in an extraordinary way. Although there was a monastery close by, he refused to go there, saying he did not want to leave a corpse for them to clean up. So we camped and pitched our tents in a circle as usual. Khandro was nursing and caring for Lama Tseten, as he was her tutor. She and I were the only two people in his tent when he suddenly called her over. He had an endearing way of calling her, "A-mi," he said tenderly, "come here. It's happening now. I've no further advice for you. You are fine as you are: I am happy with you. Serve your master just as you have been doing."

Immediately she turned to run out of the tent, but he caught her by the sleeve. "Where are you going?" he asked. "I'm going to call Rinpoche," she replied.

"Don't bother him, there's no need," he smiled. "With the master, there's no such thing as distance." With that,

---

What I remember most about the Dalai Lama was his laugh. It had a rich and deep tone. He was the only person I interviewed who laughed out loud when I asked him about death.

Oh Dalai Lama,
your laugh is all I came to hear.
It bellows from deep within.
Give me no words, I ask
no questions.
Only laugh.
If I were to describe your laugh,
it would be the fullness of living,
together with the sufferings
of Tibet.
It is a laugh of folly,
for we do the best we can,
but still,
in the end, we must laugh.

The Bible has erred.
The beginning was not the
Word.
No.
In the beginning was the Laugh.
—William Elliott, *Tying Rocks
to Clouds: Meetings and
Conversations with Wise and
Spiritual People*

he just gazed up into the sky and passed away. Khandro released herself from his grip and rushed out to call my master. I sat there, unable to move.

I was amazed that anyone who was staring into the face of death could have that kind of confidence. Lama Tseten could have had his Lama there in person to help him—something anyone else would have longed for—but he had no need. I understand why now: he had already realized the presence of the master within himself. Jamyang Khyentse was there with him always, in his mind and heart; never for one moment did he feel any separation.

Khandro did go to fetch Jamyang Khyentse. I shall never forget how he stooped to enter the tent. He gave one look at Lama Tseten's face, and then, peering into his eyes, began to chuckle. He always used to call him "La Gen," "old Lama"; it was a sign of his affection. "La Gen," he said, "don't stay in that state!" He could see, I now understand, that Lama Tseten was doing one particular practice of meditation in which the practitioner merges the nature of his mind with the space of truth. "You know, La Gen, when you do this practice, sometimes subtle obstacles can arise. Come on. I'll guide you."

Transfixed, I watched what happened next, and if I hadn't seen it myself I would never have believed it. *Lama Tseten came back to life.* Then my master sat by his side and took him through the *phowa,* the practice for guiding the consciousness at the moment before death. There are many ways of doing this practice, and the one he used then culminated with the master uttering the syllable "A" three times. As my master declared the first "A," we could hear Lama Tseten accompanying him quite audibly. The second time his voice was less distinct, and the third time it was silent; he had gone.

The death of Samten taught me the purpose of spiritual practice; Lama Tseten's death taught me that it is not unusual for practitioners of his caliber to conceal their remarkable qualities during their lifetime. Sometimes, in fact, they show them only once, at the moment of death. I understood, even as a child, that there was a striking difference between the death of Samten and that of Lama Tseten, and I realized that it was the difference between the death of a good monk who had practiced in his life and that of a much more realized practitioner. Samten died in an ordinary way and in pain, yet with the confidence of faith; Lama Tseten's death was a display of spiritual mastery.

Soon after Lama Tseten's funeral, we moved up into the monastery of Yamdrok. As usual, I slept next to my master in his room, and I remember that night watching the shadows of the butter lamps flickering on the wall. While everyone else slept soundly, I lay awake and cried the whole night long. I understood that night that death is real, and that I too would have to die. As I lay there, thinking about death and about my own death, through all my sadness a profound sense of acceptance began slowly to emerge, and with it a resolve to dedicate my life to spiritual practice.

So I began to face death and its implications very young. I could never have imagined then how many kinds of death there were to follow, one heaped upon another. The death that was the tragic loss of my country Tibet, after the Chinese occupation. The death that is exile. The death of losing everything my family and I possessed. My family, Lakar Tsang, had been among the wealthiest in Tibet. Since the fourteenth century it had been famous as one of the most important benefactors of Buddhism, supporting the teaching of Buddha and helping the great masters with their work.

The most shattering death of all was yet to come—that of my master Jamyang Khyentse. Losing him I felt I had lost the ground of my existence. It was in 1959, the year of the fall of Tibet. For the Tibetans, my master's death was a second devastating blow. And for Tibet, it marked the end of an era.

Sogyal Rinpoche is a Tibetan teacher and the author of several books including, Glimpse After Glimpse: Daily Reflections on Living and Dying, Meditation (A Little Book of Wisdom), Bringing the Mind Home, *and* The Tibetan Book of Living and Dying, *from which this story was excerpted.*

DIANA V. CULBERTSON, PH.D.

⋆ ⋆ ⋆

The Man in the Dream

On the possibility of angels.

IN THE 1930S, BEING DIAGNOSED WITH EITHER DIPHTHERIA OR scarlet fever meant quarantine for the individual and a lot of prayer by family and friends. Either of these diseases was life threatening and together it was almost a certainty that death would soon follow. As an almost five year old I had scarlet fever and diphtheria at the same time. I slipped into a coma and the doctor advised my parents that I had one chance in a million to live. My mother said she was going to ask God to give her daughter that chance.

For three weeks I lay in a coma and I had the following experience. One day a man whom I did not know came to see me. He was dressed in a white suit and shoes, quite ordinary attire for that era and summertime in hot, humid Washington, D.C. He told me he was a friend of my parents and that we were going for a walk. I took his hand, and we went outside of the hospital room and started walking down the path toward a bridge.

It was dusk and there was a lamplighter walking ahead of us, lighting the lamps and illuminating our way. At that time in Washington, D.C. there were several park areas that were still lit by gas lamps, so there was nothing unusual in this.

I kept turning to look back at the hospital and my room. It was getting harder to see as it was getting darker. The path ahead was well lit. I told the man I wanted to go back now because we were too far away and my mom might be looking for me. He asked me if I wanted to go on and told me I would see my mother and father soon. Being almost five, I protested. I told him I wanted to go back to my bed and I wanted to see my mommy now, not later.

We returned to the hospital room and the man left. He visited me several more times and each time we took the same walk and we would go a little farther away from the hospital. I kept telling him I wanted to see my mom and dad now not later. One day when he came for our walk I told him that I did not want to go on any more walks with him, I wanted to go with my mother and father and I wanted to do it now. I remember being very insistent even though I was a little scared at what my parents would say because I was brought up to be "very respectful" of my elders and not to talk back or show any signs of disrespect.

The man smiled and told me he was going away for now and that I would see my parents soon. Then he told me that we would meet again one day and take that walk together.

When I came out of the coma, I told my mother about the man and the walks. She told me that I had been very, very sick and I had a dream. That was the end of it, no more discussion. I put the entire incident in the back of my mind and we never discussed it again. But, it did not end there, not by a long shot.

Some fifteen years later it all came rushing back to me when I was involved in a head-on car accident on a winding road. I remember the car crash and the medical personnel getting me out of the car via the back door because the front was completely smashed in. I remember being put into the ambulance, and I remember hearing the attendant telling the ambulance driver that he could slow down because, "She's gone."

How could I be gone? I was here. And I was there too! I found myself on the outside of the ambulance looking through the little windows at myself. I was not holding on as the ambulance proceeded but I was on the back of the ambulance. I remember shaking my head and then I heard a voice say, "Hello, Diana." I turned my head and there riding along beside me on the outside of the ambulance was the man I had walked with when I lay comatose in the hospital some fifteen years prior.

He was dressed as before and had not gotten older as I had. He asked if I knew who he was and if I were frightened. I told him that I knew him, that he was the man who had visited me when I was a sick little girl in the hospital. I told him I was not scared. He told me that he had come back and that we were going to take another walk together. I told him I did not want to take a walk. He asked me what I wanted to do, and I told him that I wanted to go back in there, pointing to the me that was lying inside the ambulance. (I did not understand how I could be in both places but I knew I belonged in the me that was on the inside.) He asked me why; he said if I was not afraid of him or afraid of going with him then why did I not want to go? I looked at him again and I saw for the first time there was an aura of bright light surrounding him and the back of the ambulance. The road ahead was dark with only the ambulance headlights for illumination. I told him that I could not possibly go with him because there was something I had to do, it was important. He asked me what I had to do. I told him I didn't know exactly what

---

The karma theory recognizes the parallelism between events forgotten within a single life—the events of early childhood, or the things that we repress or that (in Hindu mythology) we forget as the result of a curse—and the events forgotten from a previous life. It also recognizes a similarity in the ways in which we sometimes half-recall these various sorts of events, often with a sense of déjà vu. We remember something that we cannot remember; from a lost past, through the power of the invisible tracks or traces left behind on our souls by those events; these traces the Hindus call perfumes (*vasanas*). We, too, can often smell those perfumes.
—Wendy Doniger, "Who Lives, Who Survives?" *Parabola*

it was, but I was supposed to do something and it was very important that I do it. He asked me three times if I was sure that I did not want to go with him, and I told him three more times, I did not want to go, I had something I had to do.

Then he asked me if I knew who he really was. I found myself saying, "Yes, I know who you are." "Tell me," he said and I answered, "You are my guardian angel." He smiled, nodded, and told me he would come and see me again one day, and I said, "I know."

Just as suddenly as he had come, he was gone and I was no longer riding outside the ambulance, but was inside the ambulance and back in the me that was there. I heard the ambulance personnel say, "Hey, she's back. Better speed up." A few minutes later we arrived at the emergency room of the hospital, and I was whisked inside for treatment.

It took more than six months to recover from the internal and external injuries I had suffered, but I recovered. Again my mother said I had a dream, but at age nineteen, I was less inclined to go along with her theory. But we didn't dwell on it, and once again I put it in the recesses of my mind although I could recall the incident clearly and could visualize it just as it had occurred. This was not to be the end of it, however.

Another fifteen years passed, and my uncle sent my mother some papers and photographs that he had weeded out of his collection. As we were going through them I found a picture of a man in a French Army uniform. He was the man in the hospital and on the ambulance. To my amazement I found out that he was my mother's uncle who had died on the battlefield in France during World War I. Mother had never spoken of him, and I did not know of his existence until I saw the photo. I found out that she could only remember seeing him a few times before he went off to war because she was a very young child herself at that time.

The man in the photo was the man I walked with as a four-and-a-half-year-old and the man I rode with on the back of the ambulance as a nineteen-year-old! I know in my heart and soul that one day, he'll come again, and we'll talk together and walk together and maybe the next time I'll go with him without protest. In the meantime, I'll keep searching for the "important things I have to do." Maybe I've already found them. Maybe there is more to be done. Yes, I think so.

Diana V. Culbertson, Ph.D., is a retired librarian-media specialist and educator who lives in Glendale, Arizona.

Index

Index of Contributors

Recommended Reading

Abbey, Edward. *Desert Solitaire: A Season in the Wilderness*. New York: Ballantine, 1990.

Abhedananda, Swami. *The Mystery of Death*. Calcutta, India: Ramakrishna Vedanta Math, 1953, 1967, 1978.

Atwater, P. M. H. *Beyond the Light: The Mysteries and Relevations of Near-Death Experiences.* New York: Avon Books, 1994.

Aurobindo, Sri. *The Life Divine, Vol. 19.* India: Sri Aurobindo Ashram, 1970.

Ball, Ann. *Catholic Book of the Dead.* Huntington, Indiana: Our Sunday Visitor, 1995.

Barley, Nigel. *Grave Matters: A Lively History of Death Around the World.* New York: Henry Holt, 1995.

Beattie, John. *The Breath of Angels: A True Story of Life and Death at Sea.* Dobbs Ferry, New York: Sheridan House Inc., 1997.

Berg, Rabbi Philip S. *Reincarnation: Wheels of a Soul.* New York: Research Center of Kabbalah Press, 1991.

Bernardin, Joseph Louis. *The Gift of Peace: Personal Reflections.* Chicago: Loyola Press, 1997.

Besant, Annie, and C. W. Leadbeater. *Thought-Forms.* Wheaton, Illinois: The Theosophical Publishing House, 1969.

Blackman, Sushila. *Graceful Exits: How Great Beings Die: Death Stories of Tibetan, Hindu & Zen Masters.* New York: Weatherhill, 1997.

Bogarde, Dirk. *Backcloth.* New York: Viking Penguin, 1986.

Budge, E. A. Wallis. *The Book of the Dead.* New York: Penguin Books, 1989.

Danforth, Loring M. *The Death Rituals of Rural Greece.* Princeton, New Jersey: Princeton University Press, 1982.

Dass, Ram, and Paul Gorman. *How Can I Help?* New York: Alfred A. Knopf, Inc., 1985.

Davies, Paul. *God and the New Physics.* New York: Simon & Schuster, 1983.

Davis, Stephen T. *Death and Afterlife Vol 1.* New York: St Martin's Press, 1990.

Dossey, Larry, M.D. *Recovering the Soul.* New York: Bantam Books, 1989.

Douglas, John, and Mark Olshaker. *Mindhunter: Inside the FBI's Elite Serial Crime Unit.* New York: Scribner, 1995.

Eliade, Mircea, ed. *The Encyclopedia of Religion, Vol. 13.* New York: Macmillan, 1987.

Elkin, A. P. *Aboriginal Men of High Degree.* Rochester, Vermont: Inner Traditions, 1977.

Elliott, William. *Tying Rocks to Clouds: Meetings and Conversations with Wise and Spiritual People.* Wheaton, Illinois: Quest Books, 1995.

Enright, D. J. *The Oxford Book of Death.* New York: Oxford University Press, 1983.

Evans, Laura. *The Climb of My Life: A Miraculous Journey from the Edge of Death to the Victory of a Lifetime.* San Francisco: HarperSan Francisco, 1996.

Evans-Wentz, W. Y. *The Tibetan Book of the Dead.* New York: Oxford University Press, 1960.

Fenimore, Angie, and Betty J. Eadie. *Beyond the Darkness: My Near Death Journey to the Edge of Hell and Back.* New York: Bantam Books, 1996.

Frankl, Viktor. *Man's Search for Meaning.* Seattle: University of Washington Press, 1959.

Gallenberger, Joseph. *Brothers Forever: An Unexpected Journey Beyond Death.* Charlottesville, Virginia: Hampton Roads Publishing Co. Inc., 1996.

Gallup, George, Jr. *Adventures in Immortality.* New York: McGraw-Hill, 1982.

Gonzalez-Crussi, F. *Suspended Animation: Six Essays on the Preservation of Bodily Parts.* Orlando: Harvest, 1995.

Gotshalk, Richard. *Bhagavad Gita.* Delhi: Motilal Banarsidass, 1985.

Gourevitch, Philip. *We Wish to Inform You That Tomorrow We Will Be Killed with Our Families: Stories from Rwanda.* New York: Farrar, Staus and Giroux, 1998.

Grof, Stanislav. *Beyond the Brain: Birth, Death, and Transcendence in Psychotherapy.* Albany: State University of New York Press, 1986.

Gruber, Mark, O.S.B. *Wounded by Love: Intimations of an Outpouring Heart.* Latrobe, Pennsylvania: Saint Vincent Archabbey, 1993.

Hansen, Eric. *Motoring With Mohammed: Journeys to Yemen and the Red Sea.* New York: Vintage Departures, 1991.

Herlihy, David, and Samuel Kline Cohn. *The Black Death and the Transformation of the West.* Cambridge, Massachussetts: Harvard University Press, 1997.

Hoss, Rudolf, et al. *Death Dealer: The Memoirs of the SS Kommandant at Auschwitz.* New York: Da Capo Press, 1996.

Holt, Peter. *In Clive's Footsteps.* London: Hutchinson, 1990.

Huxley, Aldous. *The Doors of Perception.* New York: Colophon Books, 1954.

Iserson, Kenneth V. *Death to Dust: What Happens to Dead Bodies.* Tuscon, Arizona: Galen Press, 1994.

Iyer, Pico. *Video Night in Kathmandu: And Other Reports from the Not-So-Far-East.* New York: Vintage Departures, 1988.

Jung, C. G. *Man and His Symbols.* New York: Doubleday, 1964.

Kaku, Michio. *Hyperspace.* New York: Anchor Doubleday, 1994.

Kanuit, Larry, and Brian Sostrom. *Cheating Death: Amazing Survival Stories from Alaska.* Kenmore, Washington: Epicenter Press Inc., 1997.

Khan, Inayat. *Sufi Teachings.* England: Servire Publishers, 1963.

Kingsolver, Barbara. *High Tide in Tucson: Essays from Now or Never.* New York: HarperPerennial, 1995.

Knox, Donald. *Death March: The Survivors of Bataan.* Orlando: Harcourt Brace, 1983.

Kubler-Ross, Elisabeth. *Death: The Final Stage of Growth*. New York: Simon & Schuster, 1997.

Kubler-Ross, Elisabeth. *On Death and Dying*. New York: Simon & Schuster, 1997.

Kung, Hans. *Eternal Life: Life after Death as a Medical, Philosophical, and Theological Problem*. New York: Doubleday, 1984.

Labro, Philippe, Linda Coverdale (translator). *Dark Tunnel, White Light: My Journey to Death and Beyond*. New York: Kodansha International, 1997.

Lewis, C. S. *A Grief Observed*. New York: Bantam Books, 1983.

Matousek, Mark. *Sex, Death, Enlightenment: A True Story*. New York: Riverhead Books, 1996.

Matthiessen, Peter. *The Tree Where Man Was Born*. New York: Penguin, 1995.

Miller, Sukie, Ph.D., with Suzanne Lipsett. *After Death: How People Around the World Map the Journey After Life*. New York: Touchstone, 1997.

Mindell, Arnold. *Coma: The Dreambody Near Death*. New York: Penguin, 1995.

Moody, Raymond A., Jr. *Life After Life: The Investigation of a Phenome-non—Survival of Bodily Death*. New York: Bantam Books, 1988.

Morris, Mary. *Nothing to Declare: Memoirs of a Woman Traveling Alone*. New York: Penguin, 1988.

Morse, Melvin, M.D., with Paul Perry. *Parting Visions: Uses and Meanings of Pre-Death, Psychic, and Spiritual Experiences*. New York: Villard, 1994. New York: HarperCollins, 1996.

Morse, Melvin, M.D., and Raymond A. Moody. *Closer to the Light: Learning from Near Death Experiences of Children*. New York: Ivy Books, 1991.

Mullin Glenn H. *Death and Dying: The Tibetan Tradition*. New York: Penguin USA, 1995.

Olsen, W. Scott, and Scott Cairns, eds. *The Sacred Place: Witnessing the Holy in the Physical World*. Salt Lake City: University of Utah Press, 1996.

Otto, Rudolf. *The Idea of the Holy*. New York: Oxford University Press, 1958.

Parkes, Colin Murray. *Death and Bereavement Across Cultures*. New York: Routledge, 1996.

Paxton, Frederick S. *Christianizing Death: The Creation of a Ritual Process in Early Medieval Europe*. Ithaca, New York: Cornell University Press, 1996.

Perkins, Robert F. *Talking to Angels: A Life Spent in High Latitudes*. Boston: Beacon Press, 1996.

Raphael, Simcha Paull. *Jewish Views of the Afterlife*. Northvale, New Jersey: Jason Aronson, Inc., 1994.

Read, Paul Piers. *Alive: The Story of the Andes Survivors*. New York: J. B Lippincott Company, 1974.

Reanney, Darryl. *After Death: A New Future for Human Consciousness*. New York: Avon Books, 1996.

Remen, Rachel Naomi, M.D. *Kitchen Table Wisdom: Stories That Heal*. New York: Riverhead Books, 1996.

Ring, Kenneth. *Heading Toward Omega*. New York: William Morrow, Inc., 1985.

Rinpoche, Sogyal, Patrick Gaffney, and Andrew Harvey, eds. *The Tibetan Book of Living and Dying*. San Francisco: HarperSan Francisco, 1992.

Ritchie, Jean. *Death's Door: True Stories of Near-Death Experiences*. New York: Dell Publishing, 1996.

Roberts, Paul William. *Empire of the Soul: Some Journeys in India*. New York: Riverhead Books, 1996.

Robinson, David. *Beautiful Death: Art of the Cemetery*. New York: Penguin Studio, 1996.

Scheper-Hughes, Nancy. *Death Without Weeping: The Violence of Everyday Life in Brazil*. Berkeley: University of California Press, 1993.

Somé, Malidoma Patrice. *Of Water and the Spirit: Ritual, Magic, and Initiation in the Life of an African Shaman*. New York: Jeremy P. Tarcher, 1994.

Steinsaltz, Adin. *The Thirteen Petalled Rose*. New York: Basic Books, Inc., Publishers, 1980.

Sterling, Richard. *Dining with Headhunters: Jungle Feasts & Other Culinary Adventures*. Freedom, California: The Crossing Press, 1995.

Straley, John. *Death and the Language of Happiness*. New York: Bantam Books, 1997.

Talbot, Michael. *The Holographic Universe*. New York: HarperCollins, 1992.

Taylor, Allegra. *Acquainted with the Night: A Year on the Frontiers of Death*. London: C. W. Daniel Company Ltd., 1995.

Tipler, Frank J. *The Physics of Immortality*. New York: Doubleday, 1994.

Turner, Alice K. *The History of Hell*. New York: Harcourt Brace & Company, 1993.

Van Praagh, James. *Talking to Heaven: A Medium's Message of Life After Death*. New York: Dutton, 1997.

Villatoro, Marcos McPeek. *Walking to La Milpa: Living in Guatemala With Armies, Demons, Abrazos, and Death*. Wakefield, Rhode Island: Moyer Bell Ltd., 1996.

Weenolsen, Patricia. *The Art of Dying: How to Leave This World With Dignity and Grace, at Peace With Yourself and Your Loved Ones*. New York: St Martin's Press, 1996.

Wolf, Fred Allen. *Star Wave: Mind, Consciousness, and Quantum Physics*. New York: Macmillan, 1984.

Yeadon, David. *The Back of Beyond: Travels to the Wild Places of the Earth*. New York: HarperCollins, 1991.

Acknowledgments

We would like to thank our families and friends for their usual forbearance while we are putting a book together. Thanks also to Lisa Bach, Susan Brady, Deborah Greco, Raj Khadka, Jennifer Leo, Natanya Pearlman, Tara Austen Weaver, Patty Holden, Tim O'Reilly, Michele Wetherbee, Emily Polk and to Sleeping Lady Retreat and Conference Center in Leavenworth, Washington, for a wonderful and supportive creative environment.

"The Bridge" by David Yeadon excerpted from *The Back of Beyond: Travels to the Wild Places of the Earth* by David Yeadon. Copyright © 1991 by David Yeadon. Reprinted by permission of the author.

"A Minor Resurrection" by Paul William Roberts excerpted from *Empire of the Soul: Some Journeys in India* by Paul William Roberts. Copyright © 1994 by Paul William Roberts. Used by permission of Putnam Berkley, a division of Penguin Putnam Inc., and Stoddart Publishing Co., Limited, Don Mills, Ont.

"Pearyland" by Barry Lopez excerpted from *Field Notes: The Grace Note of the Canyon Wren* by Barry Lopez. Copyright © 1994 by Barry Lopez. Reprinted by permission of Alfred A. Knopf, Inc. and Vintage/Random House UK.

"Tell All the Old People" by Melvin Morse, M.D., with Paul Perry excerpted from *Parting Visions: Uses and Meanings of Pre-Death, Psychic, and Spiritual Experiences* by Melvin Morse, M.D., with Paul Perry. Copyright © 1994 by Melvin Morse, M.D., and Paul Perry. Reprinted by permission of Villard Books, a division of Random House, Inc.

"Restless Ghost" by Brett Harris first appeared in *Salon.com* at www.Salon.com. An online version remains in the Salon archives. Copyright © 1998. Reprinted with permission.

"The Chalice of Repose" by Therese Schroeder-Sheker first appeared in *Lapis*, published by the New York Open Center. Copyright © 1997. Reprinted by permission of *Lapis*.

"Presences" by Sydney Lea excerpted from *Hunting the Whole Way Home* by Sydney Lea. Copyright © 1994 by Sydney Lea, published by University Press of New England. Reprinted by permission of the author.

"The Survivor" by Mark Matousek excerpted from *Sex, Death, Enlightenment: A True Story* by Mark Matousek. Copyright © 1996 by Mark Matousek.

and the author.

"More than Just a Box" by Janet Milhomme reprinted from the Winter 1994 issue of *Escape*. Copyright © 1994 by Janet Milhomme. Reprinted by permission of the author.

"*Famadihana* Diary" by Seraphine Ramanantsoa published with permission from the author. Copyright © 2000 by Seraphine Ramanantsoa.

"Mondays Are Best" by Pico Iyer excerpted from *Video Night in Kathmandu: And Other Reports from the Not-So-Far-East* by Pico Iyer. Copyright © 1988 by Pico Iyer. Reprinted by permission of Random House, Inc.

"Crossing Borders Within and Without" by Sukie Miller, Ph.D. with Suzanne Lipsett excerpted from *After Death: How People Around the World Map the Journey After Life* by Sukie Miller, Ph.D. with Suzanne Lipsett. Copyright © 1997 by Sukie Miller, Ph.D. Reprinted by permission of Simon & Schuster, Inc.

"Benares" by Mark Matousek excerpted from *Sex, Death, Enlightenment: A True Story* by Mark Matousek. Copyright © 1996 by Mark Matousek. Reprinted by permission of Riverhead Books, a division of Penguin Putnam, Inc.

"A Party at the Cemetery" by Mary Morris excerpted from *Nothing to Declare: Memoirs of a Woman Traveling Alone* by Mary Morris. Copyright © 1988 by Mary Morris. Reprinted by permission of Houghton Mifflin.

"A Grandfather's Farewell" by Malidoma Patrice Somé excerpted from *Of Water and the Spirit: Ritual, Magic, and Initiation in the Life of an African Shaman* by Maildoma Patrice Somé. Copyright © 1994 by Malidoma Patrice Somé. Used by permission of Jeremy P. Tarcher, a division of Penguin Putnam Inc.

"Last Rites" by Mark Gruber, O.S.B. excerpted from *Wounded by Love: Intimations of an Outpouring Heart* by Mark Gruber, O.S.B. Copyright © 1993 by Mark Gruber, O.S.B. Reprinted by permission of the author.

"In Normandy" by Dirk Bogarde excerpted from *Backcloth* by Dirk Bogarde. Copyright © 1986 by Labofilms S.A. Used by permission of Penguin Books Ltd., and The Peters, Fraser & Dunlop Group Ltd.

"Taken for a Ride" by Ronnie Golden reprinted from *A Woman's World,* edited by Marybeth Bond. Copyright © 1995 by Ronnie Golden. Reprinted by permission of the author.

"When It's Your Turn" by Tom Stienstra reprinted from the October 4, 1998 issue of the *San Francisco Examiner*. Copyright © 1998 by the *San Francisco Examiner*. Reprinted by permission.

"Why the Dogs of Rwanda Are Overfed" by Dorothy Leroux published with permission from the author. Copyright © 2000 by Dorothy Leroux.

"Blademaster" by Eugene Robinson published with permission from the author. Copyright © 2000 by Eugene Robinson.

"Reading the Leaves" by Peter Holt excerpted from *In Clive's Footsteps* by Peter Holt. Copyright © 1990 by Peter Holt. Reprinted by permission of the author.

"Second Sight" by Jacques Lusseyran excerpted from *And There Was Light* by Jacques Lusseyran. Copyright © 1987 by Jacques Lusseyran. Reprinted by permission of Little, Brown and Company and Floris Books, Edinburgh.

"Lists" by Sister Helen P. Mrosla reprinted from the October 1991 issue of *Reader's Digest*. Copyright © 1991 by Sister Helen P. Mrosla. Reprinted by permission

Additional Credits (Arranged alphabetically by title)

Selection from "Measures of Life: The Etiquette of the Firing Squad" by Robert M. Sapolsky reprinted from the March/April 1994 issue of *The Sciences.* Copyright © 1994. Reprinted by permission of *The Sciences.*

Selection from *On Glory Roads: A Pilgrims' Book About Pilgrimage* by Eleanor Munro (New York: Thames and Hudson, 1987) copyright © 1987 by Eleanor Munro. Reprinted by permission of Georges Borchardt, Inc. for the author.

Selection from *People of the Lie: The Hope for Healing Human Evil* by M. Scott Peck, M.D. copyright © 1983 by M. Scott Peck. Reprinted with the permission of Simon & Schuster.

Selection from "Precipice of Longing" by Thomas Handy Loon published with permission from the author. Copyright © 2000 by Thomas Handy Loon.

Selection from "Remembering *Famadihanas*" by Hilary Bradt published with permission from the author. Copyright © 2000 by Hilary Bradt.

Selection from *Talking to Angels: A Life Spent in High Latitudes* by Robert F. Perkins copyright © 1996 by Robert F. Perkins. Reprinted by permission of Beacon Press.

Selections from *Tying Rocks to Clouds: Meetings and Conversations with Wise and Spiritual People* by William Elliot copyright © 1995 by William Elliott. Reprinted by permission of Quest Books, a division of Theosophical Publishing House.

Selections from *We Wish to Inform You that Tomorrow We Will Be Killed with Our Families: Stories from Rwanda* by Philip Gourevitch copyright © 1998 by Philip Gourevitch. Reprinted by permission of Farrar, Straus & Giroux and MacMillan Publishers, Ltd.

Selection from "Who Lives, Who Survives?" by Wendy Doniger reprinted from *Parabola, The Magazine of Myth and Tradition,* Vol. XXIII, No. 4 (Winter 1998). Copyright © 1998. Reprinted by permission.

Selection from *Within Tuscany* by Matthew Spender copyright © 1991 by Matthew Spender. Used by permission of Viking Penguin, a division of Penguin Putnam Inc. and Penguin Books Ltd.

About the Editors

James O'Reilly, president and co-publisher of Travelers' Tales, wrote mystery serials before becoming a travel writer in the early 1980s. He's visited more than forty countries, along the way meditating with monks in Tibet, participating in West African voodoo rituals, and hanging out the laundry with nuns in Florence. He travels extensively with his wife Wenda and their three daughters. They live in Palo Alto, California, when they're not in Leavenworth, Washington.

Sean O'Reilly is a former seminarian, stockbroker, and prison instructor who lives in Arizona with his wife Brenda and their four small boys. He's had a life-long interest in philosophy and theology, and is at work on a book called *How to Manage Your Dick: A Guide for the Soul*, which makes the proposition that classic Greek, Roman, and Christian moral philosophies, allied with post-quantum physics, form the building blocks of a new ethics and psychology. Widely traveled, Sean most recently completed an 18,000-mile van journey around the United States, sharing the treasures of the open road with his family. He is editor-at-large and director of international sales for Travelers' Tales.

Richard Sterling is the travel editor of *Fiery Foods Magazine* and the editor of the best-selling *Travelers' Tales Food: A Taste of the Road*, winner of the Lowell Thomas Silver Award for Best Travel Book and *The Adventure of Food: True Stories of Eating Everything*. He is the author of *The Fearless Diner: Travel Tips and Wisdom for Eating Around the World* (Travelers' Tales 1998), and co-author of *The Unofficial Guide to San Francisco* (Macmillan 1998). He is at work on the first two (Vietnam and Spain) of a series of culinary guides for Lonely Planet called *World Food* to be released in 2000. He lives in Berkeley, California where he is very often politically incorrect.

TRAVELERS' TALES GUIDES

LOOK FOR THESE TITLES IN THE SERIES

FOOTSTEPS: THE SOUL OF TRAVEL
A NEW IMPRINT FROM TRAVELERS' TALES GUIDES

An imprint of Travelers' Tales Guides, the Footsteps series unveils new works by first-time authors, established writers, and reprints of works whose time has come… again. Each book will fire your imagination, disturb your sleep, and feed your soul.

KITE STRINGS OF THE SOUTHERN CROSS
A Woman's Travel Odyssey
By Laurie Gough
ISBN 1-885211-30-9
400 pages, $24.00, Hardcover

THE SWORD OF HEAVEN
A Five Continent Odyssey to Save the World
By Mikkel Aaland
ISBN 1-885211-44-9
350 pages, $24.00, Hardcover

STORM
A Motorcycle Journey of Love, Endurance, and Transformation
By Allen Noren
ISBN 1-885211-45-7
360 pages, $24.00, Hardcover

SPECIAL INTEREST

THE FEARLESS SHOPPER:
How to Get the Best Deals on the Planet
By Kathy Borrus
ISBN 1-885211-39-2, 200 pages, $12.95

THE GIFT OF RIVERS:
True Stories of Life on the Water
Edited by Pamela Michaeel
Introduction by Rober Hass
ISBN 1-885211-42-2, 256 pages, $14.95

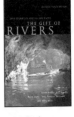

SHITTING PRETTY:
How to Stay Clean and Healthy While Traveling
By Dr. Jane Wilson-Howarth
ISBN 1-885211-47-3, 200 pages, $12.95

THE GIFT OF BIRDS:
True Encounters with Avian Spirits
Edited by Larry Habegger & Amy G. Carlson
ISBN 1-885211-41-4, 352 pages, $17.95

TESTOSTERONE PLANET:
True Stories from a Man's World
Edited by Sean O'Reilly, Larry Habegger & James O'Reilly
ISBN 1-885211-43-0, 300 pages, $17.95

THE PENNY PINCHER'S PASSPORT
TO LUXURY TRAVEL:
The Art of Cultivating Preferred Customer Status
By Joel L. Widzer
ISBN 1-885211-31-7, 253 pages, $12.95

$\mathscr{S}$PECIAL INTEREST

DANGER!
True Stories of Trouble and Survival
Edited by James O'Reilly, Larry Habegger & Sean O'Reilly
ISBN 1-885211-32-5, 336 pages, $17.95

FAMILY TRAVEL:
The Farther You Go, the Closer You Get
Edited by Laura Manske
ISBN 1-885211-33-3, 368 pages, $17.95

THE GIFT OF TRAVEL:
The Best of Travelers' Tales
Edited by Larry Habegger, James O'Reilly & Sean O'Reilly
ISBN 1-885211-25-2, 240 pages, $14.95

THERE'S NO TOILET PAPER...ON THE ROAD LESS TRAVELED:
The Best of Travel Humor and Misadventure
Edited by Doug Lansky
ISBN 1-885211-27-9, 207 pages, $12.95

A DOG'S WORLD:
True Stories of Man's Best Friend on the Road
Edited by Christine Hunsicker
ISBN 1-885211-23-6, 257 pages, $12.95

$\mathcal{W}$OMEN'S TRAVEL

A WOMAN'S PATH:
Women's Best Spiritual Travel Writing
Edited by Lucy McCauley, Amy G. Carlson, and Jennifer Leo
ISBN 1-885211-48-1, 320 pages, $16.95

A WOMAN'S PASSION FOR TRAVEL:
More True Stories from A Woman's World
Edited by Marybeth Bond & Pamela Michael
ISBN 1-885211-36-8, 375 pages, $17.95

SAFETY AND SECURITY FOR
WOMEN WHO TRAVEL
By Sheila Swan & Peter Laufer
ISBN 1-885211-29-5, 159 pages, $12.95

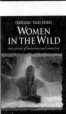

WOMEN IN THE WILD:
True Stories of Adventure and Connection
Edited by Lucy McCauley
ISBN 1-885211-21-X, 307 pages, $17.95

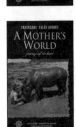

A MOTHER'S WORLD:
Journeys of the Heart
Edited by Marybeth Bond & Pamela Michael
ISBN 1-885211-26-0, 233 pages, $14.95

$\mathcal{W}$OMEN'S TRAVEL

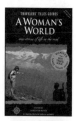

A WOMAN'S WORLD:
True Stories of Life on the Road
Edited by Marybeth Bond
Introduction by Dervla Murphy
ISBN 1-885211-06-6
475 pages, $17.95

GUTSY WOMEN:
Travel Tips and Wisdom for the Road
By Marybeth Bond
ISBN 1-885211-15-5, 123 pages, $7.95

GUTSY MAMAS:
**Travel Tips and Wisdom
for Mothers on the Road**
By Marybeth Bond
ISBN 1-885211-20-1, 139 pages, $7.95

—— ★ ★ ★ ——

*Winner of the Lowell
Thomas Award for Best
Travel Book – Society of
American Travel Writers*

$\mathcal{B}$ODY & SOUL

THE ULTIMATE JOURNEY:
Inspiring Stories of Living and Dying
James O'Reilly, Larry Habegger & Richard Sterling
ISBN 1-885211-38-4
336 pages, $17.95

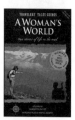

ADVENTURE OF FOOD:
True Stories of Eating Everything
Edited by Richard Sterling
ISBN 1-885211-37-6
336 pages, $17.95

ℬODY & SOUL

THE ROAD WITHIN:
**True Stories of Transformation
and the Soul**
*Edited by Sean O'Reilly, James O'Reilly
& Tim O'Reilly*
ISBN 1-885211-19-8, 459 pages, $17.95

LOVE & ROMANCE:
True Stories of Passion on the Road
Edited by Judith Babcock Wylie
ISBN 1-885211-18-X, 319 pages, $17.95

FOOD:
A Taste of the Road
*Edited by Richard Sterling
Introduction by Margo True*
ISBN 1-885211-09-0
467 pages, $17.95

THE FEARLESS DINER:
**Travel Tips and Wisdom for Eating
around the World**
By Richard Sterling
ISBN 1-885211-22-8, 139 pages, $7.95

𝒞OUNTRY GUIDES

IRELAND
True Stories of Life on the Emerald Isle
Edited by James O'Reilly, Larry Habegger, and Sean O'Reilly
ISBN 1-885211-46-5, 368 pages, $17.95

COUNTRY GUIDES

AUSTRALIA
True Stories of Life Down Under
Edited by Larry Habegger
ISBN 1-885211-40-6, 375 pages, $17.95

AMERICA
Edited by Fred Setterberg
ISBN 1-885211-28-7, 550 pages, $19.95

JAPAN
Edited by Donald W. George
& Amy Greimann Carlson
ISBN 1-885211-04-X, 437 pages, $17.95

ITALY
Edited by Anne Calcagno
Introduction by Jan Morris
ISBN 1-885211-16-3, 463 pages, $17.95

INDIA
Edited by James O'Reilly & Larry Habegger
ISBN 1-885211-01-5, 538 pages, $17.95

$\mathscr{C}$OUNTRY GUIDES

FRANCE

Edited by James O'Reilly, Larry Habegger
& Sean O'Reilly
ISBN 1-885211-02-3, 517 pages, $17.95

MEXICO

Edited by James O'Reilly & Larry Habegger
ISBN 1-885211-00-7, 463 pages, $17.95

———— ★ ★ ★ ————

Winner of the Lowell
Thomas Award for Best
Travel Book – Society of
American Travel Writers

THAILAND

Edited by James O'Reilly
& Larry Habegger
ISBN 1-885211-05-8
483 pages, $17.95

SPAIN

Edited by Lucy McCauley
ISBN 1-885211-07-4, 495 pages, $17.95

NEPAL

Edited by Rajendra S. Khadka
ISBN 1-885211-14-7, 423 pages, $17.95

COUNTRY GUIDES

BRAZIL

Edited by Annette Haddad & Scott Doggett
Introduction by Alex Shoumatoff
ISBN 1-885211-11-2
452 pages, $17.95

—★ ★ ★—
Benjamin Franklin
Award Winner

CITY GUIDES

HONG KONG

Edited by James O'Reilly, Larry Habegger & Sean O'Reilly
ISBN 1-885211-03-1, 439 pages, $17.95

PARIS

Edited by James O'Reilly, Larry Habegger & Sean O'Reilly
ISBN 1-885211-10-4, 417 pages, $17.95

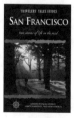

SAN FRANCISCO

Edited by James O'Reilly, Larry Habegger & Sean O'Reilly
ISBN 1-885211-08-2, 491 pages, $17.95

ℛEGIONAL GUIDES

HAWAI'I
True Stories of the Island Spirit
Edited by Rick & Marcie Carroll
ISBN 1-885211-35-X, 416 pages, $17.95

GRAND CANYON
True Stories of Life Below the Rim
Edited by Sean O'Reilly,
James O'Reilly & Larry Habegger
ISBN 1-885211-34-1, 296 pages, $17.95

SUBMIT YOUR OWN TRAVEL TALE

Do you have a tale of your own that you would like to submit to Travelers' Tales? We highly recommend that you first read one or more of our books to get a feel for the kind of story we're looking for. For submission guidelines and a list of titles in the works, send a SASE to:

Travelers' Tales Submission Guidelines
330 Townsend Street, Suite 208, San Francisco, CA 94107

or send email to *guidelines@travelerstales.com*
or visit our Web site at **www.travelerstales.com**

You can send your story to the address above or via email to *submit@travelerstales.com*. On the outside of the envelope, *please indicate what country/topic your story is about*. If your story is selected for one of our titles, we will contact you about rights and payment.

We hope to hear from you. In the meantime, enjoy the stories!